HOW I SPOKE MY MIND AND CREATED ENEMIES AROUND

ALSO BY M.P. PRABHAKARAN

What India and Virgin Mary Have in Common (2022)

Racist Bones in President Trump's Body (2020)

An Indian Goes Around the World - II:
What I Learned form My Thirty-Day European Odyssey (2016)

An Indian Goes Around the World - I:
Capitalism Comes to Mao's Mausoleum (2012)

Letters on India The New York Times *Did Not Publish* (2011)

The Historical Origin of India's Underdevelopment:
A World-System Perspective (1990)

HOW I SPOKE MY MIND AND CREATED ENEMIES AROUND

M.P. PRABHAKARAN

GOTHAM BOOKS

Gotham Books

30 N Gould St.
Ste. 20820, Sheridan, WY 82801
https://gothambooksinc.com/

Phone: 1 (307) 464-7800

© 2023 M.P. Prabhakaran. All rights reserved.

No part of this book may be reproduced, stored in a retrieval system, or transmitted by any means without the written permission of the author.

Published by Gotham Books (August 31, 2023)

ISBN: 979-8-88775-451-2 (P)
ISBN: 979-8-88775-452-9 (E)

Because of the dynamic nature of the Internet, any web addresses or links contained in this book may have changed since publication and may no longer be valid.

The views expressed in this work are solely those of the author and do not necessarily reflect the views of the publisher, and the publisher hereby disclaims any responsibility for them.

For the memory of
ADAMANTIA POLLIS,
my professor and dissertation supervisor at
The New School for Social Research, New York,
from whom I learned the importance of
speaking truth to power.

Contents

Preface		xi
1.	Bush Plays Patriotism Card to Get Democrats' Support for Iraq War	1
2.	Getting Rid of Saddam Hussein Is the Undeclared Goal of Gulf War II	5
3.	The Rush Limbaugh of the U.S. Supreme Court Reveals His Fat	11
4.	Iraq Won't Survive as a Loose Federation. India's Model Suits It Best	15
5.	*NYT* Columnist's Conservative Brother Destroys My Christmas Cheer	19
6.	Indian Communists Want to Go Back to the Days of the Bullock Cart?	23
7.	Republican Senator Calls an Indian American 'Macaca' and Makes a Monkey of Himself	27
8.	Priests at Puri Jagannath Temple Disgrace Hinduism	31
9.	The 'Hindu Taliban' May Take India Back to the Paleolithic Age	35
10.	How Clarence Thomas Played the Race Card and Lied to Get on U.S. Supreme Court	40
11.	How U.S. Democrats, Indian Communists & *NY Times* Tried to Block Indo-U.S. Nuclear Deal and Failed	47
12.	*Dear John McCain and Sarah Palin:* If You Detest Government That Much, Why Do You Want to Be Part of It?	53
13.	Monkeys in Pink Panties	60
14.	Crass Commercialization of Mother's Day in America	63
15.	Why I Didn't Survive as a High School Teacher in New York City	67

16.	An Indian American of Quisling Ancestry Ridicules Obama's Anticolonialist Ancestry	73
17.	India's War on Terror: Troubling Questions on U.S. Cooperation	77
18.	Indian Communists Are Holding On to an Antiquated Mission	81
19.	Shameless Bushies Take Credit for Bin Laden Killing	88
20.	The 'Picasso of India' Is Dead, but the 'Hindu Taliban' Continue Tarnishing His Name	90
21.	U.S. Congressmen Bought Over by Pakistan's Military?	97
22.	An Open Letter to *NYT* Columnist Thomas Friedman on Iraq War	102
23.	*NYT* Columnist's Republican Brother Insults Her Readers' Intelligence	105
24.	Cardinal Dolan Attacks Obamacare Using Jihadist Language	107
25.	Shah Rukh Khan and I Have Names that Arouse Suspicion. Why Blame Others?	113
26.	The 2008 Terrorist Attack in Mumbai Was Sponsored by Pak Spy Agency	118
27.	Chetan Bhagat's Stupid Advice to Salman Rushdie	125
28.	*An Appeal to Civilized Nations in the World:* Can One of You Come Forward to Try Iraq War Criminals?	130
29.	Triumph of Capitalism Under Lenin's Very Nose	135
30.	Nixon and Kissinger Were Complicit in the 1971 Genocide in Bangladesh	141
31.	'The Emir of NYU' Builds Abu Dhabi Campus with Petrodollars and Exploited South Asian Labor	152
32.	U.N. Pooh-Poohs Trump's Threats and Rebukes His Stance on Jerusalem	159

33.	Trump's Solution to Gun Violence in Schools: Arm Teachers with Guns	162
34.	Dinesh D'Souza, Once Ousted from Job for Adultery, Now Pardoned by President Trump	166
35.	Trump Should Be Impeached. Are There Republicans with Spine Who Will Do It?	172
36.	Hypocrisy, Thy Name Is Donald Trump!	180
37.	Trump Acting as Apologist for Saudi Prince Accused in Journalist's Murder	185
38.	A Plea to President Trump: Reenter Iran Nuclear Deal and Avoid Another Middle East War	193
39.	*NY Times* Columnist Identifies Racist Bones in Trump's Body	198
40.	Pakistan's PM Issues Nuclear Threat Over India's Latest Move on Kashmir	204
41.	Democratic-Led House Impeaches Trump; Republican-Led Senate Acquits Him	217
42.	Pro-Trump Conspiracy Theorists Blame Covid-19 on Bill Gates	223
43.	Trump Has Deplorably Failed in His First Test as Commander-in-Chief	228
44.	How to Prevent the Likes of Trump from Becoming President	235
45.	Conservative Majority on the U.S. Supreme Court May Bring Back Back-Alley Abortions	241
46.	Slow Pace of Capitol Attack Probe May Pave the Way for a Trump Comeback	246

Preface

"Your tongue is your biggest enemy." I have heard this warning from my friends on numerous occasions. My response to them has always been: "Have I ever used it to spread falsehoods knowingly?"

Most of them would smile away my response. I would then add: "If by calling a spade a spade I become an enemy to anyone, I have no problem with it."

My friends have given me similar warning with regard to my writings, too. Every time they read an article I published, which they feared could get me into trouble, they would say: "Your pen is your biggest enemy." And then, pointing to the topic of the article, they would add: "Why bother, if it doesn't affect you in any way?"

"Why bother, if it doesn't affect you in any way?" I would throw the words back at them, and then add: "History is full of examples of the disastrous consequences of this attitude. The powers that be got away with the atrocious things they did mainly because good people refused to speak up. They refused to speak up because those things did not affect them."

I often stressed my point by reminding my friends of the immortal words of the Lutheran pastor Martin Niemöller. Those words, when first published, had stirred the collective conscience of the world. The words, as translated by Bob Berkovitz, are:

> When the Nazis arrested the Communists,
> I said nothing; after all, I was not a Communist.
> When they locked up the Social Democrats,
> I said nothing; after all, I was not a Social Democrat.
> When they arrested the trade unionists,
> I said nothing; after all, I was not a trade unionist.
> When they arrested the Jews,
> I said nothing; after all, I was not a Jew.
> When they arrested me, there was no longer anyone who could protest.

After patiently listening to those words, my friends would give a pat on my shoulder and change the topic. Such gestures reassured me that at least those whose friendships I value had not joined the enemy camp my tongue and pen created. I knew their warnings were well-intentioned. They have known first-hand how the fearless use of my tongue and pen hurt my career.

To give just one example. I was still in the formative stage in journalism when I arrived in the U.S., in 1975, as an immigrant from India. A few months after my arrival, something happened in India that shocked democracy-loving people all over the world. The late Prime Minister Indira Gandhi declared a State of Emergency and brought the country under her authoritarian rule. She suspended all civil liberties and imposed strict censorship on the media.

Many of my journalist friends in India reluctantly submitted to censorship rules and continued in the profession. I could understand why they did it. To them, the alternative would be starvation. A handful of senior journalists, who defied censorship and criticized Emergency, were put in jail. I had intense admiration for some of them, and had adopted them as my role models. I looked for ways to express my detest for what Mrs. Gandhi did.

I decided to use *The Voice of India*, a monthly publication I had just started, to campaign against Emergency. Though I had started the monthly to make a living practicing my profession, it soon became an anti-Emergency publication. I paid a heavy price as a result.

The draconian measures Mrs. Gandhi introduced in India had struck terror among Indians living in the U.S., too. They didn't want to see in their living rooms a publication carrying articles with screaming headlines like "India will survive Indira and her dictatorship"; "To destroy Indira's republic is Asoka Mehta's mission"; etc. (The late Asoka Mehta was one of the opposition leaders imprisoned during the Emergency.) I also started getting phone calls threatening me with "dire consequences." With steadily dwindling circulation and advertising revenue, *The Voice of India* died a slow and painful death.

An unfortunate outcome of being the editor of a controversial publication was that, after it folded, finding a job in journalism became very, very difficult for me. Nobody wanted to hire a person who came across to them as a radical. I got a taste of this wrong perception at my very first job interview after *The Voice of India* folded. One of the writing samples I had attached to my job application was an article I had recently published. Pointing to its title, "Why He Gave Up Marx for Gandhi: The Story of an Indian Revolutionary," the interviewer asked me, "Are you that revolutionary?"

I had to explain to him that the article was about Jayaprakash Narayan, who fought side by side with Mahatma Gandhi, Jawaharlal Nehru and other political leaders, against the British, in India's freedom struggle. Ironically, the last political movement this one-time close friend of Nehru's successfully led in India was directed at Nehru's daughter and the Emergency rule she imposed. I came out of the interview, saying to myself: "This job is not for me."

Disappointing job interviews like this reminded me that the possibility of my being branded a radical was what my friends had in mind when they warned me about my tongue and pen. I soon realized that if I am keen on staying in journalism, I had to launch my own ventures, like the one just folded. To keep the wolf from the door, I even did non-journalistic work.

The next journalistic venture I launched was *South Asia Newsspecial*, a feature syndicate. It was followed by *The East-West Inquirer*, an online monthly, published at www.eastwestinquirer.com.

The book I am presenting to you now is a compilation of articles that appeared in *The East-West Inquirer* over the past two decades. The contents of the book may give you the impression that my friends' warnings have had no effect on me. I can't help it. Speaking truth to power is something that comes to me naturally. If by doing it I am able to keep a critical voice alive against the wrongs done by those in power, I will have accomplished something. And that's my primary goal in bringing out this book.

•

I want to thank my friend Haresh Advani, formerly of *Economic & Political Weekly*, published from Mumbai, India, for reading most of the articles, at the manuscript stage, and making some valuable suggestions. The book is a slightly edited and expanded version of what was published earlier under the title *Racist Bones* in *President Trump's Body*.

1

Bush Plays Patriotism Card to Get Democrats' Support for Iraq War

October 15, 2002

The right to dissent is a laudable feature of democracy. It is more so in a political system like that of the United States which discourages ideological pluralism. The U.S. has only two political parties that matter, the Democratic Party and the Republican Party. Both hold identical views on most everything.

The absence of ideological pluralism notwithstanding, the American political system has a reputation for being so vibrant. The main factor that accounts for that vibrancy is the fearlessness with which a few politicians persist in exercising their right to dissent from powers that be in the country and in their own party. They have to be fearless because, on matters they dissent, they often find themselves taking unpopular positions and pitted against a tyrannical majority. Their courage of conviction has been the envy of many, even of those who are opposed to them politically. Alas, they are fast becoming an endangered species, thanks to the relentless attack on their integrity by paleolithic conservatives (paleocons) and, sometimes, even by non-conservatives.

Last Refuge of a Scoundrel

If the issue is related to economy, these conservatives try to stifle the dissent by calling the dissenters liberals, which, unfortunately, has become a dirty word in America. If the issue involved is national security, the attackers take the low road of challenging the dissenters' patriotism. One is reminded of what Dr. Samuel Johnson said about patriotism over two centuries ago. "Patriotism," he said, "is the last refuge of a scoundrel." These self-styled standard-bearers of patriotism should know that systematic stifling of dissent can lead to a one-party political system that will not be much different from the dictatorship of Saddam Hussein which they deplore.

That brings us to the present debate on the invasion of Iraq to rid that country of weapons of mass destruction, which the George W.

Bush administration says it has. Even President Bush stooped to the level of taking refuge in patriotism to silence his critics and turn the debate to his advantage. The Republican president accused Democrats who are opposed to the idea of going to war with Iraq of not being serious about the nation's security. That was enough to do many Democrats in. Even those who had earlier taken a bold, principled position and argued on the inadvisability of launching a preemptive strike against Iraq, which was what the president was campaigning for, started looking for excuses to rally behind him. Columnist Frank Rich of *The New York Times* described the somersault in their position thus: "They challenged the administration's arrogant and factually disingenuous way of pursuing its goal, then beat a hasty retreat to sign on to whatever fig-leaf language they could get into the final resolution." Their performance, to say the least, was pathetic.

The underlying theme of the president's campaign that led to the resolution was that the gravest threat to the nation's security now comes from Saddam Hussein's Iraq. Many around the world, though they detest Saddam Hussein, do not agree with the president's contention. A lot of them even question the timing of his raising the issue. The world has been living with threats from Saddam Hussein for quite some time, they say. If there has been any new development that makes those threats more imminent now, the president has not produced any evidence of it. In the absence of such evidence, they have every right to question his intentions in raking up the issue just a few weeks before the congressional election.

Machiavellian Tactic

They argue that if the election is fought on the real issue confronting the country today, the electorate will overwhelmingly vote against the president's Republican Party. The real issue is the shrinking economy and the people's lack of confidence in the economic system itself. Some of the corporate crooks responsible for bringing the economic system to the brink of collapse happen to be the president's buddies. There is no hope of getting the present trend reversed anytime soon. And the president has not come up with any concrete plan to reverse it. Hence his resort to the Machiavellian tactic of diverting people's attention from the problems at home to the imaginary threats emanating from abroad.

Americans refuse to live in fear, President Bush repeatedly said during his campaign to win congressional authorization for use of force against Iraq. Unfortunately, the authorization has only added to that fear. Since the terrorist attacks of September 11, 2001, they have been fearing more such attacks from the same group that was responsible for them. The group, of course, is Osama bin Laden's Al Qaeda. The passing of the resolution by Congress, on October 10, 2002, authorizing the president to use force against Iraq, has given them reason to fear attacks from one more group: Saddam Hussein and his henchmen.

All that matters to Saddam is his own survival, personal and political. He has proved to the world time and again that, if he perceives any threat to his survival, he would do just anything to eliminate that threat. The resolution, which the president bulldozed through Congress, has sent him a message that his days are numbered. Even if he had no plan to attack America before, he has reason to expeditiously put together one now. The attack from him could be to preempt the preemptive strike, which he fears President Bush is contemplating against him. Or it could be to avenge the strike if America launches it first. In either case, he won't have any qualms about using the most lethal weapon he has in his arsenal. If he is sure that he is going down, he will not hesitate to take with him as many as he can.

Yes, to repeat what Bush said, Americans refuse to live in fear. But that is true only in normal circumstances. Having brought them to the brink of a catastrophe, he cannot expect them to live in anything other than utter fear.

Here is something the president can do to mitigate that fear and, if lucky, avoid the catastrophe: Stop the bravado and muscle flexing. Doesn't he know the simple truth that one advantage of being a superpower is that it doesn't have to keep rubbing in on others that it is a superpower. At the same time, it is worth bearing in mind that even a superpower is not invincible. If there is one lesson that the world learned from 9/11, it is this: It doesn't take a superpower to humiliate a superpower. A bunch of disgruntled youths can do it, if they are given the wherewithal and fired up by fanaticism.

The president will be doing America and the rest of the world a big favor if he leaves the job of looking for and destroying weapons of mass destruction, which he says Saddam Hussein has in his arsenal, to the United Nations. If Saddam has such weapons, it should be the concern of the whole world. Let the world's representative body address that concern.

Dialogue with Saddam

There is also a need to open a dialogue with Saddam, no matter how dangerous and despicable he is. He needs to be convinced that he has only two paths before him: the path of self-destruction and the path that will save his life, along with the lives of many Iraqis and Americans. He must be told that he would be allowed to take the latter path only if he abides by all the resolutions the U.N. Security Council passed in the wake of the 1991 war against his country.

Saddam can be expected to agree to this dialogue if he is given a modicum of recognition that any head of state deserves and if the dialogue is given the semblance of being one between two equals. The need here is of nuancing diplomacy. It can be achieved only if the U.S. steps aside for the time being and lets the U.N. play the role it is mandated to play.

Let the U.N. be represented by no less a person than its secretary general, Kofi Annan. I can also think of an American Saddam will grab the opportunity to have a dialogue with. His name is Jimmy Carter, the 39th U.S. President and the winner of the 2002 Nobel Peace Prize.

In conclusion, here is my appeal to President Bush: Please pause and think about these options before you order the first strike. It is a question of saving thousands of lives, American as well as Iraqi.

2

Getting Rid of Saddam Hussein Is the Undeclared Goal of Gulf War II

December 31, 2002

The warmongers in the Bush administration may soon act out their threat to attack Iraq. Fifty thousand ground troops are being readied for dispatch to the Gulf region to join the 60,000 air force and navy personnel who are already there. The alarm the administration has raised gives one the impression that the missiles mounted with weapons of mass destruction (WMD) are about to be launched by Saddam Hussein toward the shores of America. Apart from preempting such a launch, the impending war – call it Gulf War II – also has the hallowed goal of destroying all weapons of mass destruction the administration says Saddam has in his arsenal and of making the world safe from them. That, by the way, is only the declared goal of the war.

There is also an undeclared goal, a hidden agenda, which we don't hear much about: destruction of Saddam Hussein himself. It is hidden in what is euphemistically presented to the public as "regime change." As far as President George W. Bush is concerned, there is a filial aspect to this goal and, as such, it is very personal and more important than the declared goal. It must stay hidden because assassinating a foreign head of state is against American and international laws. It has to be accomplished in the course of fighting a war whose goal is couched in noble-sounding words. The goal of ridding a murderous dictator of the weapons of mass destruction he is said to be in possession of does sound noble. But while that goal can be achieved through diplomacy, war is the only means by which the undeclared goal of eliminating him can be achieved. Hence the insistence by the president on seeking a war solution, not a diplomatic solution, to the threat posed by WMD, which he says Saddam Hussein has. More about the filial aspect of the war in a little bit.

If Iraq is in possession of weapons of mass destruction, it certainly is in violation of U.N. Security Council resolutions. But there are procedures put in place, under the aegis of the U.N. that can deal with such situations. The U.N. Charter clearly prohibits any state to take upon itself the responsibility of punishing another state for any violation, unless approved by the Security Council.

If violations of Security Council resolutions or international law were the real problem, all that President Bush had to do was get the U.N. to put its machinery at work. Why was he so reluctant in the beginning even to approach the U.N.? As we all know, it took a good deal of persuading by some level-headed men in his administration, notably Secretary of State Colin L. Powell, to get him to fulfill that legal requirement. Bush's constant refrain, which betrayed his disdain for international laws and norms, was that it was not a requirement.

Disdain for the U.N.

This disdain explains why, even after bringing the matter to the U.N., he kept threatening that he would go it alone if the world body was unwilling to go along with his wishes. (Correction: His threat was more arrogant and uncouth than that. What he said was that he would attack Iraq with or without U.N. approval.) Repeated warnings from legal scholars and, more importantly, from U.N. Secretary General Kofi Annan, that any attack by one country on another, unless undertaken in self-defense, would be a violation of international law had no effect on him.

To the Security Council's credit, it did not succumb to his threat. But it expressed its willingness to accommodate his wishes within legal bounds. Though his approach was crude and bombastic, it couldn't ignore the fact that he was the leader of the only superpower left in the world and of the country that is the largest contributor to the U.N. budget. Also, it was willing to go to any extent to avoid a war. The result was Resolution 1441 (2002), which the council passed unanimously on November 8, 2002.

It is laughable to see many in the Bush administration boast that, but for the president's repeated threat to go to war alone, if necessary, the resolution would not have received the support of all 15 council members. Equally laughable is their interpretation of the resolution as a carte blanche for their war plans. At best, the resolution puts Saddam Hussein on notice that the rest of the world is losing its patience with him. It gives him one more chance to abide by all the resolutions the U.N. has passed concerning his country since the end of the 1991 Gulf war. If he is found in "material breach" of any of them, the latest resolution says, the consequences will be severe.

Contrary to the actual intent of the "material breach" provision in the resolution, the Bush team has been interpreting it as an authorization for automatic triggering of war, if the breach occurs. And it has been overanxious to find "material breach" in every action and omission of Iraq since the passage of Resolution 1441.

The latest case in point is the administration's rush to judgment on the report and declaration Iraq submitted to the U.N. on December 7. As required under Resolution 1441, Iraq declared the report to be a true and complete dossier of its weapons and weapons programs. Hans Blix, executive chairman of the United Nations Monitoring, Verification and Inspection Commission (Unmovic), which is currently combing Iraq to determine whether Saddam Hussein was hiding any of the banned weapons anywhere, is expected to give the commission's assessment of Iraq's December report on January 9. But the Bush team has no patience to wait until then. It issued its verdict on the report on December 19, finding Iraq in "material breach." It did so even before some members of the Security Council had finished reading and evaluating the 12,200-page report. Those members and many around the world found the way the administration handled the issue and rushed to judgment disgusting. Syria, one of the 10 nonpermanent members of the Security Council, returned its copy of the report to the council and refused to participate in its discussion.

Iraq's response to the U.S. verdict came through Gen. Amir al-Saadi, Saddam Hussein's top adviser on weapons. He said: "We have only heard politicians talk like that. We haven't heard any reputable weapons expert come out and pick out the holes in our declaration."

U.N. weapons inspectors, sent back to Iraq to resume their work that had been suspended in 1998, have been doing as thorough a job as possible. They have been looking in every nook and cranny of the country. They are fully aware that Saddam had lied in the past and will lie again. They have the expertise to determine whether the dossier of weapons Iraq submitted to the U.N. truly represented realities on the ground. No smoking gun has been found during the search of 200 suspicious sites they have so far completed. We will wait and see whether they find any during the search of the remaining 100 sites on their list. The inspectors are expected to submit their report to the U.N. on January 27. One hopes that the trigger-happy in the Bush camp would wait at least until that date before deciding to pull the trigger.

If they want to pull the trigger right now, they must come forward with hard evidence to prove that Iraq is hiding weapons of mass destruction. As the Russian ambassador to the United Nations said, "To say 'We know, but we won't tell you,' is not something that is persuasive, frankly speaking. This is not a poker game, when you hold your cards and call others' bluff."

Why a Different Approach to North Korea?

That brings us back to these questions: Is the President really serious about disarming rogue states of weapons of mass destruction? And is war the only means of achieving it? If so, why isn't he making war preparations against North Korea which already has one or two nuclear bombs and is well on its way to making more? Also, in a tone that can be construed as a challenge to the Bush administration, North Korea announced on December 27 that it would restart its nuclear fuel reprocessing laboratory, which was shut down under its 1994 agreement with the U.S. Though the proclaimed purpose of the restarting is to produce electricity, which that impoverished nation badly needs, the actual purpose experts say is to produce weapons-grade plutonium. At this writing, North Korea has also ordered all international nuclear inspectors out of the country. Which means that there will be no outsiders to monitor what goes on in that isolated country hereafter. It has been in isolation from the rest of the world for over 50 years. The scenario is scary.

What is the Bush administration's response to all this? It says it would seek a diplomatic solution, working through the U.N. Suddenly it has realized that the U.N. is not all that irrelevant. "We want to make it clear that this is now an international problem, not just a problem between the United States and North Korea," according to a senior administration official, quoted in a December 28 story in *The New York Times*.

Mark this: The Bush administration is willing to treat North Korea's actual possession of nuclear weapons as an international problem, deserving diplomatic approach. But Iraq's alleged possession of nuclear and biological weapons is a national problem that calls for military approach. Why this double standard?

Real Threat Comes from Pakistan

If there is any state whose possession of weapons of mass destruction poses a real problem for the United States, it is neither Iraq nor North Korea. It is a state that helped North Korea develop its clandestine nuclear weapons program. It is a state that is allied with the U.S. in its ongoing war against terrorism. The state is Pakistan.

That Pakistan possesses nuclear weapons is no secret. The possibility of some of them, or at least some portable nuclear warheads, falling into the hands of terrorists cannot be ruled out. The victory that the U.S.-led coalition achieved in Afghanistan over the Taliban and Al Qaeda has proved to be ephemeral. Reports are pouring in daily that both are regrouping in two Pakistani provinces bordering on Afghanistan and preparing for the next strike. Hereafter, they will be able to conduct their activities with impunity because the governments that came to power after the recent elections in those provinces, Baluchistan and Northwest Frontier Province, are controlled by coalitions of hardcore, anti-American Islamist parties. They openly support the Taliban and Al Qaeda. The central government's control over these provinces, vast areas of which are still governed by tribal laws, is very tenuous.

The situation at the center, Islamabad, is not all that encouraging either. The coalition of parties that took over the administration there may profess support to President Pervez Musharraf, a friend of the Bush administration. But the coalition enjoys only a wafer-thin majority over the opposition Islamist parties. May of the Islamist parties are ardent supporters of the Taliban and Al Qaeda. The latter, thanks to that support, could gain access to Pakistan's nuclear arsenal. And if they do, they will use it against the U.S. with a vengeance and with great relish.

President Bush has a military plan to deal with the perceived threat from Iraq. He has a diplomatic plan to deal with the possible threat from North Korea. Does he have any plan to deal with the probable, perhaps more imminent, threat coming from Pakistan? None that we know of.

Filial Obligation of a Son

If that is the case, why is he so obsessed with Iraq? More to the point, why is he so obsessed with Saddam Hussein? The answer has to be sought in what we set out to examine in the beginning: the filial obligation of a son to punish the man who tried to kill his father.

In mid-April 1993, there was an attempt on Bush Sr.'s life by Saddam Hussein's agents. Thank God, he escaped unhurt. Under a legal system like America's, the perpetrators of the crime could easily be brought to justice. Not under the Iraqi system. Under the latter, the law is what Saddam Hussein says it is. President Clinton's decision to mete out the punishment that would fit the crime has to be seen in that context.

On June 26, 1993, U.S. Navy ships launched 23 Tomahawk missiles against the headquarters of the Iraqi Intelligence Service. According to Clinton, it was a "firm and commensurate" response to Iraq's plan to assassinate Bush Sr. There was a reason for the choice of the target: The assassination plot was "directed and pursued by the Iraqi Intelligence Service," Clinton said in a speech on the day he ordered the attack. The missile attack did some damage to Iraq, all right. But it did nothing to the man who contrived the crime.

No son would be at ease seeing the man who made an attempt on his father's life go unpunished. Bush Jr., after nursing the grievance for as long as he could, has decided to act, it seems. Unfortunately, he doesn't seem concerned that the action he is contemplating is going to hurt others more than the person at whom it is directed. It is quite possible that Saddam would survive the next war also.

There is one more thing that may be rankling this proud son. The government-owned hotel in Baghdad, Al Rashid, which is a symbol of Iraq's modernity and status as a secular state, was mostly destroyed in the Gulf War I bombings. Soon after the war, Saddam Hussein rebuilt and restored it to its original grandeur. But the restoration was done in such a way that no guest can now enter the hotel without stepping on Bush Sr.'s face. The face is imprinted on the tiles that make up the mosaic in the foyer of the hotel. Which son won't be angered by such an insult done to his father?

So, Bush Jr.'s anger and determination to get rid of the man who disgraced his father is understandable. But should that anger be translated into the undeclared goal of a war in which thousands of people, soldiers as well as civilians, Iraqis as well as Americans, are going to be killed? The whole civilized world will be happy if it is rid of Saddam Hussein. But the way President George W. Bush is trying to accomplish it will have disastrous consequences.

3

The Rush Limbaugh of the U.S. Supreme Court Reveals His Fat

March 27, 2004

Associate Justice Antonin Scalia of the U.S. Supreme Court and talk radio host Rush Limbaugh have a few things in common. Both look strikingly alike. Both have several extra pounds of fat at wrong places. And both are paleolithic conservatives (paleocons, for short). Progressives find their views too primitive to stomach.

Until recently, I had mistakenly thought that the similarity between the two ended there. But the 21-page memorandum that Scalia issued on March 18, justifying his decision not to recuse himself from the soon-to-be-heard Supreme Court case involving his longtime buddy, Vice President Dick Cheney, has persuaded me to conclude that it didn't.

The Supreme Court case arises from an appeal by the Bush administration against a lower court decision in favor of the Sierra Club, an environmental group, and Judicial Watch, a public-interest law group. The two groups had initiated the case in the lower court when Vice President Cheney, who headed the Bush administration's energy task force that formulated its now-controversial energy policy, refused to reveal who the members of the task force are and to disclose details of its meetings. Dick Cheney is the chief defendant in the case.

Usually, judges withdraw from cases voluntarily when they suspect that their participation in them would appear improper for any reason whatsoever. They don't even wait for a request for withdrawal to come. They don't waste time writing memorandums – of even one page, let alone 21 pages – mocking at the people who ask for their withdrawal. Mere appearance of impropriety has been good enough reason for most judges to step aside.

But then, paleocons, whether in politics or in judiciary, are a different breed. Questions of concern for ordinary mortals don't bother them because they think God is always on their side. They also think that, in doing what they do, they are carrying out the will of God.

Duck-Hunting Trip

The Sierra Club had filed a petition requesting Scalia's recusal from the case. The reason for the request was that his recent duck-hunting trip to Louisiana with Dick Cheney and his acceptance of free rides on Air Force Two for himself, a son and a son-in-law could be characterized as favors, thus undermining "the prestige and credibility" of the Supreme Court. Several newspapers in the country have written editorials expressing the same view.

It is important to note here that Dick Cheney and George Bush owe their positions as vice president and president, respectively, of the country to Scalia and the other four conservative justices on the Supreme Court, including Chief Justice William Rehnquist. There are many who still believe that but for the 5-to-4 Supreme Court decision in the 2000 Bush v. Gore election case, Al Gore and Joe Lieberman would be sitting in the White House today as president and vice president. The Supreme Court decision stopped the recounting of the vote that had been ordered in a Florida county. (Remember the controversial "hanging chad" on the ballot, which had made the earlier count questionable and because of which a recount was ordered?)

The plaintiffs in the present case cannot be blamed if they suspect that Scalia's decision in the case could be swayed by a desire to offer a "Quid Pro Quack." (The quote is from Maureen Dowd's recent *New York Times* column on the controversy. One cannot think of a better play on the "quid pro quo" phrase in this context. The "quid" is a decision by Scalia in favor of the vice president for the "quo" of the duck-hunting trip aboard Air Force Two he and his entourage had received from Cheney.) Even a 2,100-page memorandum from the judge, asserting his ability to be impartial and nonpartisan, wouldn't remove the suspicion the plaintiffs raised.

Scalia is unmoved by such reasoning. "The motion is denied" is his arrogant and contemptuous response to the recusal request. He doesn't stop at that. He stoops to the level of besmirching the character of the person who sent him the recusal request. It was sent by Alan B. Morrison, in his capacity as the lead counsel representing the Sierra Club.

Morrison is also a longtime friend of Scalia's. On October 28, 2003, he had written a very warm, personal letter to his "Dear Nino." (Nino is Scalia's nickname, which only his close friends use). The purpose of the letter was to share with his friend what was happening in his life, especially the joy he felt over the prospect of taking up a teaching position at Stanford. Morrison ended the letter thus:

"Assuming we [Morrison and his wife] go to Stanford, we will be around until the summer, and perhaps we can get together before then. But if not, perhaps you will come to visit there for a few days and talk with my students: imagine the reaction if they found out we actually agree on some issues! Best to Maureen [Scalia's wife]."

At the height of the controversy over his refusal to recuse, Scalia leaked the letter to *The Wall Street Journal* which, as was expected, printed it with great relish. It did it in its March 19, 2004, issue. To enhance the effect, it was printed beside an editorial that applauded Scalia for "eviscerating their case until there's nothing left but its naked partisanship." According to the editorial, Morrison's asking Scalia to speak to his students was an invitation to "his own version of a 'hunting trip'" The editorial also gleefully declares that "Scalia's memo explaining why he won't recuse himself from [the] case … is a smackdown for the ages."

Maybe so to the *Journal* editorialists and their ilk. But to those who believe that true friendship transcends partisan politics, the leaking of the letter from a trusted friend of 30 years, especially to a paper that specializes in character assassination of people who don't subscribe to its paleolithic worldview, is the betrayal of the century.

Perception Is Important

None has ever questioned Scalia's right to be friends with people in high places. He didn't have to dig into history and cite examples – like Justice Harlan F. Stone "toss[ing] around a medicine ball with members of the Hoover administration" and Chief Justice Fred M. Vinson playing poker with President Truman – to justify his friendship and socializing with Vice President Cheney. He didn't have to go into silly details of what he did during the hunting trip – "Sleeping was in rooms of two or three, except for the vice president, who had his own quarters"; "I never hunted in the same blind with the vice president"; "none of us saved a cent by flying on the vice president's plane"; etc., etc. – to prove his ability to be impartial in the upcoming case. The question here is one of appearance of impropriety, one of perception. As an adage goes, Caesar's wife should not only be above suspicion but appear to be so, too. In other words, when the conduct of public officials is at issue, how others perceive it is what matters, not what the officials profess.

Justice Scalia's adamant refusal to step aside from this case will have the effect of its outcome being viewed as biased. It will also tarnish the image of the Supreme Court. As *The New York Times* says in its editorial of March 20, "Justice Scalia, having lowered the bar for judicial ethics by refusing to acknowledge the reasonableness of questions about his impartiality, has guaranteed that the Supreme Court will end up embarrassed, no matter which way it rules."

4

Iraq Won't Survive as a Loose Federation. India's Model Suits It Best

August 30, 2005

Iraq's draft constitution, in the form in which it is heading for referendum, is deeply flawed. If approved, it could set the stage for that country's disintegration. The consequences will be disastrous to the region and to the United States.

The proposed new constitution leaves almost untouched the autonomy the Kurds have been enjoying in the north since the early 1990's. It also contains language that would allow the majority Shiites to set up a vast autonomous area in the oil-rich south. The Sunnis of Iraq, who constitute barely 20 percent of the population, will be left to fend for themselves in the resources-poor central region. It will be only a matter of time before the Sunni region collapses as a viable political entity. No wonder all the 15 Sunni members of the constitutional committee refused to endorse the draft.

The Kurds and the Shiites on the committee decided to go ahead with the referendum plan, over the Sunnis' protests. Obviously, they have everything to gain by getting the draft approved. They also relish the idea of hurting the Sunnis who had been ruling over them until the collapse of the Saddam regime. The fate of the draft constitution will be known on October 15, 2005, when Iraqis vote on it. Those who want to see Iraq survive as one nation and prosper hope that this flawed constitution would be rejected.

President George W. Bush called it a milestone in Iraq's history and a document containing "far-reaching protections for fundamental human freedoms." His paeans of praise should not surprise anyone. Anything that makes his getting out of the mess he has created in Iraq faster is welcome to him. What comes as a surprise to most well-wishers of Iraq is that even some perceptive analysts of Iraqi politics and of Bush's policies in Iraq have found the document praiseworthy. One of them is Peter W. Galbraith, a former United States ambassador to

Croatia, a scholar and currently a senior fellow at the Center for Arms Control and Non-Proliferation.

I am disheartened to learn that the possibility of Iraq's unraveling in the course of implementing this constitution doesn't bother Mr. Galbraith. "It's not a problem if a country breaks up, only if it breaks up violently," he said, according to David Brooks's August 25, 2005, column in *The New York Times*. Even more disheartening is the reason he gives why Iraq's unraveling should not be of great concern: "Iraq wasn't created by God. It was created by Winston Churchill."

This is the kind of language that arrogant and conceited neocons and paleocons in the Bush administration are wont to use. One doesn't expect it from a person of Mr. Galbraith's caliber. Doesn't he know that the same can be said, *mutatis mutandis*, about most countries in the world, including the United States, that are former colonies?

The most laudable feature of the new constitution, according to Mr. Galbraith and its other supporters, is its emphasis on a "loose federation" for Iraq. But the critics of the document see in the very same "loose federation" idea the seed of the country's eventual breakup. Iraq is already loose as a political entity, thanks to the American invasion, say these critics, and a constitution providing for a loose federation will only reinforce that looseness. It will serve as a catalyst for disintegration. For a loose federation to survive, it should have attained some level of political maturity. It is not advisable for an infant nation, the critics say.

What Iraq needs today is a tight federation, one with a strong center. Surprisingly, the demand for it came from the representatives of the Sunni minority who joined the constitutional committee and participated in its deliberations much later. The Shiite majority and the pro-Western Kurds decided to draft at least 15 members of the Sunni community into the committee only when pressured by the Bush administration.

The Shiites and the Kurds rejected the Sunni demand for a strong center, arguing that a federation with centralized power wouldn't be different from what it was under Saddam Hussein's dictatorship. Most of the Sunni members of the panel, it may be added, were members of the Baath Party of Saddam Hussein that ruled Iraq for decades. However, their past association with the Baath Party, and its misrule, does not in any way diminish the validity of the case they make – that the right form of government for Iraq at this critical juncture is federation with a strong center.

They are not talking about a centralized authority with all powers vested in one individual or a coterie of individuals. They are talking about a system in which the central government will be stronger than the governments in the provinces; in which decisions will be made by democratically elected representatives of the people, not by a dictator; in which the rights of minorities will be protected from the tyranny of the majority; and so on. Fair-minded Iraqis owe it to their country to pay heed to these points. They owe it to their country to put pressure on their elected representatives to revise the draft of the constitution accordingly before it is put to referendum on October 15.

I also want to suggest to them that there is a vibrant constitution they can use as a model – the Indian Constitution.

Strong Center Needed

The challenge Iraq is facing today is one of binding together three ethnic groups – the Shiites, the Sunnis and the Kurds. The challenge India faced in 1947, the year in which it gained independence from Britain, was one of binding together hundreds of ethnic and linguistic groups belonging to all leading religions of the world. The founding fathers of India met the challenge by adopting a constitution, federal in nature, and adapting it to accommodate the realities of the time.

For a country like India, with more centrifugal forces than centripetal ones, keeping the country together called for a strong center. The document, which India's constituent assembly adopted on January 26, 1950, after deliberating upon it for over two years, provided for a strong central government and comparatively weak provincial governments. Looking back, it can be said that, but for that provision in the constitution, India would have splintered into as many independent entities as there are linguistic, ethnic and religious divisions in the country. Iraq would do well to emulate India's example.

There is one more point of comparison between India and Iraq. If Iraq was created by Britain's Winston Churchill, as Mr. Galbraith told Mr. Brooks, rightly if sarcastically, the political entity called India as we know it today was a creature of British rule. Before Britain began to rule India, it was a land of constantly warring kingdoms, not vastly different from what Europe was until the Second World War. If Iraq happened by design, the political entity called India happened by default. But both happened in furtherance of British interests.

True, unlike the Iraq of today, India was fortunate to have a philosopher-statesman of Plato's description to guide it in its nascent stage. It is not out of place to mention here that this philosopher-statesman, Mohandas Gandhi, was once ridiculed by Winston Churchill as a "half-naked fakir." Thanks to the guidance provided by the "half-naked fakir" in its incipient stage, India in time evolved into a developed polity and the largest democracy in the world.

Iraq may not have a Gandhi to guide it. But the Iraqis can certainly seek inspiration from his teachings and learn from India's experience.

5

NYT Columnist's Conservative Brother Destroys My Christmas Cheer

December 31, 2005

Columnist Maureen Dowd of *The New York Times* is a rarity among today's journalists. Apart from being a bold and perceptive political and social commentator, she is also an equal opportunity ego-smasher. Movers and shakers of America – be they part of the politically correct (P.C.) crowd on the left, the religiously correct (R.C.) crowd on the right, or the crafty fence-sitting variety – become eligible to receive her barbed darts, once their egos get bloated and their actions and utterances produce disastrous results. For those reasons, I became an avid reader of her column ever since it began to appear in *The Times* over a decade ago. But the one that appeared on Christmas Eve this year turned out to be a disappointment. It nearly destroyed my Christmas cheer. The fault is not entirely Maureen's, though.

President George W. Bush and Vice President Dick Cheney have been at the receiving end of her attacks more often than others. On Christmas Eve this year, in true Christmas tradition, she decided to be nice to Bush because of the gargantuan problems he has lately been facing both at home and abroad. She decided not to write anything and invited her conservative-Republican brother Kevin to fill her column space with his thoughts. To entice the president to read what her brother wrote she captioned the December 24, 2005, column "Hey, W., It's Safe! Read This."

W., on his own admission, doesn't read newspapers. But it's quite possible that he made an exception in this case and was happier for it. Kevin has poured paeans of praise on the religiously correct right for its railing against the politically correct left in the recent "Merry Christmas" versus "Happy Holidays" controversy. As we all know, the president, a born-again Christian, has always been at the forefront of the R.C. crowd. But in the process of making the president and his cronies happy, Kevin has disgraced his sister. Maureen, I have reason to believe, detests both crowds. The only redeeming feature in Kevin's piece is this line: "To Hillary [Clinton]: A hearty welcome to the Republican Party." Maureen may have had a good laugh reading that line. And there begins and ends anything good that I can say about what her brother has written.

It is very mean of Kevin to bracket Judge Jones of Pennsylvania with the P.C. crowd. What provoked Kevin to do this was Judge Jones's decision in a recent case, declaring the Christian conservatives' attempt to force schools to offer "intelligent design" as an alternative to the theory of evolution, in biology classes, as unconstitutional. The federal judge was only reaffirming the fact accepted all over the world that religion belongs in religion classes and science in science classes. One should not be taught in lieu of the other. There is nothing P.C. or R.C. about his decision. Would Kevin like to go back to the pre-Darwinian age, when his sister could as well be thinking of hitching a ride on the next space shuttle?

Too Late to Stay the Course in Iraq

It is just laughable that Kevin, in his over-enthusiasm to please President Bush, should appeal to him to "Stay the Course" in Iraq, when the whole country knows that a decision has already been made to reduce the number of American troops fighting there. Even a complete troop withdrawal is being talked about now. Until recently, such talk was considered unpatriotic. Kevin should know that "Let's fight them [terrorists] there instead of here…" was a cliché which the warmongers who instigated Iraq invasion uttered ad nauseam to justify their mission. They stopped uttering it when evidence became irrefutable that the "there" they had been referring to was the outcome of mostly faulty, and partly fabricated, intelligence analysis. When they realized that the cliché wouldn't wash with the public any longer, they stopped mouthing it. One finds it difficult to understand what prompted Kevin to revive that worn-out cliché.

Also, he is contradicting himself when he asks the president to stay the course and "bring our troops home with honor as soon as possible," in the same breath. The president has learned the hard way that if he stays the course indefinitely, there will be little honor and few troops left to bring home.

I wonder whether Kevin, before he decided to launch his tirade against the P.C. crowd for the position it took in the "Merry Christmas" versus "Happy Holidays" controversy, had read what Nicholas D. Kristof wrote in his December 11, 2005, column in *The Times*. The column, presented in the form of an imaginary dialogue at the Pearly Gates between President Bush and St. Peter, is not an endorsement of the P.C. crowd's position, though the R.C. crowd often brands him as a liberal. Kristof, like many of us, knows that the P.C. crowd was stretching its belief in secularism too far, when it demanded that the White House "Christmas Tree" be renamed "Holiday Tree" from this year onward and that, in all government-initiated season's greetings, "Merry Christmas" be replaced with "Happy Holidays."

What Kristof's imaginary dialogue does is remind the president and the rest of the R.C. crowd – "religious blowhards," as he calls them – that Christmas is not about the number of greeting cards sent out and the kind of words used in them. "It's more about feeding the hungry, clothing the naked and housing the homeless." Kevin may be pleased to know that for making pithy comments like this one, Kristof was called a "left-wing ideologue" by the standard-bearer of the R.C., Bill O'Reilly of Fox News Channel.

Kristof's Challenge to O'Reilly

[In his December 18, 2005, column, Kristof threw a challenge to O'Reilly to leave the studio of Fox News and cover a real war, like the one in Darfur, not the nonexistent "War on Christmas." "War on Christmas" was the title Fox News gave to what Kristof calls its "crusade against infidels who prefer generic expressions like 'Happy Holidays'" and to which it devoted "58 separate segments in just a five-day period."]

I am bringing up O'Reilly here for another reason: Kevin's kissing up to him. Yes, he is kissing up to O'Reilly when he says, "Thank you for dragging the P.C. crowd into the open. Maybe they will learn that America doesn't want to be de-Godded."

Doesn't Kevin know that matters Godly and O'Reilly don't go together? The man who solicited phone sex from his female coworker, and then turned around and besmirched her name when she sued him for sexual harassment, should not be pontificating on God, Christmas and subjects of that kind. According to him, anyone who disagrees with the self-righteous spin he puts on every item he presents in his Fox News program is part of the P.C. crowd deserving condemnation. Print journalists whom he dislikes are "a bunch of vicious S.O.B.'s." Such spins notwithstanding, he calls "The O'Reilly Factor," his prime-time program, "The No-Spin Zone."

O'Reilly's calling his program "The No-Spin Zone" is very much in line with Fox News's calling its entire presentation "Fair and Balanced." The network even had the audacity to claim trademark rights for its "Fair and Balanced" slogan.

Fox News trademarking "Fair and Balanced" is as laughable as a prostitute trademarking "Chastity."

6

Indian Communists Want to Go Back to the Days of the Bullock Cart?

February 18, 2006

The Industrial Revolution had bypassed India. Though the bypassing happened for no fault of Indians' – their economic and political destiny at the time was controlled by foreign powers – they were made to pay a heavy price because of it. The price was: When the West soared into the jet age, India remained in the bullock cart age.

By contrast, India has been at the forefront of the information technology (IT) revolution that began over two decades ago. It is now racing on the "information technology superhighway," ahead of many other nations. This phenomenal achievement has earned the country plaudits from around the world. The achievement was made possible mainly by the economic reforms initiated, in the 1990s, by Manmohan Singh. Dr. Singh, India's prime minister now, was finance minister at the time. But there is a danger of the country's going back to the days of the bullock cart if Indian Communists and their fellow-travelers don't give up their obscurantist attitudes toward the Manmohan Singh government's efforts to modernize India. Their obstructionist tactics are threatening to wipe out all the gains the country has made in the past two decades.

My immediate reason for raising this alarm is the four-day strike the Communists organized all over India early this month, in protest against the government's decision to privatize and modernize the international airports of New Delhi and Mumbai. In India, as we all know, taking any entity away from the control of the government is an essential first step toward modernizing it and making it work efficiently. There is no denying that the two airports – for that matter, most airports in India – badly need modernizing. Even some bus stations in advanced countries are better-looking and more efficiently run than international airports in India. But Communist and other leftist leaders in India, to whom preserving their control over airport workers is more important than making airport operations efficient and economically viable, wanted to thwart the government plan. Prodded by them, 22,000 employees at 126 airports across the country struck work for four days. If they had hoped that their action would halt the entire air traffic in India and force the government to cave in, they were disappointed. The government had a contingency plan ready to ward off any possible disruption in traffic. Airport operations continued with minimal inconvenience to passengers.

Airports Turned into Garbage Dumps

But the strikers and their leaders can take pride in having accomplished one thing, though: they "turned airports across the country into huge garbage dumps," to quote from *The Times of India* of February 5, 2006. Most of those who went on strike were cleaners and other ground workers.

Thanks to government's firm resolve, the strike fizzled out. To quote from *The Times*, again, the strikers "clutched at the straw of a written assurance from the government – to look into the issue of workers' job security and future of AAI [Airports Authority of India] in view of privatization of Delhi and Mumbai airports – to justify their retreat." Quite an "embarrassment for their political patrons, the Left."

While Prime Minister Singh personally intervened and appealed to the workers to end the strike, he made it clear to them that there was no going back on the government's decision to modernize the airports. Most Indians, and well-wishers of India around the world, applauded the prime minister for the firm stand he took. They all knew that it was not easy, given the precarious position he is in: The Congress Party to which Dr. Singh belongs does not enjoy majority in the Indian Parliament. It was able to form a government, after the 2004 general election, only when Communist and other leftist parliamentarians offered the Congress Party their support from outside, without joining the government. The Communists have been extracting a price for that support ever since: Every time they put forth a demand in furtherance of their agenda, they would preface it with a threat to withdraw their support.

The last time they did it was on September 29, 2005. To force the Singh government to abandon the plan it had drawn up to speed up its economic reforms, they led a one-day strike of airport workers, bank employees, and employees of insurance companies and of central and state governments. The strike nearly paralyzed public services in India and the government gave in by temporarily shelving the reform plan.

Six of the seven trade unions to which the strikers belonged were affiliated with parties that profess Marxism or some variant of it. It is ironic that, in India, one can still come across loud-mouthed Marxists, while in Russia and many other countries that were formerly part of the Soviet Union, which practiced Marxism for over seven decades and failed, most people despise it. The Communists in those countries have become an endangered species.

Bankruptcy of Leftist Politics

Most mainstream newspapers in India condemned the airport strike. According to *The Indian Express* of September 30, 2005, the strike showed "the sheer bankruptcy of Left politics" in India. "And what is it that the seven trade unions ... actually want?" asked *The Times of India* of the same day, in a well-balanced editorial criticism of the strike. "They want no asset sales in profitable PSUs [public sector undertakings], a lowering of overseas investment caps in sectors like telecommunication and aviation, and a restriction on foreign direct investment [FDI] in insurance, banking and retail – which could be opened up to FDI soon."

The *Times* editorial went on to explain why the trade unions' demands were short-sighted: "India's recent history shows that sectors which have received large doses of overseas capital – manufacturing, telecom, banks and financial services – have done much better than those that have not.... And the unions' Left sponsors should look to China, which attracted over 10 times the $3.4 billion FDI that India has received so far this year [2005], for clues about what posture to adopt on economic policy."

The suggestion to leftist union bosses to look to China for guidance on economic policy is well meant, I am sure. But that's the last thing they would want to do. They, like the rest of the world, know full well that China has been able to attract heavy doses of foreign capital and become the fastest-growing economy in the world today, because of its Janus-faced policy: While adhering to authoritarian communism in political and social spheres, it has been practicing crude capitalism in the economic sphere. Workers are prohibited from adopting any posture that would even remotely suggest a threat of strike. Any violation of that prohibition entails imprisonment. Can anyone expect Indian

Communists, who strike work at the drop of a hat, to look to China for inspiration?

It is laudable that India has become the second-fastest-growing economy in the world, despite the abundance of freedom its people enjoy, including the freedom of workers to strike work. None should grudge them that freedom, which is bestowed on them by India's democratic constitution. The question is: Should that freedom be misused by those who have been enjoying the benefits of the economic progress the country has been making to engage in activities that would reverse that progress?

In today's world, the best way to champion the cause of workers is to equip them to be part of the ongoing technological revolution, not instigate them to resort to counterrevolutionary tactics, to borrow a phrase from the leftist lexicon. It's about time the Indian Communists and socialists of all hues who masquerade as champions of India's working class recognized that the technological revolution that is underway in India is irreversible.

7

Republican Senator Calls an Indian American 'Macaca' and Makes a Monkey of Himself

September 5, 2006

Politicians are very good at hiding their personal prejudices and undesirable private thoughts. They do it with sugarcoated words and affectation of compassion and culture. But once in a rare while they blab, giving others a chance to peek into their true selves. In the case of Republican Senator George Allen of Virginia, that rare moment came on August 11, 2006.

He was in the small southwestern town of Breaks, campaigning to be a second-term senator from his state. Pointing to the only dark-skinned person in an otherwise all-white crowd of about 100 people, he said, "This fellow here, over here with the yellow shirt, Macaca, or whatever his name is. He's with my opponent. He's following us around everywhere. And it's just great."

His audience had a hearty laugh. A beaming Mr. Allen, who had begun his speech saying that he was "going to run this campaign on positive, constructive ideas," then went on to articulate ideas that were totally destructive and racist: "Let's give a welcome to Macaca, here. Welcome to America and the real world of Virginia."

The young man whom Mr. Allen singled out for ridicule was S. R. Sidarth, an Indian American and a fourth-year student at the University of Virginia. Sidarth could as well have turned around and told Mr. Allen, "Welcome to Virginia, you Californian carpetbagger in cowboy boots." Allen was born in California and is said to be fond of wearing cowboy boots. Sidarth, though of Indian descent, was born and brought up in Virginia. Admirably, the 20-year-old lad did not stoop to the level of the 55-year-old U.S. senator. The great-grandson of a man who had accompanied Mahatma Gandhi, as his secretary, to the famous 1931 Round Table Conference in London, held in response to Indians' demand for self-rule, he is too cultured to do that.

One can think of only two reasons why Sidarth was picked as a target for ridicule: he looked different from the rest of the crowd; and he was working for James Webb, Allen's Democratic Party opponent in the senate race. As a volunteer for the Webb campaign, he had been following the Republican senator around with a video camera, recording his travels and speeches. As we all know, it is an accepted practice in American politics.

Colored Immigrant

What does Macaca mean? It could mean different things, depending on the context in which it is used. It could mean a monkey. Or, in the sense in which it is used in France and some other European countries, it could mean a colored immigrant, the equivalent of wog. Senator Allen, the son of an immigrant mother who grew up as a French Tunisian, certainly knew what the word meant when he used it. He should know that he was making a monkey of himself when, in an effort to put out the firestorm his gaffe had created, he repeatedly said that he did not know what it meant.

He told Managing Editor Aziz Haniffa of *India Abroad* that he "would have spelled it m-e-k-a-k-a." In his interview with Mr. Haniffa, published in the weekly's September 1, 2006, edition, he also said that if he "actually knew it was an insulting phrase or word, of course, I would not have used" it. Thank God he didn't say he meant it as a compliment.

An educated person who has two university degrees under his belt, a lawyer by profession, a former governor of a state, a former member of the House of Representatives and current member of the U.S. Senate using a word the meaning of which he did not know? Whom is he trying to fool? And nobody believed, either, the explanation he gave to the "Welcome to America and the real world of Virginia" part of his insult. This is what he said he meant: "Just to the real world. Get outside the Beltway and get to the real world."

What a belabored explanation! He should know that the camera doesn't lie. The glee and scorn with which he uttered those words made it clear that he welcomed the young Indian American as though he were someone from another planet.

Mr. Allen's communications director, John Reid, came up with a creative explanation for the senator's use of the word Macaca: Allen campaign workers had nicknamed Mr. Sidarth "Mohawk" because he would not disclose his name. They came up with that name because of his hairstyle. According to Mr. Reid, the senator was playing on the word Mohawk when he called Sidarth Macaca, not trying to stamp a "foreigner" label on him.

The explanation, apart from being stupid, was a lie. It was stupid because Sidarth's hairstyle is a mullet, tight on top, long in the back. It was a lie because Sidarth had already been introduced to Mr. Allen and others in his campaign. In an interview with CNN, Sidarth said that he remembered the senator making special effort to pronounce his name correctly, when he was introduced to him. Jessica Smith, press secretary for the Webb campaign, also confirms the fact that Mr. Sidarth had been introduced to the senator prior to the incident and that his staff knew who he was.

Because of twisted explanations and lies like these, the apology he has been offering lately – a direct apology to Sidarth was offered only 12 days after the incident – carried little weight. Many people even find it insincere. They say it is a desperate attempt to win back the support he lost in the wake of the controversy. Let's see whether he succeeds.

There are other reasons, too, why people find it difficult to accept his apology as sincere. Even as he was profusely apologizing, his campaign staff was trying to silence the critics with the accusation that they were blowing it out of proportion. According to them, the controversy was the handiwork of the liberal media, Democrats and Internet bloggers.

The performance of Mr. Allen's campaign manager, Dick Wadhams, also contributed a great deal to making the senator's apology appear insincere. A few hours before he first apologized to Sidarth, through *Washington Post* staff writers, Tim Craig and Michael D. Shear, Mr. Wadhams had dismissed the whole episode with an expletive, and insisted that the senator had "nothing to apologize for." In a memo sent to fellow Republicans, which was signed on August 19, 2006, and titled "Notes on a tough week," he said that the Webb campaign and the news media had ganged up "to create national news over something that did not warrant coverage in the first place." Wadhams blamed them for "[l]iterally putting words into Senator Allen's mouth that he did not say...."

If that is so, people are asking, why did Mr. Allen apologize? And why should anyone take that apology seriously?

Racist Past

This would have been dismissed as a faux pas, had there been no racist blots on Mr. Allen's past. There are quite a few: He had once hung a noose in his law office (when pointed out, he said it had "nothing to do with lynching"); in 1984, as a member of the Virginia House of Delegates, he had opposed creating a state holiday honoring the Rev. Martin Luther King Jr.; he had voted against changing a racially offensive state song; he had displayed the Confederate flag on several occasions; he had featured the flag in his first statewide television ad in Virginia; after being elected governor of Virginia in 1993, he had signed a Confederate Heritage Month proclamation that described the Civil War as "a four-year struggle for independence and states' rights"; he had opposed the 1991 Civil Rights Act; and, as recently as 2002, during the Trent Lott controversy over his praise of segregationist Strom Thurmond's 1948 presidential candidacy, he first defended Senator Lott, but became a critic only after Lott's ouster as senate majority leader became certain.

The important question Virginians have to ask themselves when they vote in the November election is: Does a man with such a racist past, and is not completely cured of it yet, deserve to be their senator, again? And, since his name has been bandied about as a possible Republican presidential candidate in the 2008 election, all Americans must ask themselves: Should such a man be even dreaming of becoming the president of the United States at a time when its popularity around the world has sunk to the lowest point?

8

Priests at Puri Jagannath Temple Disgrace Hinduism

March 13, 2007

All progressive-minded Hindus must have hung their heads in shame at the news: that the priests of Puri's Jagannath Temple fined an American for the 'sin' he committed of having entered the temple. The questions they all must now be asking are: Are there no legal authorities in India to challenge the audacious act of those priests? Who in the world gave them the authority to impose fine on anyone? Are they getting fattened and battened by the offerings of devotees, many of whom are from abroad, to bring disgrace to Hinduism? Where in the Hindu scriptures is it said that a devotee cannot enter a Hindu place of worship simply because he was born into a different religion or nation? For that matter, where in the scriptures is the word Hindu used or defined?

Ever since a few 18th century British visitors to the Jagannath Temple, in the Indian state of Orissa, described in astonishing terms the spectacle they witnessed, it became a place of great attraction for Westerners. The spectacle the Britons witnessed was the annual Ratha Yatra (chariot procession) the temple is famous for. They were wonderstruck at the sight of the 45-foot-tall, multi-ton chariot carrying the idol of Jagannath (literally meaning the Lord of the Universe), which is one of the synonyms of Lord Vishnu, being pulled by devotees; and at the sight of some of them even throwing themselves in front of the chariot. They described what they saw as "juggernaut," which was how the word Jagannath came across to them. Their description also gave birth to a new word in the English language.

The etymological origin of the word and exaggerated stories about the chariot procession made Jagannath Temple very popular in the West. It owes a great deal of its fame and prosperity to its Western visitors. In denying entry to it to one such visitor, the priests have disgraced not only the temple and India, but also Hinduism. As C.N.N. Nair, a reader of *The Asian Age*, a popular Indian daily, says in his letter, published in the March 5, 2007, edition of the paper, "It is ironic that this denial of entry is practiced by the followers of a Lord [Lord Krishna] who had categorically proclaimed, 'To me all beings are equal; I have no favorites, nor enemies.'" Mr. Nair's quote is from the *Bhagavad Gita*. Do the priests believe in what is said in the *Gita*?

It's the all-embracing nature of Hinduism, its adaptability, its tolerance, and its absolute respect for individuality and individual freedom that enabled it to survive years of onslaught by foreign invaders. The most admirable feature of the religion is that one can choose one's own path and still reach Him. "You can reach Him through football," said Swami Vivekananda, the famous Indian sage who introduced Hinduism to the United States, in the 19th century. Religious labels have no place in Hinduism. It is the way of life one chooses that qualifies or disqualifies him or her for entry into God's premises. The American who traveled thousands of miles to be on the premises of a temple dedicated to the Lord of the Universe more than qualifies for it. In saying that his presence made the premises "impure" and punishing him for that reason, the priests of Puri have stooped to the level of Osama bin Laden, the number one terrorist in the world today.

The main reason given by bin Laden for instigating the carnage his followers committed in America on September 11, 2001, was that Americans' presence on the soil of Saudi Arabia polluted Islam's holy places in that country. Not for a moment did he pause to think that Saudi Arabia owes its security and prosperity, which in turn enabled his family to amass immense wealth by doing business in that country, to Americans' presence there.

So also, the Jagannath Temple of Puri and famous temples elsewhere in India owe their prosperity and fame partly to the generous contributions and writings of Americans and other foreigners. There are collection pots placed on the premises of almost all temples. Why don't the priests put warning labels on those pots prohibiting foreigners to put their "impure" money into them? They won't because they know their potbellies will begin to shrink when contributions from foreigners stop.

Traveling around the world is one of my passions in life. If the place I am in is also home to a famous temple, church, mosque, or pagoda, I make it a point to visit that religious site. It is intellectual curiosity and a fascination for history, more than anything else, that draw me to it. At no time and in no place have I ever been asked by the authorities of that place what religion I belong to. And in no place have I seen any warning sign put up preventing people belonging to certain religious denominations from entering that place. Except, of course, in some Hindu temples of India. It's about time the authorities of those temples gave up their medieval mentality of treating everything foreign as *mlechha* (impure). Most foreigners who come to Hindu temples come there with more admiration and respect than many Hindus I know have.

Tamil Tigers Roam Rameshwaram

The *Asian Age* letter referred to above goes on to ask: "Aren't there any atheists, criminals and other anti-social elements in Hinduism who enter the temple? Why aren't they stopped?"

The questions remind me of a brief conversation I had with an assistant at the famous Rameshwaram Temple, in the southern Indian state of Tamil Nadu, during my recent visit there. The assistant asked my name while guiding me through the temple's labyrinthine complex. When I told him "Prabhakaran," his face lit up.

"That name is very popular around here. He is a hero to many," he said.

"So, you like Velupillai Prabhakaran, eh?" I asked.

"Of course, who doesn't? He is a good man," he replied.

Mark it: Velupillai Prabhakaran, head of the Liberation Tigers of Tamil Eelam (LTTE), a terrorist organization in Sri Lanka that has been fighting to create a separate homeland for the Tamil minority in that country, is a very popular figure in the holy city of Rameshwaram. The inlet of the Bay of Bengal between Sri Lanka and Rameshwaram, it may be noted, is less than 16 miles wide. Rumors are rife that many wanted terrorists belonging to the LTTE have crossed over to the city and are roaming the premises of Rameshwaram Temple. Both the city and the temple are named after Lord Rama. Legend has it that the temple was founded by Lord Rama himself.

To throw in an aside, a few days after my visit to Rameshwaram, I ran into a German at the airport at Madurai, another holy city in Tamil Nadu. She told me, during our brief conversation, that she excluded Rameshwaram from her itinerary because of the rumors of Tamil Tigers' presence there.

It is a shame that the priests who act in the name of God have problem allowing law-abiding foreigners on the premises of their temple, but none whatsoever when it comes to terrorists. All they are concerned about is the Hindu stamp on the visitors' faces.

Biggest Sinners Are the Priests

In entering a temple dedicated to the Lord of the Universe, the American did not commit any sin, the Puri priests may note. The Lord embraces all who come to Him, as long as they come with no evil intentions. The biggest sinners here are the priests who punished him. And they made their sin unforgivable when they destroyed the food that was prepared as *prasada* for thousands of devotees. The reason for doing it, according to their sick minds, was that a Christian's presence inside the temple had made the food "impure." As Mr. Nair says in his *Asian Age* letter, "The food could have been given to the hundreds of beggars around the temple complex." That would have expiated their sin of punishing a devout visitor to the temple, I may add.

"*Loka Samasta Sukhino Bhavanthu* [Let happiness happen to the entire world]," says the famous Hindu prayer. My request to Puri priests is: Please stop chanting it unless you want hypocrisy to be added to the list of sins you have already committed.

9
The 'Hindu Taliban' May Take India Back to the Paleolithic Age

June 8, 2007

The Muslim Taliban who ruled Afghanistan from 1996 to 2001 nearly succeeded in taking that country back to the Neolithic Age. The 'Hindu Taliban,' those who have been masquerading as the guardians of Hindu culture, could take India further back, to the Paleolithic Age, unless they are stopped right now. The initiative to stop this motley crowd, belonging to the Bharatiya Janata Party, the Vishwa Hindu Parishad, the Shiv Sena, and such other Hindu-sectarian organizations, must come from progressive-minded Hindus. The latter, fortunately, are in a majority. Unfortunately, however, the authorities in India often act as the enablers of the obscurantist minority among Hindus. A few recent cases would substantiate the point.

We all know that Hollywood actor Richard Gere loves India, visits the country several times a year, and is a driving force behind many worthy causes aimed at helping India. Combating AIDS is one of those causes. Indians will always be indebted to him for the efforts he has been making to bring India's AIDS problem to the awareness of the rest of the world. They want him to know that those who reacted unreasonably to what he did at a rally in New Delhi on April 15, 2007, are in a tiny minority.

The Fuss Over a Kiss

The rally was organized to promote AIDS awareness among India's truck-drivers. With him on the stage, holding his hand, was Bollywood actress Shilpa Shetty. In a playful moment, he turned toward Ms. Shetty, embraced her, twisted and turned her, and kissed her on the cheek. Ms. Shetty played along, and the crowd enjoyed it. But the 'Hindu Taliban' took offense to it. According to them, it was un-Indian to kiss in public. They held protest rallies and burned effigies of Gere and photos of Shetty. Mr. Gere's "sincere apology" and his explanation – "my clumsy attempt at a 'Shall We Dance' dance move was a naïve misread of Indian customs" – did not pacify them. Nor were they restrained by Ms. Shetty's calling them a "lunatic fringe" and her wish that they had focused on "AIDS awareness, and not three pecks on her cheek."

More than the behavior of the moral brigade, it's the performance in this connection of a judge in a court in Jaipur, Rajasthan, that most people find laughable. The judge was deciding on a citizen's complaint filed by a member of the moral brigade. Instead of dismissing the complaint as a baby's cry for attention, Dinesh Gupta, the judge, characterized the kiss as "highly sexually erotic" and even criticized Ms. Shetty for not resisting it. He charged the couple with "obscene behavior" and issued warrants for their arrest. It's a shame that a judge in India, a country which has a movie theater at every other street corner, showing movies with love scenes that leave nothing to the viewers' imagination, should find a playful kiss of a man on the cheek of a woman "highly sexually erotic." The noble cause the man and the woman were promoting did not mean anything to the judge.

A Celebrated Painter Goes into Exile

The case mentioned above and the judge's verdict on it bring to mind the numerous other cases that are now pending in various Indian courts against the celebrated Indian painter M. F. Husain. Those cases, too, stemmed from the moral outrage of the 'Hindu Taliban.' The most recent case, filed in a court in the state of Gujarat, pertains to a painting by Mr. Husain, captioned "Bharat Mata [Mother India]."

The painting depicts a nude woman, with the names of Indian states scribbled on various parts of her body. The judge presiding over the case ordered that Mr. Husain's house in Mumbai be confiscated as punishment for his non-appearance in court on the day of the hearing. Mr. Husain responded that he was not aware of any summons requiring his court appearance. The laughable thing about the court order is that the house in question is no longer in Husain's name. [It has since been reported that the Supreme Court of India has stayed the Gujarat court's order.]

The main charge against Mr. Husain in almost all cases – there are about 900, Mr. Husain told a reporter recently – is that he has been portraying Hindu gods and goddesses in the nude. For doing that, in 1988, the Bajrang Dal, a Hindu-extremist group, attacked his house and destroyed his artworks. In February 2006, he was arrested and charged with "hurting sentiments of people." One Hindu group even offered a reward of $11.5 million to anyone who would murder Mr. Husain.

Harassment by the 'Hindu Taliban' and a legal system that willingly cooperates with them forced Husain to go into exile. The 91-year-old artist, whom *Forbes* magazine had once called the "Picasso of India," now spends his time between Dubai and England. Though he has told journalists who met him that he is feeling "extremely homesick" and that "I am missing my country," he has been advised by his lawyers to stay away from India for the time being.

The editorial in the May 8, 2007, edition of *The Hindu*, an Indian daily known for its balanced opinion on social issues, speaks for all right-minded people when it says: "There is something terribly amiss about a social order that coerces a law-abiding 91-year-old artist – India's most celebrated painter – into leaving the country because of harassment by rank communalists and moral vigilantes. There is also something lopsided about the priorities of a criminal justice system that orders the attachment of his properties when cases against hardened criminals drag on interminably."

The editorial ends with this profound observation: "There is little doubt that the criminal cases against Mr. Husain will fail. But the mischief-makers may have already succeeded – because the process has become the punishment, especially for a nonagenarian free spirit."

Another Victim of the Moral Brigade

The most recent victim of the Hindu moral brigade is a young graduate student. In this case, too, the brigade is from Gujarat State. As part of the course requirements for his master's degree in fine arts from the state's prestigious Maharaja Sayajirao University, Srilamathula Chandramohan, the graduate student, had submitted a digital enlargement of a painted work depicting a female form with many arms, wielding weapons and giving birth. Obviously, the work alluded to a Hindu goddess. It was later exhibited on the wall of the university's art department.

A Hindu fanatic by the name of Neeraj Jain, who is a lawyer by profession and belongs to the Bharatiya Janata Party, found the work offensive to Hindu culture. Accompanied by police officers and television news teams, he barged into the art department and got Mr. Chandramohan arrested and sent to jail on the charge of "deliberately offending religious sentiments."

Reporting on the incident in the May 19, 2007, edition of *The New York Times*, Somini Sengupta, the paper's New Delhi correspondent, quotes Mr. Jain as saying: "I cannot tolerate any insult to our culture and to our gods and goddesses."

The question most Hindus have for this vigilante lawyer is: Who in the world made him, a fellow with a primitive view of Hinduism, *the* spokesman for Hindu culture? The message I have for him is: Go get a life. Leave my religion alone.

A lawyer-politician craving for publicity – why else did he take TV news teams with him? – acting and speaking in this manner doesn't surprise most people. According to them, he and his fellow goons marched into the university and seized the student's artwork in pursuance of their political and personal agendas. But they do ask: Doesn't the head of a university have a responsibility to stop them, if, in the process of pursuing their agenda, they interfere with the university's academic activities and destroy its reputation? Regrettably, vice chancellor Manoj Soni of the university did nothing to stop them. In fact, according to news reports, he extended his full cooperation to the hooligans and urged the police to arrest his student. Most people find Mr. Soni's behavior despicable.

His despicable behavior did not stop at that. In protest against Chandramohan's arrest, many other students had held an exhibition of several artworks, which they pulled out from the archives of the art department and which they knew would offend the self-styled champions of Hindu morals. The vice chancellor approached the acting dean of the department and demanded an apology and ordered him to close the exhibition. Shivaji Panikkar, the acting dean, refused. And for that, he lost his job.

The courage and integrity of Mr. Panikkar, who has given 27 years of his life to the university and its art department, have earned him admiration and applause from academics, artists and art lovers around India. Rallies held in various cities condemned the university authorities, police and the Hindu chauvinists responsible for the ugly incident.

Mr. Chandramohan, after spending five days in jail, was released on bail. Fearing further harassment from Hindu activists, he went into hiding.

Meanwhile, Neeraj Jain, the chief architect of the ugly incident, is reported to be basking in the glory of his success. There is no denying that Mr. Jain's arrogance and conceit come from the fact that Maharaja Sayajirao University is a state-run institution; that the state that runs it is Gujarat; and that the elected government which is in power in Gujarat is led by the Bharatiya Janata Party to which he belongs. He doesn't realize that, very often, the activities he and his ilk are engaged in, in the name of preserving Hindu culture, go against the very tenets of that culture. He doesn't accept the basic principle that a piece of art is beheld in as many ways as there are beholders and interpreted in as many ways. Instead of basking in glory, he must be ashamed that it was his warped interpretation of the student's artwork that started the storm, which in turn destroyed the reputation of a university.

Freedom of Worship in Hinduism

Gods and goddesses in the Hindu pantheon have been portrayed from time immemorial in as many forms and shapes as the imagination of the portrayer permitted. They have been portrayed naked and they have been portrayed fully clothed. Hinduism gives one the freedom to choose and worship any, or all, of them. Hinduism also gives one the freedom to reject all of them and worship a shapeless, formless cosmic spirit. One who worships nothing at all, and seeks guidance only from reason, is also a Hindu. There is no excommunication in Hinduism.

There are Hindus who worship Linga (penis). There are Hindus who worship Yoni (vagina). There are temples, dedicated to Lord Krishna, which have sculptures, paintings and carvings showing him in every imaginable form of sexual activity with his Gopis. Among the many things that earned India fame around the world are the erotic sculptures in the temples of Khajuraho and uninhibited sexual acts described in *Kama Sutra*. The world should thank itself that there were no 'Hindu Taliban' at the time these masterpieces were created.

10

How Clarence Thomas Played the Race Card and Lied to Get on U.S. Supreme Court

October 16, 2007

Clarence Thomas (left) and Anita Hill, being sworn in for testimony at the 1991 Senate Judiciary Committee hearings on Thomas's nomination to the U.S. Supreme Court. At the hearings, Prof. Hill gave a graphic description of the kind of sexual harassment by Thomas she had endured, when she worked under him, first at the U.S. Department of Education, and then at the Equal Employment Opportunity Commission. The all-male, all-white Judiciary Committee refused to take her allegations seriously. Thomas was confirmed as an Associate Justice of the Supreme Court by a narrow 52-48 majority in the full-Senate vote. (*The picture is reproduced courtesy Eric Ortiz*/NBC News/bing.com.)

•

"What's the difference between a low-tech lynching and a high-tech lynching?" asks Frank Rich, in his October 7, 2007, column in *The New York Times*. He answers the question himself: "A high-tech lynching brings a tenured job on the Supreme Court and a $1.5 million book deal. A low-tech lynching, not so much."

The book Mr. Rich is referring to is the U.S. Supreme Court Justice Clarence Thomas's recently published autobiography, *My Grandfather's Son: A Memoir*. Rich is right: Mr. Thomas owes his elevation to the Supreme Court to his colorful, if angry, characterization of the Senate Judiciary Committee hearings on his nomination as "a high-tech lynching."

The racially charged characterization came during his rebuttal of the accusation of sexual harassment made against him by his one-time subordinate, Anita Hill. At the time of the 1991 Senate hearings, Ms. Hill was a professor of law at the University of Oklahoma and Mr. Thomas a federal appeals court judge in Washington, D.C.

In her testimony before the Senate committee, presented on October 11, 1991, Ms. Hill gave a graphic description of the nature of the sexual harassment she was subjected to by Mr. Thomas, while working as his assistant in 1981-83. She worked with him first in the Department of Education and later at the Equal Employment Opportunity Commission, both in the Republican administration of President Ronald Reagan. She testified that Mr. Thomas used to make her feel "extremely uncomfortable" by persistently asking her out, despite her saying no, and by talking to her about the size of his penis and about things of that nature. "He spoke about acts that he had seen in pornographic films, involving such matters as women having sex with animals and films showing group sex or rape scenes. He talked about pornographic materials depicting individuals with large penises or large breasts involved in various sex acts. On several occasions Thomas told me graphically of his own sexual prowess," Hill told the committee.

Judge Thomas denied "unequivocally, uncategorically [sic] ... each and every single allegation." At one point in his lengthy, angry rebuttal, he did something which neither the senators who questioned him nor the public at large who watched the proceedings on TV had expected: He played the race card. "This is a circus," he said. "It is a national disgrace. And from my standpoint, as a black American, as far as I am concerned, it is a high-tech lynching for uppity blacks who in any way deign to think for themselves, to do for themselves, to have different ideas, and it is a message that, unless you kowtow to an old order, this is what will happen to you, you will be lynched, destroyed, caricatured by a committee of the U.S. Senate rather than hung from a tree."

That did it. Until then, at least the Democratic members of the committee had been asking probing questions on Prof. Hill's accusations. Once Thomas compared what they were doing to the lynching the blacks in the country suffered, until not long ago, at the hands of the Ku Klux Klan, even they felt uncomfortable continuing their probe. Remember, it was an all-white Senate panel. Republican senators, on their part, accused Hill of "erotomania" and perjury. Senator Orrin Hatch of Utah even accused her of making up her testimony from her reading of *The Exorcist*.

Those of us who watched the Senate hearings had thought that "high-tech lynching" was a phrase Mr. Thomas uttered extempore in an angry outburst. His autobiography proves us wrong. The phrase was deliberately incorporated in the rebuttal, which he had prepared at his mentor Senator John Danforth's office, with the senator "watching over me like a guardian angel." This is how he says it happened:

"Jack had been writing down possible points for me to make.… [T]he thoughts that had been running through my head for the past half-hour crystallized into a single phrase. 'Jack,' I said, 'this is a high-tech lynching.'

"'If that's what you think,' he replied, 'then say it.'

"I took his pad and scrawled 'HIGH-TECH LYNCHING' under his list of talking points.

"Somewhere in the back of my mind, I must have been thinking of *To Kill a Mocking Bird*, in which Atticus Finch, a small-town southern lawyer, defends Tom Robinson, a black man on trial for the rape of a white woman."

Mr. Thomas is wrong in one important respect, though: In this case, both the accuser and the accused are black. One of them spoke the truth and the other one lied. No other human being had witnessed what happened between the two. I hope Mr. Thomas, who invokes God and the Bible at the drop of a hat, wouldn't have problem accepting this: God has witnessed what happened between him and Anita Hill and, one day, the truth will out.

No Opinion on Roe v. Wade?

However, we don't have to wait until then to point out that he was not being truthful in answering some of the questions put to him at the hearings. For example, every time he was asked to give his opinion on a woman's right to an abortion under the U.S. Constitution, his stock reply was that he had not given sufficient thought to the subject and so had not formed any opinion on it. In response to Senator Patrick Leahy's questions, he even went to the extent of saying that he had never discussed Roe v. Wade, the most important case on the subject ever taken up by the U.S. Supreme Court. When asked whether the fetus has status as a person under the Constitution, he paused for long, keeping the senators in suspense, and then came up with the answer: "I cannot think of any cases that have held that."

Millions of viewers around the country were quite surprised that a nominee to the Supreme Court was allowed to get away with the kind of answers he gave. When the Supreme Court issued its landmark decision in Roe v. Wade, upholding a woman's constitutional right to terminate her pregnancy if she so chooses, millions of women in the country had heaved sighs of relief. However, the January 22, 1973, decision instantly became controversial and stirred heated discussions among academics, lawyers and in the media. Even high school students participated in those discussions. Mr. Thomas, who at the time was a student at Yale Law School, one of the prestigious law schools in the country, had not participated in any such discussions? Whom was he kidding?

Equally shocking was the answer he gave to the question whether the fetus has constitutional status as a person. The historic verdict in Roe v. Wade, written by Justice Harry Blackmun, had held that "the word 'person,' as used in the Fourteenth Amendment [to the Constitution], does not include the unborn." If not anyone else, a federal appeals court judge was expected to know this pivotal point in the verdict. Instead of saying no and reaffirming what Justice Blackmun said, Thomas gave a noncommittal reply that he "cannot think of any cases that have held that." He dared not utter a word that would antagonize the ultraconservative anti-abortion lobby in the country.

The question came up again during his interview on CBS's "60 Minutes," on September 30, 2007. When asked by Steve Kroft, the CBS correspondent who conducted the interview, about the answers he gave on abortion and the status of fetus, during the 1991 Senate hearings, he said: "The issue was abortion. That's the issue today. That was the elephant in the room." Many people who had watched the 1991 Senate hearings had come away with the feeling that Thomas was not being truthful in answering the questions put to him by senators. His "60 Minutes" interview has now proved them right.

Toward the end of the interview, Steve Kroft pointed out what struck him as "One of the most surprising things" in Mr. Thomas's autobiography: "'Like most Americans,'" Mr. Kroft read from the book, "'I had mixed emotions about abortion. I wasn't comfortable telling others what to do in that difficult circumstance.'"

Justice Thomas's response: "There are tough decisions we have to make in life. And of course, we all feel about that. People think that because you might agree or disagree with them on certain things, that you don't have that concern about people who are left with tough choices. You do have that concern. But none of that had anything to do with what's in the Constitution. The point is simply this. The Constitution is what matters. Not my personal views, whatever they may be. And I don't go around expressing them on that issue."

If that's the case, why didn't he say so during the confirmation hearings? Why did he confuse and frustrate the senators who questioned him on the subject, and millions of those who watched the hearings, with his convoluted, evasive, and untruthful answers?

Narrow Victory Prompts Hasty Swearing-In

Even after his "high-tech lynching" accusation intimidated some senators into switching sides and voting to confirm him – though by a narrow 52-48 margin – his joining the Court could not be guaranteed until he was administered the oath of office by the chief justice.

The White House hastily held an unofficial swearing-in ceremony on its South Lawn, on October 18, just three days after the Senate vote. The date for the official ceremony which it had decided earlier, with the consent of Chief Justice William Rehnquist, was November 1, full 17 days after the senate vote. Anything could happen in the interim. The media were still at work, trying to prove or disprove Hill's charges and Thomas's denial. Supporters of Hill were also busy collecting evidence to substantiate her charges. Because of all this, White House officials wanted to move the oath-taking to a date earlier than November 1. But they had a problem: Chief Justice Rehnquist was in mourning. His wife had died on October 17. They agonized for some time over what to do.

Finally, as legal analyst and TV commentator Jeffrey Toobin says in his recent best-seller, *The Nine: Inside the Secret World of the Supreme*

Court, they "decided the stakes were high enough to risk offending Rehnquist, so they asked him to administer the oath to Thomas only days after Nan Rehnquist's death. The chief agreed, and the swearing in took place on Oct. 23 in a conference room at the Court, the first such private ceremony in fifty years. The official explanation for the speeded-up procedure was to allow Thomas's secretaries and clerks to get on the Supreme Court payroll."

Bah! What a convincing explanation! It's as convincing as what Mr. Thomas says in his book about the episode: that he "had wrongly supposed that the White House ceremony was sufficient."

Mr. Thomas can thank the Holy Ghost, whose name has been invoked several times in his book, that the White House expedited the official oath-taking. To quote from Mr. Toobin's book, again, "That same day, according to Jane Mayer and Jill Abramson, three reporters for the *Washington Post* 'burst into the newsroom almost simultaneously with information confirming that Thomas' involvement with pornography far exceeded what the public had been led to believe.' They had testimony from eyewitnesses and the manager of a video store where Thomas rented such fare. But since Thomas had been sworn in, the *Post* decided not to pursue the issue and dropped the story."

It's hard to tell what would have happened if those reporters had come up with the information a day earlier and if *The Washington Post* had published the story. What is important is that Clarence Thomas officially became an associate justice of the Supreme Court of the United States, on October 23, 1991.

Considering what he went through during the confirmation process, even his critics had no problem granting him his legitimate right to declare victory and to savor it. But they had also expected him to be magnanimous in victory. They had expected the man, who never tired of tom-toming to the world how deep his faith in God was, to forgive his enemies and move on. But the muckraking he has done in his book, and during his TV network tours to promote it, has let them down. They have realized, to their utter disappointment, that he still harbors hatred for those who opposed his nomination.

Anita Hill, the main target of his hatred, has already responded to the "litany of unsubstantiated representations and outright smears that Republican senators made about me when I testified before the Judiciary Committee," which Mr. Thomas has repeated in his book. "The Smear

This Time," her article in *The New York Times* of October 2, 2007, in which she gave her response, also addresses the derisive remarks Mr. Thomas made about her religious conviction. He had remarked, during his "60 Minutes" interview, that "She was not the demure, religious, conservative person that they [high-tech lynching mob?] portrayed."

She calls it "a particularly nasty blow" and goes on to prove how unfounded it is: "Perhaps he conveniently forgot that he wrote a letter of recommendation for me to work at the law school at Oral Roberts University, in Tulsa [Oklahoma]." She had taught there for three years. Would she have survived as a teacher for three years, at an evangelical Christian university, unless she was religious and conservative?

Conclusion

A democracy, it can be said, is a marketplace for varied ideas – political, social and economic. Sometimes those ideas conflict with one another. But democracy also has institutions that provide means for resolving such conflicts. The most revered and authoritative among those institutions is the court of law. In America, the most powerful democracy in the world, we now have sitting on the highest court of law a justice who portrays people with ideas that are at variance with his as part of a lynch mob. God save America!

11

How U.S. Democrats, Indian Communists & *NY Times* Tried to Block Indo-U.S. Nuclear Deal and Failed

October 4, 2008

After a three-year journey, often on bumpy roads, the Indo-U.S. civilian nuclear cooperation agreement is set to become law. With its passage in the U.S. Senate by an 86-to-13 vote, on October 1, 2008, the only thing left to be done is the signing of it by the president. President George W. Bush has said that he is enthusiastically looking forward to doing it.[*]

The tenacity with which the Bush administration pursued it and the tirelessness with which Indian Americans and American well-wishers of India worked on it have now been rewarded. The administration can be justifiably proud of having achieved a rare foreign policy victory. With this achievement, President Bush has also established a strong personal bond with India.

Criticisms of the deal and attempts at blocking it came from India as well as the U.S. Those that came from India did not surprise anyone. They were orchestrated by that endangered species called the communists. That the ultimate goal of the deal is to quicken the pace of India's march to prosperity did not appease them one bit. Anything that has to do with capitalist United States is anathema to Indian communists.

---

[*]*UPDATE: President Bush signed the nuclear agreement into law, at a ceremony at the White House, on October 8, 2008. Among those who attended the ceremony were more than 100 Indian Americans, whose hard work was a significant factor in bringing the agreement to its fruition. To the applause and cheers of all who attended the ceremony, the president declared: "This agreement sends a signal to the world: Nations that follow the path of democracy and responsible behavior will find a friend in the United States of America. The American people are proud of our strong relationship with India. And I am confident that the friendship between our two nations will grow even closer in the years ahead." The agreement became operational on October 10, when it was signed and sealed by India's External Affairs Minister Pranab Mukherjee and U.S. Secretary of State Condoleezza Rice.*

Do they realize that China, the country they look up to as their Mecca, has no problem entering into all sorts of deals with the United States and other capitalist countries? Have they heard any criticism from the Chinese of any deal their country wants to conclude with any other country or have already concluded? If there was any, the Chinese leadership had seen to it that it was silenced forever. That's why nobody heard about it.

Indian Communists Live in a Vibrant Democracy

The fact that such a fate hasn't befallen the Indian communists is a testimony to India's being a developed democratic polity. Where else can we see political ideologies that are totally opposed to one another functioning side by side? Indian communists should be grateful that they are living in a vibrant democracy, not a stifling dictatorship like China. Mark this: When this agreement with the U.S. eventually yields the intended benefits, the communists will be the first in line to grab them.

The Indian communists' behavior did not surprise those who were determined to push the agreement to its conclusion. But they were surprised, even appalled, by the criticism that came from within the U.S. More than the criticism, it was the sources of that criticism that the supporters of the deal found appalling. Most of the politicians who criticized the deal and tried hard to block it belonged to the Democratic Party. And the leading media critic of the deal was *The New York Times*.

Historically, it has been the Democratic, not the Republican, Party that supported India on matters that are vital to its well-being. The Indian Americans overwhelmingly voted Democratic in all past elections. They were shocked to learn that if Democrats had their way, this deal would have died in U.S. Congress.

In the House of Representatives, which passed it on September 27, 2008, 107 of the 117 votes that were cast against it came from Democrats. Thanks to the Republican members of the House, 178 of whom voted for the agreement, it passed by a comfortable 298-117 margin. A two-third majority is a constitutional requirement for the passage of all international agreements.

When the Senate passed the agreement by an 86-to-13 vote, on October 1, 2008, Indian Americans were ecstatic. But the Democrats among them felt let down when they learned that all 13 dissenting votes came from senators belonging to their party. We will know the extent of their wrath when those senators are up for reelection. That goes for the members of the House who voted against the agreement, too.

Performance of the Media

Indians and friend of India also found the performance of some of the media very disappointing. Making the disappointment bitter was the fact that at the forefront of the media that tried to block the deal was their favorite newspaper, *The New York Times*. The paper wrote editorial after editorial, trashing the deal at every step of its making. The editorials indirectly equated nuclear India with the few rogue nations in the world that possess nuclear weapons.

The deal had been stuck for some time at the 45-nation Nuclear Suppliers Group (NSG), based in Vienna. Approval of the deal by the NSG was a legal requirement. It took a great deal of effort on the part of the Bush administration to get that approval. Once the NSG approval came, in the first week of September, *The Times* came out with an editorial, taking the administration to task. According to the paper's September 9, 2008, editorial, entitled "A Bad Deal," "The administration bullied and wheedled international approval of the president's ill-conceived nuclear deal with India." The editorial asked U.S. lawmakers to "hold off considering the deal."

The lawmakers knew better. Once the House of Representatives passed the deal, on September 27, *The Times* became desperate. It knew that its only hope now lay in the Senate. If the Senate also passed it, the paper feared, there was no stopping of it from becoming law. On September 30, 2008, in a last-ditch attempt to thwart the deal, it published another editorial, this one entitled "A Bad India Deal." If the earlier one was an appeal to the members of the House to "hold off considering the deal," the later one was an appeal to the Senators to "postpone action until the next Congress can figure out how to limit the damage from this deal." The lawmakers gave each appeal the treatment it deserved. They pooh-poohed it.

A *New York Times* Addict

I am a *New York Times* addict. I have been reading it since the time it was sold for a dime. Whenever I found this favorite paper of mine erring factually or, in my opinion, judgmentally, I have sent a letter to its editor. I lost track of the number of letters I sent over the past quarter century. The paper was gracious enough to publish at least five of them.

I did send letters in response to the two editorials mentioned above, too. Needless to say, they weren't published. Let me reproduce below what I said in the letter sent in response to *The Times*'s Sept. 30 editorial:

To the Editor:

Re "A Bad India Deal" (editorial, Sept. 30, 2008):
Every time you come out with an editorial opposing the U.S.-India civilian nuclear cooperation agreement, you are strengthening the hands of Indian communists, who have been at the forefront of those trying to block it since its very inception.

The communists' opposition to the deal nearly brought down the Congress Party-led coalition government in India. Prime Minister Manmohan Singh put his prestige and the survival of his government on the line in pursuance of the deal. The reason? India, the second-fastest-growing economy in the world, badly needs it to meet its ever-growing energy needs.

Let's agree with you, for argument's sake, that over 30 years ago, "India used its civilian nuclear program to produce a bomb." Is that good enough reason to punish India now? Is the world of today the same as that of 30 years ago?

India produced a bomb in 1974 because that was the only way it could ward off the threat posed by its neighbors, Pakistan and China. China already had nuclear weapons and Pakistan was armed to the teeth by the United States. [Let me insert here a portion from the letter I sent to *The Times* in response to its Sept. 9 editorial, "A Bad Deal": "It was the height of the Cold War period. Throughout that period, the United States had armed Pakistan to the teeth, in pursuance of its Cold War goals – to fight communism and prevent Soviet expansionism. While not a single shot had been fired by Pakistan toward that goal, it found U.S.-supplied weapons very handy in two of the three wars it fought against India before 1974."] Coincidentally or consequently, it was about that time that these two adversaries of India started wooing each other and the U.S. started making friendly overtures to China. Admittedly, the two developments added to India's worries. That is, India's making of the bomb over three decades ago had something to do with the policy pursued by the U.S. in that part of the world, at that time.

Since then, international relationships and the centers of power in the world have dramatically changed. Now, India is well on its way to becoming a world power. It is in recognition of this reality that the Bush administration "chose to build a new relationship with India." The assurance given by the Manmohan Singh government – that the fuel and technology bought under the deal would be used only for peaceful purposes – is good enough for the administration and for the overwhelming majority in the U.S. House of Representatives who approved the agreement. But not for *The New York Times*. It seems you want to punish India for something it did, in its national interest, 34 years ago.

The Indian communists want to punish the Singh government for an entirely different reason. The reason given by them for public consumption is that the deal would be a sellout of Indian sovereignty to American imperialism. The actual reason, however, is different. They know that if the agreement is finally approved, there is a possibility of India's emerging as a balancing power to rising China. The Indian communists find the idea of their motherland becoming a balancing power to their 'holy land' inconceivable.

If the U.S. Senate, whose approval is the only step that needs to be taken for the agreement to become a reality, listens to you and rejects it, the communists will be dancing on the streets of New Delhi. Will that make you happy?

Fortunately, that did not happen. In a way, in passing the agreement with a landslide, U.S. Congress was sending a message to *The Times* that the Bush administration was right in making the agreement the centerpiece of America's new relationship with India. I would like to draw the paper's attention to what Richard G. Lugar, Senator from Indiana and the ranking Republican on the Senate Foreign Relations Committee, said during the debate on the agreement: "The national security and economic future of the United States will be enhanced by a strong and enduring partnership with India. With a well-educated overall middle class that is larger than the entire United States population, India can be an anchor of stability in Asia and an engine of economic growth."

I don't know what the *Times* editorialists' next move will be. But as far as the Indian communists are concerned, it's quite possible that they are sulking in some dark corners of New Delhi, plotting other ways to bring down the Manmohan Singh government.

12

Dear John McCain and Sarah Palin:
If You Detest Government That Much, Why Do You Want to Be Part of It?

October 25, 2008

"Government is not the solution to your problem, government is the problem." This is the slogan Republican presidential candidate John McCain and his running mate Sarah Palin have been repeating ad nauseam on the campaign trail. If that is so, one may legitimately ask: Why do you want to be part of such a government? In fact, they are campaigning tirelessly, not just to be part of it, but to be its top leaders. And the way they have been campaigning shows that they are prepared to stoop to any low to achieve that goal.

Their contempt for government is in striking contrast to the attitude of Barack Obama, the Democratic Party nominee for president. "Government cannot solve all our problems," he said in August, while accepting his party's nomination, at its national convention, in Denver, Colorado, "but what it should do is that which we cannot do for ourselves: protect us from harm and provide every child a decent education; keep our water clean and our toys safe; invest in new schools and new roads and new science and technology."

It is obvious that McCain and Palin are mouthing the slogan that belittles government with a view to appeasing the far right in their party. Those on the far right call themselves Reagan Republicans. John McCain never misses an opportunity to identify himself as one of them. The slogan was first coined and popularized by Ronald Reagan himself. During the late president's term in office (1980-88), the conservative movement in the country gained in strength and popularity and the word "liberal" began to be treated with derision. Anything the government was supposed to be doing for the benefit of the disadvantaged in society was considered part of a liberal agenda and received scant attention. Many in the conservative wing started using the word liberalism interchangeably with socialism. Some even went to the extent of using it interchangeably with communism, thus making it sound un-American and anti-democratic. That is, "liberal" became a dirty word in America, much to the amusement of the rest of the world.

Theory of Liberalism

The 19th century political philosopher John Stuart Mill, who propounded the theory of liberalism, with the humane purpose of extending the benefits of democracy to disadvantaged minorities in society, may be turning in his grave when conservative Republicans equate liberalism with socialism and communism. The theory was born out of Mill's concern that democracy being the rule of the majority, there was a danger of its degenerating into a "tyranny of the majority." The theory makes it obligatory on the part of a democratically elected government to provide for the protection of minorities in the country. Conservative politicians who condemn liberals as "socialists" and "communists" are either ignorant of this fact or deliberately ignoring it. Deliberately, because they know that in America, attaching a "commie" label to a person is the surest way of destroying that person's career. Remember McCarthyism?

It is sickening to see McCain and Palin resorting to such dirty tactics. Having failed to make an impact on the electorate on issues that are important to them, the two have now sunk to the level of portraying their Democratic opponent as a socialist. "No, I wouldn't call him a socialist," Sarah Palin made a small concession, while responding to a reporter's question. But, she hastened to add, the tax plan he proposed was socialistic.

Obama's tax plan calls for a modest tax cut for the middle class and a slight tax increase for those who make over $250,000 a year. The plan would also permanently stop the tax cut the Bush administration has been giving to the richest 1 percent in the country. The administration did it in the hope that the benefits accrued to the richest would trickle down to the middle class and the poor. It has proved to be a pious hope. More than anything else, it was the provision in the Obama plan to stop the tax cut which the richest in the country have been enjoying that annoyed conservative Republicans.

In spreading the Obama-is-a-socialist canard, Palin has been more voluble than McCain. The person who started the canard has become the poster boy for the McCain-Palin campaign. He is a plumber's assistant, by the name of Samuel J. Wurzelbacher, who lives in Ohio.

On October 12, 2008, Obama was campaigning in Holland, Ohio, when this "big, bald man with a goatee," as Athena Jones of NBC puts it, approached him and said that he was ready to buy the plumbing company he had been working for. Once he bought it, he said, he could be making $250,000 a year. "Your new tax plan is going to tax me more, isn't it?" he asked Obama.

It might, Obama said. The two argued for some time and at one point, Obama told the prospective entrepreneur, "And I do believe for folks like me who have worked hard, but frankly also been lucky, I don't mind paying just a little bit more than the waitress that I just met over there who ... can barely make the rent. Because my attitude is that if the economy's good for folks from the bottom up, it's gonna be good for everybody. If you've got a plumbing business, you're gonna be better off ... if you've got a whole bunch of customers who can afford to hire you, and right now, everybody's so pinched that business is bad for everybody ... and I think **when you spread the wealth around, it's good for everybody** [my emphasis].... But listen, I respect what you do, and I respect your question, and even if I don't get your vote, I'm still gonna be working hard on your behalf because small businesses are what create jobs in this country and I want to encourage it."

It's the words that I highlighted that gave the Republican camp the ammunition to attack Obama. During the third and last presidential debate, on October 15, 2008, McCain invoked the plumber's name – he called him "Joe the Plumber" – over two dozen times to accuse Obama of waging "class warfare." Thanks to McCain and Palin, and right-wing journalists like the ones who work on the *Wall Street Journal* editorial page and for the Fox News Channel, a plumber's assistant, who turned out to be a tax-evader and who doesn't even have a license to plumb, let alone acquire a plumbing business, became an overnight celebrity. Reporters and talk-show hosts sought him out for interviews.

Father of Modern Capitalism

What had Obama done to deserve the accusation that he was waging a class war? Do McCain and his amen crowd think that spreading wealth to benefit all sections of society occurs only under socialism? Doesn't Ronald Reagan's "trickle-down economics," which McCain and his ilk endorsed enthusiastically, mean the same thing? That the trickling down of wealth never happened is a different matter.

And that Reagan saddled the country with the largest debt known until then is something conservatives seldom talk about.

The underlying principle of what Obama said can be traced to Adam Smith, the father of modern capitalism, says Steve Coll, in his "The Talk of the Town" column, in the October 27, 2008, issue of *The New Yorker*. He quotes the following passage from Smith's *The Wealth of Nations* (1776) to substantiate his point:

"The necessaries of life occasion the great expense of the poor. … The luxuries and vanities of life occasion the principal expense of the rich, and a magnificent house embellishes and sets off to the best advantage all the other luxuries and vanities which they possess. … It is not very unreasonable that the rich should contribute to the public expense, not only in proportion to their revenue, but something more than in that proportion."

Every time McCain and his running mate call Obama a socialist for suggesting that the rich in society help out the poor, they are insulting the memory of the man who laid down the theoretical foundation of modern capitalism. Or they are betraying their ignorance of the basic principles of capitalism.

Spreading wealth doesn't incite class war, Mr. McCain may please note. Undue concentration of wealth in the hands of a few, to the detriment of the rest, does. The pertinent question is: How can you create wealth to run the government and pay for at least the most essential services it is supposed to provide, if you give tax cut to the rich and refuse to raise the tax on any? Gone are the days when stronger countries generated wealth by looting weaker ones. For modern nation-states, the main source of wealth is tax.

Obama has spelled out how he intends to create wealth: by taxing the rich, avoiding waste, eliminating departments that don't work, abolishing the tax cut that President Bush gave to the richest in the country, and so on. McCain, it seems, knows only one way of creating wealth: by eliminating pork-barrel spending. He keeps harping on it even after he was told that the entire pork-barrel spending accounts only for $18 billion. What is $18 billion in a $3 trillion budget? On his own admission, economics is not his cup of tea. But what we are talking about here is simple arithmetic. By saving $18 billion, McCain won't be able to pay even for the Bush tax cut which he has vowed to make permanent, if elected.

Paying Tax Is Not Patriotic, Says Sarah Palin

Another fact relevant to the running of a state is worth examining here. When the tax collected by the state is insufficient to pay for unavoidable services, it borrows money from other states and from private sources. Though continuous borrowing for an unreasonable length of time erodes the state's strength and prestige, there is no other way it can meet its obligations. The unsavory condition the U.S. is in right now is partly the result of reckless borrowing and profligate spending. Right now, its overall debt is over $10 trillion, and it is ballooning by an addition of $3.88 billion a day. Half of the debt is owed to foreign countries. China is the second-largest creditor of the U.S., the largest being Japan. If the leader of the capitalist world has come to the sorry pass of borrowing from a communist country, there is something wrong with the way that leader is conducting its business. The steepest rise in debt in the post-World War II period occurred in the past eight years. The tax policy of the Bush administration and its misadventures abroad, both of which McCain supported, have something to do with it.

Lately, some conservative Republicans have even started ridiculing those who suggest that making sacrifices by paying higher taxes to help the country out of a crisis is the patriotic duty of a citizen. Prominent among the ridiculers is the star of the Republican ticket, Sarah Palin. She has been making fun of her Democratic counterpart Joe Biden for having made such a suggestion. She first did it during her debate with Biden, on October 2, 2008, and has since been repeating it at every other campaign rally. During the October 2 debate, she turned to Biden and said:

"Now you said recently that higher taxes or asking for higher taxes or paying higher taxes is patriotic. In the middle class of America which is where Todd [her husband] and I have been all of our lives, that's not patriotic. Patriotic is saying, 'government, you know, you're not always the solution. In fact, too often you're the problem so, government, lessen the tax burden and on our families and get out of the way and let the private sector and our families grow and thrive and prosper.' An increased tax formula that Barack Obama is proposing in addition to nearly a trillion dollars in new spending that he's proposing is the backwards way of trying to grow our economy."

Though she outdoes President Bush in affronting English grammar, one can gauge the essential point of what she said: paying tax is not patriotic. Does she think evading tax is? "What an awful statement," says Thomas L. Friedman, in his October 8 column in *The New York Times*. "Palin defended the government's $700 billion rescue plan [which the Bush administration pushed through Congress to bring the biggest financial institutions in the country from the brink of bankruptcy]. She defended the surge in Iraq, where her own son is now serving. She defended sending more troops to Afghanistan. And yet, at the same time, she declared that Americans who pay their fair share of taxes to support all those government-led endeavors should not be considered patriotic."

Millions of Americans would agree with Mr. Friedman. He goes on to list a few questions he wishes the moderator of the debate or Biden himself had asked Palin. Questions like: "Do you think borrowing money from China [to pay for those endeavors] is more patriotic than raising it in taxes from Americans?"

'Get Government Off People's Back'

There is one more campaign slogan which McCain and Palin have been repeating to please their ultra-conservative base in the party: that they are going to Washington to "get the government off people's back." (This phrase also was borrowed from Ronald Reagan). The point they are trying to make is that the government has no business to get involved in people's activities, especially economic activities. That brings us back to the question with which we started this discussion: If that is so, why do they want to be part of that government and add to the burden on people's back?

Reagan translated the slogan into action by removing governmental regulations in the economic arena. The process begun by him was quickened by the present administration. The result is here for all to see: a financial meltdown, the disastrous consequences of which the U.S. and the rest of the world are going to suffer for years to come. And to prevent a complete collapse of the economy, those who detested governmental intervention all these years have now come out with the biggest form of it. The Bush administration's $700 billion bailout plan is precisely that. It is the biggest form of governmental intervention in the private sector, in the history of the U.S. This could have been avoided, if the administration had not dismantled the regulatory mechanism built into the system over years.

Impartial Umpire

Yes, free-market competition is the lifeblood of capitalism. That doesn't mean that the government has no role to play in it. For any competition to be fair, certain rules and regulations have to be followed. The role of the government is first to formulate those rules and regulations and then to enforce them as an impartial umpire. Freemarket competition, in the absence of governmental regulations, can lead to a free-for-all. Some economists call it "predatory capitalism." And some others call it "social Darwinism." What we have witnessed in the past few years – instances of giant corporations swallowing up small ones – is precisely that. It's the removal of governmental regulations that facilitated the swallowing. Not surprisingly, McCain was at the forefront of senators who argued for the removal. Deregulation has been their way of getting the government off people's back.

It is not enough that McCain, Palin and their supporters proclaim their patriotism by shouting "Country First" at the drop of a hat and by festooning their campaign rallies with posters and banners carrying the "Country First" slogan. Patriotism also means respecting the government that a country lawfully establishes. It also means respecting the machinery the government lawfully sets up to bring some order in the country. The alternative to order is anarchy. Are John McCain and Sarah Palin going to Washington to usher in an era of anarchy?

13
Monkeys in Pink Panties

February 16, 2009

On January 24, 2009, some 40 misguided men barged into a pub at Mangalore, a cosmopolitan town overlooking the Arabian Sea, in the southern Indian state of Karnataka, and attacked some young women who were relaxing there over a drink. The men called themselves Rama Sena (the army of Rama) and said they did it because the women were "violating traditional Indian values."

True believers among Hindus were outraged that those who engaged in hooligan activities should call themselves the army of Rama, a revered god in the Hindu pantheon. Believers look up to Rama as an embodiment of manly virtues and righteousness. Attack on women, they say, will find no justification in Hinduism, a religion that teaches its followers to address older women as *mataji* (respected mother) and younger ones as *behanji* (respected sister). By engaging in hooliganism, those who masquerade as the army of a Hindu god have only besmirched Hinduism, true Hindus argue.

Non-believers among Hindus and those belonging to other religions were outraged, too. They condemned the despicable act as a disgrace to their country which is well on its way to becoming a superpower in the world. Modern women of India have made invaluable contribution in moving the country toward that status. If some of them enjoy their well-deserved freedom by visiting a pub after their day's hard work, that's something no right-minded Indian would grudge them.

A minister in India's federal government also joined the chorus of criticism and condemnation that poured in from various parts of the country. The minister, Renuka Chowdhury, who at the time was India's Minister for Women and Child Welfare, said that Mangalore was "being Talibanised." It was an appropriate characterization. But the mayor of the city reacted to it in a stupid way. He sued the minister, charging her with causing disrepute to the city.

The mayor, Ganesh Hosabettu, belongs to the Hundu-nationalist Bharatiya Janata Party. Would he mind answering this question: Is it the failure on the part of the Mangalore City administration to protect women from the attack on them by some rowdies that brought disrepute to the city? Or is it the federal minister's characterization of the attack as Taliban-like that did it? The mayor may please note that, by suing the minister, he is giving moral support to the goons who are acting as self-appointed champions of "Indian values." By the way, was the suit aimed at giving moral support to the goons?

The controversy did not shame the Rama Sena activists into silence. Pramod Muthalik, the founder-leader of the organization, threatened to continue his campaign. The next phase of it was supposed to be launched on February 14, 2009, Valentine's Day. Observance of Valentine's Day is not permissible in terms of his paleolithic interpretation of Indian values. Well before the day, he unleashed the following threat:

"Our activists will go around with a priest, a turmeric stub and a *mangalsutra* on February 14. [Hindus consider the color of turmeric holy; and *mangalsutra* is the sacred thread, usually made of gold, the tying of which around the neck of a bride by the bridegroom is supposed to solemnize a Hindu wedding.] If we come across couples being together in public and expressing their love, we will take them to the nearest temple and conduct their marriage."

They Haven't Found a Manly Cause

I don't think that Mr. Muthalik and his gang of goons would have dared to include in their threat a demonstration as to how to consummate the marriage. Now that they have proved to the world that they haven't found any manly cause to live for, it is reasonable to assume that the relevant part of their body is incapable of rising to the occasion.

A few daring women came up with a novel way of responding to the Rama Sena threat. Styling themselves as Love Sena, they organized what they called a "Pink Panties Campaign." Their plan was to send cartloads of pink panties to the Sena chief Muthalik's office, on Valentine's Day. The idea was the brainchild of the main organizer of the campaign, Nisha Susan. Women all over India enthusiastically responded to Susan's call and sent her lots of pink panties. On the eve of Valentine's Day, however, the authorities rounded up Muthalik and his men and kept them in preventive custody. The women were disappointed that they could not accomplish their mission.

I have one request for these women, especially their leader who thought up the ingenious way of expressing their outrage: Please keep the panties intact. The next time the Rama Sena or any sena challenges your basic rights, please force them to wear those panties and parade them in public. Please also force them to change the name of their organization to Vanara Sena (the army of monkeys). You can bet that media outlets around India will report the event the next day, with the headline: "Monkeys in Pink Panties."

14

Crass Commercialization of Mother's Day in America

May 10, 2009

Today is Mother's Day in America. For several days now, the electronic and print media in the country have been carrying advertisements and special programs associated with the day. Most of them remind you of the importance of remembering your mother, at least on this day, and of letting her know how much you love her.

I was bemused by the one that appeared on my Internet home page. My Internet provider is AT&T. Usually AT&T gives the latest news of the day as the lead item on its customer home page. The one that appeared on April 28, 2009, which I mistook for a news item, started with the headline, "1 CT Sapphire and Diamond White Gold Ring – Only $175." The text below the headline read:

"This Mother's Day, show her how much you really care by treating her to a unique ring design that bears a timeless appeal. Crafted in lustrous 10K white gold, this delicate accessory showcases a breathtaking 1-carat blue sapphire centerpiece framed by intricate diamond filigree ornaments. Offer her a treasure she will cherish forever. Every mother deserves her time to shine!"

The ad kept repeating, with the gold ring shown in it replaced now and then with one of a slightly different design. But the message of the ad was the same: It "is bound to take [your mother's] breath away."

AT&T has every right to make money by selling space on its customer home page. And any company that has a product to sell will look for ways of selling it to any customer. The question is: Should it be at the cost of commercializing one's love for his or her mother? Who in the world told the manufacturer of this ring – ICE (I don't care to know what the three letters stand for) – that a mother's love is something that can be bought over with a gift, no matter how attractive?

The question may be out of place in the modern era in which even the holiest of all holidays, Christmas, has been commercialized to a sickening level. And in terms of crass commercialization, Mother's Day has come to occupy a place second only to Christmas.

The Origins of Mother's Day

While celebration of motherhood is the underlying theme of the holiday, different countries observe it on different days. In the U.S., where it is celebrated on the second Sunday of May, its origin is different from how it began in Europe. The origin in Europe has been traced to the 16th century Christian practice of a person's visiting his or her mother's church once a year. In England, the practice later evolved into what came to be called Mothering Sunday. It came to be called so because, when the industrial era began, it became customary for masters of trades and homes to release on that day young men and women working under them as apprentices and servants, thus enabling them to reunite with their mothers. In England and Ireland, Mothering Sunday, which lately have been called Mother's Day, is observed three weeks before Easter Sunday. Though the day got secularized in due course, there are churches in those two countries which still observe it with ceremonies dedicated to Mary, mother of Jesus, and with those invoking the concept of Mother Church.

The origin of Mother's Day in the U.S. has no religious trappings. It has been traced to the work done by a young Appalachian homemaker called Anna Reeves Jarvis. She started her work, initially aimed at improving sanitation, in 1858. Throughout the Civil War period, she organized women and tried to bring better sanitary conditions on both Union and Confederate sides. In 1868, she even tried, without success, to reconcile the two sides.

Her work inspired a social activist called Julia Ward Howe who, after the Civil War, started a campaign to unite women against war. Howe, it may be added, was the author of the "Battle Hymn of the Republic." In 1872, she initiated and promoted what was called Mother's Day for Peace, to be observed on June 2. Women in 18 cities across America celebrated the day the following year. Women of Boston continued the celebrations for another decade. But the celebrations phased out eventually when Howe stopped underwriting their cost. Her source of inspiration, Anna Reeves Jarvis, died in 1905.

Her daughter, Anna Jarvis, refused to let the noble cause her mother worked for die with her. At her mother's grave, she took a vow not to rest until she realized her mother's lifelong dream. The dream was to create a national day to honor all mothers.

In 1907, she started a campaign to achieve that goal. In the beginning, the campaign was in the form of handing out white carnations to those who went to worship at her mother's church, in Grafton, West Virginia. A year later, responding to her request, the church held a special Sunday service in honor of all mothers. Churches in 46 states followed suit the next year. From then onward, Anna Jarvis dedicated herself to a full-time letter-writing campaign, imploring politicians, clergymen and civic leaders to institute a national day for mothers.

Her tireless work was rewarded in 1912, when West Virginia, her home state, adopted an official Mother's Day. The ultimate triumph came two years later, on May 9, 1914, when President Woodrow Wilson, signed a resolution passed by the United States Congress, declaring the first national Mother's Day. The resolution was a victory for, and in celebration of, motherhood. Ironically, Anna Jarvis, the greatest proponent of motherhood in the U.S., and to whom the country owes the Mother's Day holiday, was not a mother.

The joy Anna felt at seeing her mother's dream come true did not last long. She was upset by the way Mother's Day soon got commercialized. "I wanted it to be a day of sentiment, not profit," she lamented. She died on November 24, 1948. One wonders what her reaction would be if she were alive today and exposed to the deplorable advertisements that have been coming out on the eve of Mother's Day.

It is mainly to share Anna's lamentation and disgust that I decided to write this piece, not with any hope of getting the commercialization of Mother's Day stopped. Some of the advertisements, if anything, are a disgrace to motherhood.

Belittling Motherhood

There are those who don't commercialize it, but guilty in a different way. They are guilty of belittling motherhood. The belittling comes in the form of motherhood being treated in a formulaic manner. Treating things in a formulaic manner is an essential American trait.

On last year's Mother's Day, I was upset when I noticed that trait even in my favorite *New York Times* columnist, Thomas Friedman. He had dedicated his column on that day to appealing to his readers to "Call Your Mother." Disappointed, I sent a letter to *The Times* (which, understandably, the paper didn't publish). My letter said:

The sentiments expressed by Thomas L. Friedman in his May 11 column are touching. I would go a step further and implore *Times* readers to call their mothers as often as they can, not just on Mother's Day, and keep her in their thoughts all the time.

Calling Mother on Mother's Day and Father on Father's Day is very much an American custom, given rise to by the American way of life. As more and more old parents began to be shipped to nursing homes, it became necessary to remind the children to connect with their parents at least once a year. Thus began the practice of their calling, or sending flowers to, parents on Mother's Day or Father's Day. Whoever thought the practice that arose out of such a noble purpose would over time become so formulaic and commercialized?

There is a way out: Take care of your parents all the time. If for reasons beyond your control they must be put in a nursing home or are living away from you, visit them as often as you can. If you are not in a position to do either, call them as frequently as possible. Don't wait for an Internet provider, telephone company or flower shop to remind you of the importance of doing it.

Sure, those commercial enterprises have every right to make money. But let them look for other ways of doing it, not by cashing in on one's love for one's parents.

15

Why I Didn't Survive as a High School Teacher in New York City

May 23, 2010

Nearly two decades ago, I became a social studies teacher at an inner-city high school in New York. I took up the job for two reasons: one, I desperately needed a job; and two, I enjoyed teaching.

I had thought that having done college-level teaching for some time (after I completed my Ph.D. in 1988, I had worked for several semesters as an adjunct professor of political science, at the City University of New York), high-school teaching would be very easy. It turned out to be anything but easy. In fact, it has been the hardest job I have ever done in my life. It lasted only one semester.

I used to put the entire blame on myself for its being short-lived. I used to blame it on my inexperience and lack of skill in dealing with inner-city children. Many of those children came from broken homes and most of them were raised by single parents. The single parent, in every case I had a chance to contact, was the mother.

Lately, however, I have been able to be less hard on myself. The perennial discussion that has been going on around the country on how to improve the school system and measures taken now and then toward that end have convinced me that I am only partly to blame for what went wrong. There were systemic problems over which I had no control.

Let me start with my own shortcomings. If a person with a Ph.D. decides to become a teacher in an inner city, the reason can be that he either has no other source of income or that he has a burning desire to do something for the less fortunate in society. Or both. In my case, though I am not totally devoid of the latter, my immediate reason for taking up the job was the former. Anyone living in New York City, who has gone through the humiliating experience of not being able to pay the bills, would be able to appreciate my situation.

My inexperience and lack of patience in dealing with inner-city children stood in the way of my building a rapport with them. Most of my students were African American. Even a casual remark or wrong choice of words by someone who is not one of their own could be misconstrued as stemming from insensitivity to their values and heritage. I learned it early in the semester.

One day, I asked the class to name a country other than the United States. "Africa," most of them said.

"Africa is not a country," I told them.

"Why, you don't like Africa?" some of them shouted. "Don't you know that we are proud of being African American?"

My students' ignorance of a simple geographic fact did not bother me that much. Their mistaken notion that I, because of my being from a different country and ethnic background, was disrespectful of their proud heritage not only bothered me, it also hurt me. The incident reinforced the point that it is not only important that a teacher must be above prejudice, but he must also be perceived as such by his students. As that clichéd adage goes, Caesar's wife must not only be above suspicion, but also appear to be so.

While those personal shortcomings were within my power to overcome, there were problems with the school system as a whole which I could do nothing about. Let me start with what they call, in public school parlance, tracking – grouping students of every grade on the basis of their performance in the previous grade. The school where I taught was one of the many in the country that enthusiastically introduced this 'innovation.'

Under tracking – to quote Jeannie Oakes, who at the time was considered "the country's best-known expert on tracking" and is now director of education and scholarship at the Ford Foundation – "you find low-track teachers with a classroom full of students who have a history of school difficulties, school failures, or misbehavior."

Ms. Oakes's words aptly describe the situation I was in. Being the junior-most, I ended up as the lowest-track teacher at the high school's lowest grade, ninth grade. And most students in my class had "a history of school difficulties, school failures, or misbehavior." My experience with them made me a firm believer in what some school reformists call heterogeneous grouping: mixing 'bright' students with 'slow' ones, so that the former get an opportunity to encourage the latter and the latter to emulate the former. As one such reformist puts it, "Peer models are more effective than teachers in influencing self-efficacy beliefs of low-achieving children."

Misbehavior Problem

I was faced with the misbehavior problem on the very first day in the job. As I entered the class, a few students said in a derisive tone, "Oh, another substitute!" I was to learn later that the class had been without a regular teacher, whom they call class teacher, though nearly a month had elapsed since the new semester began. I also learned in time that students did not take substitute teachers seriously. In fact, they often pushed them around.

"No, I am not a substitute," I told them. "I will be your class teacher from today onward."

Two girls in the class were working on the hairdo of a third one. After staring at them for a minute or so, I asked them to stop it. They wouldn't. I went near them and said, "Young ladies, this is not a class on hairdressing, this is social studies class."

"Go f... [expletive] yourself," one of them said. I was shocked.

"Would you talk like that to your parents?" I asked her.

"You are not my parent," she said. "You are not my father."

"Next to your parents, your teacher is the most important person in your life at this stage," I told her.

"Leave me alone, Mister," she shouted.

I didn't know how to handle the situation. I requested a security guard who was passing by to take the three girls to the assistant principal's office. "Please tell him that I will come there and explain everything at the end of the period," I told him.

"For me to take the students out, you have to write up a referral," he said and handed me a form.

That was another procedure that I was not familiar with. For any student to be disciplined by higher-ups in the department, he or she had to be sent with a referral.

To fill up the referral form, I needed the names of the three girls. They wouldn't give their names. Nor would any student in the class help me with their names. I stood there, not knowing what to do. The guard left with a smirk on his face. The three girls laughed and resumed their hairdressing job.

I spent the rest of the period, pleading with the rest of the class to listen to me. After a good deal of persuading, I was able to get at least four students – out of the class of 35 – to pay attention to what I was saying.

At the end of the period, on the advice of a fellow teacher, I brought the hairdressing incident to the attention of one of the deans in the department. The dean discussed the matter with the girls' parents. The parents were so decent and apologetic, and the girls' behaviors shouldn't be blamed on their upbringing, the dean told me. He suggested that the girls be allowed to continue in the class. All three girls were raised by single parents, mothers.

The situation was not much different the rest of the semester. I could see that the handful of students who were serious about their studies were as frustrated as I was. "Why did I spend all those hours last night, poring over the textbook, maps and journals?" I would ask myself in utter dejection.

There were days when, at the stroke of the bell that started the school day, I found myself alone in the class, staring at the walls, waiting for the first student to walk in. It took a while for me to realize that absenteeism, especially in the first period, was not a problem that only a low-track teacher like me faced. It was prevalent throughout the school system. An article that appeared in *The New York Times*, on January 14, 2008, convincingly makes the case for starting the school day not as early in the morning as it is done now. "[T]he first class of the morning is often a waste," says Nancy Kalish, the author of the article titled "The Early Bird Gets the Bad Grade." Drawing on the results of a National Sleep Foundation survey, the article goes on to say: "Some [students] are so sleepy they don't even show up, contributing to failure and dropout rates."

Social Promotion

No matter what the failure and dropout rates, at the end of the semester, I was supposed to pass certain number of students, irrespective of their performance. The school's eligibility to get grant from government depended upon that, I was told. "How can I pass those whom I have not seen in my class even once, let alone take any exam or do any assignment?" I asked my supervisor who chastised me for not following the time-honored tradition in the public school system.

I had the foregoing episode in mind when I wrote a letter to *The New York Times*, in response to an article by its op-ed columnist, Nicholas D. Kristof. The article appeared on April 24, 2007, under the title "In Its Match With China, India Penalizes Its Own Team." In the course of condemning – justifiably, I should say – the kind of education imparted in some schools in the rural areas of India, Mr. Kristof wrote that "when it came time for exams, the teachers wrote the answers on the blackboard for students to copy so the exam results wouldn't embarrass the school." His source for this information was a sixth grader in a school in Gujarat State.

My response to his piece, which *The Times* did not publish, said: "What the teachers did is laughable and unconscionable. But I don't think it is as unconscionable as what I was asked to do when I worked as a teacher at an inner-city high school in New York several years ago. ... I am bringing this up only to drive home that disgusting, questionable practices prevail not only in public schools in the 'bimar [sick]' states in India, but in advanced states of America, too."

In America, the practice is euphemistically called "social promotion." My refusal to follow the practice was one of the factors that contributed to the premature termination of my job. However, years later, when the New York City public school system, on the initiative of Mayor Michael Bloomberg, abolished the abominable practice, I felt vindicated.

Constant carping by the supervisory personnel about my performance made me very diffident. I even started questioning my ability to do the job. I was able to get over the diffidence when I shared my frustration with some fellow teachers. As the semester was coming to a close and I was not sure whether I wanted to continue working as a teacher, I asked one of them, "Don't you think one semester is long enough time for one to know whether he is teacher material?"

His reply was: "After teaching for ten years, I am still not sure whether I am teacher material. Don't be so hard on yourself."

In contrast to well-meaning teachers like him, there were also those for whom the main attraction of the job was the power it gave them in a classroom situation. I had made the mistake of listening to the 'advice' of some of them, too. "Let the kids know who is in charge," these self-styled 'veteran' teachers told me.

I should have known that there are many ways of letting the students know who is in charge, without making it stridently obvious. As B. McElroy-Johnson says in "Teaching and practice: Giving voice to the voiceless," an article published in *Harvard Educational Review* (1993), what the students want is "an authoritative, not authoritarian, teacher, a sensitive, helpful, and knowledgeable person who provides a disciplined, supportive environment for student learning."

I have been happy to note lately that the issue of carping I referred to above has been addressed by some education reformists in the country. They have expressed disgust over the way teachers' performances are evaluated by their superiors. Many of those superiors are unfit to make such evaluation. I had the misfortune of having a couple of them.

Principal's Evaluation

One day, toward the end of the semester, the principal of the school came to my class to "observe" me. It was the first period and, fortunately, three students had already ambled into the class by the time the principal arrived. The "unsatisfactory classroom observation" report he submitted a few days later was just formulaic. I could see that he had ferreted out a boilerplate and made some changes here and there. What made me sick was the fact that some of the observations he made had no bearing on what happened in the class.

To give just one example: His report reprimanded me for not carrying out a recommendation, made in a different context by the supervisor of the department, that "the class be broken up into cooperative learning groups." In my point-by-point rebuttal, I told the principal that while the supervisor's recommendation was well taken, it was not applicable to the class he observed. "When you came in, there were only three students in the class," I said in my rebuttal. "How many groups can three students be broken into? Groups of one each?"

My rebuttal concluded thus: "I do not resent criticisms and suggestions as long as they are well-meant and constructive. Unfortunately, most of your criticisms point to the apparent lapses on my part that are the outcomes of systemic shortcomings. To the extent that I am part of the system, I take responsibility for them. The question is: Are you not part of the system, too?"

I was not surprised that after reading the rebuttal, he decided not to renew my contract. Two years later, I learned to my relief that I was not the only one who gave the principal a bad grade. During a surprise visit to the school by the New York City school chancellor, he was summarily dismissed from the job. The chancellor at the time was Rudy Crew.

16

An Indian American of Quisling Ancestry Ridicules Obama's Anticolonialist Ancestry

September 21, 2010

Dinesh D'Souza's diatribe against President Barack Obama, in the September 27 issue of *Forbes* magazine, portrays anticolonialism as evil. Obama "is the last anticolonial," he says in the magazine's cover story, titled "Obama's Problem With Business." The online version of the story is titled "How Obama Thinks."

If anticolonialism is evil, Mahatma Gandhi of India, Jomo Kenyatta of Kenya and even the founding fathers of the United States were guilty of having espoused an evil ideology. Unfortunately for D'Souza and other defenders of colonialism, the rest of the world doesn't think that way. The rest of the world is indebted to Gandhi, Kenyatta and others who exposed the evil of colonialism and freed their respective countries from it.

Colonialism lasted as long as it did mostly because of the support the colonial powers received from a tiny section of the population in their colonies. Jawaharlal Nehru, who was one of Gandhi's trusted lieutenants in India's struggle for freedom from colonialism and who became the first prime minister of free India, used an apt word to describe those supporters. The word is "quisling." The word, which is now a synonym for "traitor," owes its origin to Vidkun Quisling, the Norwegian politician who betrayed his country to the Nazis.

Britain, which ruled most of India for 200 years, left the country in 1947; France left Pondicherry, its colonial enclave in India, in 1954; and Portugal, which clung to its colonial possessions – Goa, Daman and Diu – even after Britain and France left, was expelled by the Indian army in 1961. Of all the quislings the colonial powers created in India, those created by the Portuguese were more obeisant to their masters than the rest. The first generation of Portuguese-created quislings consisted of those who converted to the colonial masters' religion for a few pieces of silver. The later ones played the quisling role by acting as props for the colonial administration. Their descendants still talk in eulogizing terms about the colonial masters of yore and in bitter terms about India for what it did to those masters. Many of these descendants have D'Souza as their last name.

Singing Praise of Conservatism

When Dinesh D'Souza immigrated to the U.S. over three decades ago, he witnessed a strong wind of what was called Reagan conservatism blowing across the country. He tested the wind and decided that singing the praise of conservatism was the surest way of advancing his career. Since then, he has been doing an excellent job of that. He reaped the rewards for it in the form of steady rise up the career ladder. Very often, he also acted as the conservative lobby's self-appointed spokesman. His primary qualification for the spokesman's job was that he was more eloquent than most American conservatives in expressing contempt for Third World countries (former colonies of Europe) and their anticolonialist ideology. Being a person of quisling ancestry, it didn't take much effort for him to acquire that qualification.

According to D'Souza, all policies Obama adopted and actions he took in pursuance thereof, since he became president, have to be attributed to the anticolonialist trait in his character, which he inherited from his Kenyan father. "Clearly," he says in the *Forbes* piece, "the anticolonial ideology of Barack Obama Sr. goes a long way to explain the actions and policies of his son in the Oval Office. And we can be doubly sure about his father's influence because those who know Obama well testify to it."

The use of the word "those" makes it obligatory for D'Souza to produce more than one testimony in support of his outrageous accusation. But he produces just one, that too from Obama's grandmother – "not his real grandmother but one of his grandfather's other wives," as D'Souza sarcastically puts. He quotes what the grandmother told *Newsweek*: "I look at him and see all the same things – he has taken everything from his father. The son is realizing everything the father wanted. The dreams of the father are still alive in the son."

These are affectionate words, the kind of words any grandmother would use while talking about her grandchild. But no serious writer would quote them as a testimony to the character of a person. This is not to say that there is anything wrong with Obama's father's dream, if ending colonialism was part of that dream. But I don't think a woman who spoke only the Luo dialect used in Kenya (formerly East Africa) was referring to that part of the dream.

I wish D'Souza had quoted something from what Obama's white American grandparents, from his mother's side, said about him and his father. *Dreams from My Father*, which D'Souza has used as a source material for his character-assassination piece, contains a lot of references to them. Unlike his Kenyan step-grandmother, whom Obama met only once, that too as an adult, his maternal grandmother Tutu had played a significant role in raising him. She "has been a rock of stability throughout my life," Obama says in the dedication page of his other book, *The Audacity of Hope*.

Being a compassionate person and a history buff, Obama may have a streak of anticolonialism in him. It is something that he can be proud of and most people in the world would applaud him for. But to say that he inherited it from his father, whom he knew "only through the stories my mother and [maternal] grandparents told," is quite a stretch. Unless, of course, you believe what D'Souza insinuates – that Obama got it genealogically or through reincarnation.

Absence of a Father Figure

Obama has stated on numerous occasions about the impact on his life of the absence of a father figure. His father had left him and his mother when he was only two years old. The absence of a father figure had created a void within him, and he sought to fill that void partly through spiritual pursuits. This is what Obama wrote about his visit to his father's grave in Kenya and weeping over it:

"When my tears were finally spent, I felt a calmness wash over me. I felt the circle finally close. I realized that who I was, what I cared about, was no longer just a matter of intellect or obligation, no longer a construct of words. I saw that my life in America – the black life, the white life, the sense of abandonment I'd felt as a boy, the frustration and hope I'd witnessed in Chicago – all of it was connected with this small plot of earth an ocean away, connected by more than the accident of a name or the color of my skin. The pain that I felt was my father's pain. My questions were my brothers' questions. Their struggle, my birthright."

These are touching words. All of us find in them a son's warm tribute to the memory of his father whom he "had never truly known." But D'Souza finds in them a vindication of his claim that Obama is living his father's dream.

Obama's father had many flaws, as all of us have. But his struggle to end colonialism in Kenya was not one of them. While D'Souza can find only flaws in this anticolonialist, Obama's American grandparents found in him qualities worthy of being their son-in-law. One of the many anecdotes involving Obama's absent father, which his grandfather used to regale him with, ends thus: "Now there is something you can learn from your dad. *Confidence*. The secret to a man's success." Obama himself has forgiven all the flaws in his father, which had caused a lot of agony to him and his mother. But D'Souza, who never tires of talking about Christian values, uses them to conduct a character-assassination campaign against the dead man's son.

He says in the *Forbes* article: "Obama takes on his father's struggle, not by recovering his body but by embracing his cause. He decides that where Obama Sr. failed, he will succeed. Obama Sr.'s hatred of the colonial system becomes Obama Jr.'s hatred; his botched attempt to set the world right defines his son's objective. Through a kind of sacramental rite at the family tomb, the father's struggle becomes the son's birthright."

If a son takes upon himself, as his birthright, the task of continuing the struggle started by his father, and if the struggle was aimed at ridding the world of the evils of colonialism, it is an admirable thing. Only the descendants of worshipers of colonialism would ridicule the son for doing it.

In the last paragraph of the article, which sounds like an ominous warning to all Americans, D'Souza says, "Incredibly, the U.S. is being ruled according to the dreams of a Luo tribesman of the 1950s. This philandering, inebriated African socialist, who raged against the world for denying him the realization of his anticolonial ambitions, is now setting the nation's agenda through the reincarnation of his dreams in his son. The son makes it happen, but he candidly admits he is only living out his father's dream. The invisible father provides the inspiration, and the son dutifully gets the job done. America today is governed by a ghost."

And Dinesh D'Souza is governed by the ghosts of his quisling ancestors.

17

India's War on Terror: Troubling Questions on U.S. Cooperation

October 20, 2010

A front-page story in *The New York Times* of October 17, 2010, has raised some troubling questions. "U.S. Had Warnings About Plotter of Mumbai Attack," says the headline to the story. The most troubling of the questions it has raised are: Will the U.S. take terror warnings seriously only when its own interests are threatened? Are there people in the U.S. government interested in protecting known terrorists? Haven't they learned anything from the mistake they made prior to 9/11?

What was the mistake they made prior to 9/11? It is known to all by now that in the summer of 2001, the authorities had a clear warning about the imminent danger of a terrorist attack. If only they had taken the warning seriously and acted on it, more than 3,000 lives would have been saved; the United States wouldn't be in the mess in which it finds itself today; and the world would be a much safer place now. The warning was unambiguous: Osama bin Laden was determined to attack inside the United States. What did those who were supposed to take precautionary measures to prevent the attack do? Nothing.

Thanks to three enterprising reporters of *The Times*, Jane Perlez, Eric Schmitt and Ginger Thompson, we now learn that U.S. authorities had clear warnings about the man who masterminded the terrorist attack that took place in Mumbai, India, on November 26-28, 2008. If only they had taken the warnings seriously and shared them with India, the Mumbai tragedy could have been averted. And 166 lives could have been saved. American authorities decided to ignore the warnings. Why?

Lashkar-e-Taiba Is a Creature of ISI

Soon after the Mumbai attack, Indian investigators were able to establish, mainly by interrogating the only surviving member of the terrorist group which carried out the attack, that it was the handiwork of Lashkar-e-Taiba (the army of the pure). The militant group was created by Pakistan's powerful military-intelligence agency, the Inter-Services

Intelligence (I.S.I.), several years ago. Its undeclared goal was, and still is, to destroy India. The investigators were also able to establish who the mastermind behind the Mumbai attack was. He was David C. Headley, the son of a Pakistani diplomat by his American wife. The *Times* report reveals that he had been known to American authorities for a long time. A criminal who did his time for drug trafficking, he later became a paid informant for the U.S. Drug Enforcement Administration, in Pakistan. His dual citizenship and roots in both Pakistan and the U.S. put him in the best position to do the job.

The most shocking part of the *Times* report is that the authorities did nothing, even after they received credible information that the man who worked as their paid informant was also a terrorist who worked for Pakistan's spy agency and its terror outfit. They received the information from not just any person. They did it from the terrorist's two former wives – two of the three wives he has had so far. One of them is an American and the other a Moroccan. His third wife is a Pakistani. We don't know at this point whether he is still married to her. For a man who masqueraded as a devout Muslim named Daood while in Pakistan (though as an American playboy named David while in India), having three wives was not a problem.

As early as 2005, the *Times* story says, Headley's American wife had informed federal investigators in New York that her husband was a member of Lashkar-e-Taiba. She had also told them about his shameless boasting that he was working as an American informant, while also training with the Pakistani terrorist outfit.

Lashkar-e-Taiba has been responsible for many terrorist attacks in India. India had made that fact known to all who would listen. What did U.S. authorities do when they heard that the person who was working for them was also a member of a terrorist group? It was not just any terrorist group, but one that had been outlawed by their country years earlier. According to the *Times* reporters, "Federal officials say that the State Department and the F.B.I. investigated the warnings they received about Mr. Headley at the time, but they could not confirm any connections between him and Lashkar-e-Taiba."

Does that explanation sound familiar? It is frighteningly similar to the explanation the authorities gave for their decision to ignore the warnings they received prior to 9/11. The explanation was that Osama bin Laden had not mentioned any specific targets.

Two years later, Faiza Outalha, Headley's Moroccan wife, alerted the authorities on her husband's link to terrorism. Twice in 2007, says the *Times* story, she approached American officials at the United States Embassy in Islamabad, Pakistan's capital, and told them that Headley had many friends who were known members of Lashkar-e-Taiba. She also told them that he was passionately anti-Indian and made them aware that he "traveled to India all the time for business deals that never seemed to amount to much," according to the *Times* story. The story adds, "She [Headley's Moroccan wife] claims she even showed the embassy officials a photo of Mr. Headley and herself in the Taj Mahal Hotel, where they stayed twice in April and May 2007. Hotel records confirm their stay."

Warnings from Terrorist's Wife Ignored

Mumbai's Taj Mahal Hotel, a marvelous piece of architecture, was one of the places the terrorists attacked, and partly destroyed, during their November 2008 attack. It came to light soon after the attack that the actual purpose of Headley's travels to India was to scout targets for the attack Lashkar-e-Taiba was planning to launch.

"I told them, he is either a terrorist, or he is working for you," the *Times* story quotes Headley's Moroccan wife as saying. What was the final outcome of the two sessions she had with embassy officials? "Indirectly, they told me to get lost."

The least the officials could have done with this valuable piece of information was to add Headley's name to the international terror watch list and share it with other nations, especially India. The lonely battle against terrorism, which India has been fighting for years, had gone largely unappreciated by the U.S. until 9/11. But, at least after 9/11, India had expected full American cooperation in that battle.

Numerous terrorist training camps have been operating in Pakistan for a long time now. The whole world knows it. It is also known that the primary target of the terrorists who came out of those camps all these years has been India. The C.I.A. and other intelligence agencies in the U.S. are fully aware of this. What is surprising is that, years after Pakistan joined the U.S. in its war on terror, those camps are still in operation. That is, Pakistan is fighting terrorism on one hand – or it has at least proclaimed to be doing so – while producing terrorists on the other. The revelation in *The Times* that the U.S. did nothing about it, even after it was told that a person who had once been on its payroll received terrorist training in one of those camps, is indeed appalling.

That brings us to another important question: Were there people working at C.I.A., the F.B.I. and the D.E.A. keen on protecting this drug-trafficker-turned informant? Pakistan's spy agency, the I.S.I., is a close ally of the C.I.A. It's quite possible that each has friends in the other. The terrorist outfit Lashkar-e-Taiba is a creature of the I.S.I. As stated in the *Times* report, citing Mr. Headley's testimony to Indian investigators as its source, it was one Major Iqbal, an I.S.I. officer, who sent Headley on a reconnaissance mission to India prior to the Mumbai attack. He "handed Mr. Headley $25,000 in early 2006 to open an office and set up a house in Mumbai to be used as a front during his scouting trips." The I.S.I. officer "served as the supervisor of Lashkar's planning, helping to arrange a communications system for the attack, and overseeing a model of the Taj Mahal Hotel."

It is reasonable to suspect that the $25,000 given to Headley might have come from the billions of dollars America has been pouring into Pakistan as a reward for its promised cooperation in the war on terror. Did the C.I.A. and other affiliated agencies decide to ignore the warnings about Headley and the terror plot against India he and Lashkar-e-Taiba were hatching because they did not want to displease the I.S.I., whose cooperation they badly needed in their fight against Al Qaeda and the Taliban? If so, it was a very shortsighted decision. The country that suffered its consequences is India.

This time, the I.S.I. sent a terrorist to India armed only with some cash, $25,000. The next terrorist it sends could be armed with nuclear weapons. There are rogue elements in the I.S.I capable of doing such things. As said earlier in this article, to destroy India is Lashkar-e-Taiba's mission. And Lashkar-e-Taiba takes orders from the I.S.I. American authorities may want to think twice before they ignore any warning they receive in the future about anyone even remotely connected with Lashkar-e-Taiba.

18

Indian Communists Are Holding On to an Antiquated Mission

November 1, 2010

A Communist Party-controlled trade union hall in Kolkata, India.
(*The picture is reproduced courtesy* The New York Times.)

•

An article that appears in the October 22, 2010, edition of *The New York Times* is titled "Communists in India Fight to Hold On to a Mission." After reading the article, written by the paper's New Delhi-based correspondent Jim Yardley, and especially after seeing the picture that goes with it, most Indians would go a step further and say that the mission the Indian communists are holding on to is an antiquated one. We'll get to the article in a little bit. The bigger story here is the picture (see the one printed above).

It is that of a Communist Party-controlled trade union hall in Kolkata, the capital of West Bengal. West Bengal is one of the two Indian states where the communists control the provincial governments. The other state is Kerala. Take a closer look at the picture. Hung on the wall are the portraits of Stalin, Marx, Lenin, Engels, Mao and Ho Chi Minh. The first question that anyone would ask is: Can't Indian communists think of a single Indian leader whose portrait is worthy of being displayed alongside those of foreigners?

I am not talking about nationalist leaders like Mahatma Gandhi and Jawaharlal Nehru. Those leaders, though respected all over the world, were treated with contempt by Indian communists. When India's struggle for independence from Britain was steadily gaining momentum, the communists had done everything they could to discredit it. Why? The answer is not that simple.

Time was when World War II had just broken out in Europe and the Soviet Union, ruled by the Communist Party under dictator Josef Stalin, was on the brink of being overrun by Nazi Germany. Stalin realized that the only way he could save his country from the Nazis was by entering into an alliance with Britain. He did it. He also ordered communists all over the world to support Britain in the war. Indian communists dutifully obeyed.

Though Britain was fighting Hitler's and Mussolini's forces in Europe, which was laudable indeed, in India, it was fighting one more battle: the battle for independence from Britain led by Indian nationalists. Stalin, who was the unchallenged leader of communists all over the world at the time, ordered the Communist Party of India to cooperate with the British in that fight, which it did. Throughout India's independence struggle, the leaders of the Indian Communist Party were pitted against the nationalist leaders of the country. So, if their followers today decided not to honor Gandhi, Nehru or any other nationalist leader the way they did Stalin and other foreign communist leaders, it should not surprise anyone. But what about the Indian communist leaders of that period? After all, they were the ones who brought communism to India. Doesn't any of them deserve any respect from the present-day Indian communists?

More important, do the communists of Kolkata realize that the portraits they have put up on the wall of their union hall are of those who have already fallen from grace in their own countries? The only exception is Ho Chi Minh of Vietnam. The Vietnamese still revere him. But not as a man who brought communism to their country, but as one who liberated it from French colonialism and later humbled the most powerful military in the world, the American military. Though Vietnam is theoretically under communist rule now, capitalist enterprises are thriving there.

The Soviet Union, once the leader of the Communist World, is now non-existent. It disintegrated under the weight of communism. Russia and other countries, which were parts of the Soviet Union before its disintegration, have discarded communism as unsuited for the modern era. This is the era of global economy, which emphasizes decentralization, individual enterprise and openness. It is so laughable that the Indian communists are still holding on to an ideology whose time has passed.

Fate of Lenin's Embalmed Body

"Lenin's statue still rises near the center of the city [Kolkata], and portraits of Stalin and Marx still hang inside the biggest union hall," says the *Times* article. While Lenin's statue still rises in Kolkata, the authorities in Moscow are debating, though not openly, what to do with his embalmed body that lies in his mausoleum there. It is even rumored that what one sees in Moscow's Lenin Mausoleum now is a look-alike in wax of the original body. The original was quietly carted away and buried elsewhere some time ago, goes the rumor. I heard it from a woman from Siberia during my visit to Moscow in the summer of 2009. Though I instantly dismissed it as a rumor, its subtext struck me as important. The subtext is that in his own country, Lenin's name is no longer sacrosanct. When he was alive, even rumors like this were unthinkable.

None of the youngsters I spoke with, while in Russia, had a good word to say about their country's communist past. A young Russian who was sitting next to me during my flight from St. Petersburg to Moscow said, "We may not become as open as America anytime soon. But there is no going back on the openness we are enjoying now. The same is true of the democratic process that is evolving in our country. There is no question of reversing it."

The sentiment expressed by her was shared by another member of her generation. It was my last day in Moscow. On my way to the airport, I met a young man, maybe in his late teens or early twenties. An undergraduate student at the Moscow State University, he was on his way to Rome to attend a summer camp. "We were a closed society," he told me. "It is slowly opening up. It will take years for us to catch up with Western Europe. Thank God for the internet. The authorities may block the sites they don't like. But we can still access some sites and find out what is happening in the rest of the world." He was able to secure an invitation to the two-week program in Rome "because of my habit of web surfing."

Lenin's statue may stand in Kolkata and other places in West Bengal, as long as the communists are able to cling to power in that state. But in Moscow itself, it is only a question of time before the statues of Lenin, Stalin and other pioneers of the communist movement came down from their pedestals. Going by the attitude of the younger generation in Russia, I could tell that the time won't be too long.

While that is the case with Russia, in countries that were formerly known as Soviet satellites, the process is already underway. In Budapest, the Hungarian capital, the city authorities removed the statues of Lenin, Stalin and other communist leaders, which had stood tall in city squares until the collapse of communism, and dumped them in a faraway place, some time ago. The place has since been named the Statue Park. It is presented to tourists as a relic of Hungary's past status as a Soviet satellite.

While in Warsaw, during the same 2009 tour, I had an interesting conversation with another college student. She was working part-time at the hostel where I was staying. She spoke good English and I told her so. When I asked her whether she also spoke Russian as fluently as she spoke English, she threw a contemptuous look at me. "No," she said. "And I don't want to do it either. I will learn French. I will learn German. I am already taking classes to improve my English. My parents were forced to learn Russian. For that reason alone, I refuse to learn it."

"What a shame," I said to myself. "People hating a beautiful, rich language because of what the communists have done to their country!"

Stalin's Gift to Poland

I had a similar experience on another day, while still in the Polish capital. I was at the Palace of Culture and Science, which tour companies in Warsaw tout as a must-see place. The 33-story, 757-foottall building is known as Stalin's gift to the Polish people. Its 30th floor has an observation deck. The Warsaw I observed from the deck would make Stalin turn in his grave. Not just because many of the buildings that came up in recent years dwarf the one built to preserve his memory. Those buildings also bear testimony to the triumph of capitalism over communism. They house the Warsaw offices of Western multinational corporations. The logos of those corporations decorate the skyline. As I was coming down by elevator, I said, to no one in particular, "After all, Stalin did something good for the Polish people."

A middle-aged woman, who was in the elevator, gave me a nasty look and said, "What do you mean?"

"This wonderful building," I replied.

"This is the only good thing he did for us." She followed it with a gesture of wiping sweat from the forehead with her index finger. It made most people in the elevator laugh.

That is the fate that has befallen Stalin, Lenin and others, in countries that were once bastions of communism.

China Is Janus-Faced

The only communist country of any clout that exists today is China. It is called communist only because its leaders insist on doing it. In reality, it is neither truly communist nor truly capitalist. It is Janus-faced. While it presents its political face as communist, its economic face is capitalist. China decided to make its economic face capitalist when the brand of communism imposed on it by its founder, Mao Zedong, proved to be a disaster.

Millions of people perished when Mao put the country through his ambitious, but shortsighted, experiments known as the Great Leap Forward and Cultural Revolution. Thanks to the pragmatic approach of those who came after him, especially Deng Xiaoping who became the de fact leader of the country after Mao's death in 1976, China is now the fastest-growing economy in the world. Last month, it also became the second-largest economy in the world, next to the U.S. The theoretical foundation of that economy is not Maoist or Marxist. If anything, it is close to Keynesian.

Credit for making China Janus-faced also goes to Deng Xiaoping. He allowed the political face to continue to preach communism, while forcing the economic face to practice capitalism, though in its crude form. Those who followed Deng, after his death on February 19, 1997, decided to keep the pattern intact. Keeping the political face communist has enabled Chinese leaders to exercise their power, with no challenge from followers. Unfortunately, it is such unchallenged exercise of power that has made the capitalist face look crude.

Modern capitalism means free enterprise and free-market competition. No enterprise can be completely free unless the individuals engaged in it enjoy total freedom. Yes, the political side can curb it, when it is absolutely necessary. But its role should be limited to that of an umpire, one who makes sure that the competition among the players is governed by fair and impartial rules. In other words, modern capitalism and individual freedoms go hand in hand. So, China has a long way to go before it becomes truly modern and truly capitalist.

China uses state machinery to manipulate the market and curb individual freedoms. Activities demanding democratic reforms and human rights are ruthlessly crushed. We all know what happened to the pro-democracy activists, mostly students, who staged a sit-in in Beijing's Tiananmen Square, in 1989. The number of those killed when the military cracked down on the activists is still a state secret. At this writing, Liu Xiaobo, a veteran pro-democracy advocate in China is serving an 11-year prison term. His crime? He wrote essays and helped draft a manifesto, which later came to be called Charter 08, demanding political reform, human rights guaranty and an independent judicial system. When the Norwegian Nobel Committee declared him winner of this year's Nobel Peace Prize, the Chinese authorities called it "obscenity" and lambasted the committee.

Economically, however, China is on a roll. The results of the decision to put the country on a capitalist path, which Deng Xiaoping made in 1978, are obvious everywhere. During my visit to Shanghai and Beijing, in the spring of 2002, I saw more pictures of Colonel Sanders at public places than that of Mao Zedong. Colonel Sanders, it may be added, was the founder of the American fast-food chain, Kentucky Fried Chicken (KFC). KFC and McDonald's were the most crowded eating places I saw during my visit.

I am bringing up all this to emphasize the fact that in countries that were once communist strongholds, communism now exists only in theory. Those countries are now bustling with capitalist activities. While in Shanghai, I took a night cruise down the Huangpu River. On both sides of the river, the night sky was lit up by neon signs advertising products and services sold by multinational corporations of the West. Not a single Mao picture or Mao thought was displayed by any of those signs. I remember telling an American tourist who was with me on the cruise, "If anyone wants to see Mao still being eulogized, he has to go to West Bengal or my home state Kerala, in India."

The picture and the article in *The New York Times* corroborate my point, belatedly though. "Marxist politics has come to a critical juncture" in India, the article quotes a leftist minister in the West Bengal Government as saying. I would go a step further and say that it is on the verge of extinction.

19

Shameless Bushies Take Credit for Bin Laden Killing

May 10, 2011

In locating and killing Osama bin Laden, President Obama has accomplished something no other U.S. president has done in a long, long time. According to a *New York Times*/CBS News poll, his approval rating suddenly went up by 11 points.

However, as Charles M. Blow says in his column in *The New York Times* ("The Bin Laden Bounce," May 7, 2011), the temporary "uptick" in Obama's popularity doesn't mean anything. The mass is fickle. The uptick turning into down-tick is only one wrong presidential decision away. Also, as Mr. Blow reminds his readers, "the right and its corporate overlords will work tirelessly and spend endlessly to ensure that Obama's accomplishment is diminished. They're already tripping over themselves to credit George W. Bush in Bin Laden's demise, and Glenn Beck, that paragon of political distortion and delusion, went so far as to call the president's trip to ground zero 'disgusting,' 'obscene' and 'grotesque.'"

The whole world knows that the country is in this mess mainly because of the pig-headed policies adopted by the Bush administration in the war on terrorism. It also knows that, but for its diverting of attention and resources from Afghanistan to Iraq, Bin Laden would have been captured or killed long ago.

President Obama announced Bin Laden's death on the night of Sunday, May 1, 2011. The Bush spin machine and the right-wing media were at work the very next day to take the credit for what happened away from Obama and give it to Bush. According to them, it was the information extracted from abused prisoners that "directly led" to Bin Laden's hiding place. If that was the case, says *The New York Times*, in its May 5 editorial ("The Torture Apologists"), "why didn't the Bush administration follow that trail years ago?"

But Bush was busy looking for ways to get rid of Saddam Hussein. This is what he said on March 13, 2002, just a few months after the hunt for Bin Laden began: "I don't spend much time worrying about [Bin Laden].... I truly am not concerned about him."

On Sunday, May 8, 2011, Bushies were busy on all leading television talk shows, peddling the line that it was the enhanced-interrogation policy (read torture) the Bush administration put in place that enabled Obama to achieve what he did. Prominent among the peddlers were Vice President Dick Cheney and Secretary of State Condoleezza Rice. Who can forget the immortal phrase Ms. Rice used to justify the Iraq war? The Bush administration could not afford to wait, she said, until Saddam Hussein's "smoking gun turns into mushroom clouds." The smoking gun (read weapons of mass destruction) soon proved to be nonexistent.

Let's hope that President Obama would neither be carried away by the well-deserved praise he has been receiving for killing the most wanted terrorist in the world nor be discouraged by the campaign Bushies have already launched to belittle his historic achievement. Let's also hope that he would take this temporary uptick in popularity as an incentive to clean up the economic mess left behind by the Bush administration.

20

The 'Picasso of India' Is Dead, but the 'Hindu Taliban' Continue Tarnishing His Name

June 15, 2011

Maqbool Fida Husain, whom *Forbes* magazine once called the "Picasso of India," died in London in the early hours of Thursday, June 9, 2011. Alas, this proud son of India, who won for his country accolades from around the world, died in exile a non-Indian!

The foregoing may not be news any longer. All leading media outlets in the world have already reported it. Indian newspapers splashed the news of his death across the front page. What is still news, though, is that Hindu extremists in India, who forced this world-renowned painter into exile and were instrumental in his dying a non-Indian, have not stopped besmirching his name even after his death.

While alive, he was persecuted by them on the warped charge that his portrayal in the nude of Hindu deities denigrated Hinduism. I call them the 'Hindu Taliban' of India. Like the Taliban of Afghanistan and Pakistan, they have proved to the world that they are incapable of appreciating what a good piece of art is. They may masquerade as custodians of Hindu and Indian values. But by tormenting a man who drew inspiration from Hindu mythology in his artistic pursuits and whose life-long work was a testament to his love for India, they have proved to be a disgrace both to Hinduism and India.

They try to justify their action by asking why Husain never caricatured holy men and women of Islam. Husain might have been born into Islam. But he never identified himself as belonging to any religion. It was Indian ethos that guided him in his work. His search in Hindu mythology for artistic inspiration must be viewed from this perspective. In providing artistic and other creative inspirations, Hindu mythology ranks with Greek mythology. There is nothing comparable to that in Islam.

Moreover, Husain was one of those rational human beings who believed that none should be either proud or ashamed of what he or she was born into. Pride and shame should be associated with what one consciously and deliberately does in one's life. Husain could be justifiably proud of what he did in his life as an artist. And as an Indian artist who won praise for his country from around the world, he also did India proud. But the 'Hindu Taliban' refuse to acknowledge it. Their shallow minds couldn't see anything beyond the nudity in Husain's portrayal of Hindu gods and goddesses.

Lord Krishna's Sexual Activities

May I ask these Hindu prudes: What about the numerous temples in India that have sculptures and pictures showing gods and goddesses in the nude? What about the temples dedicated to Lord Krishna which have paintings and carvings showing Krishna in all kinds of sexual activities? What about the Hindus who worship Linga (penis) and those who worship Yoni (vagina)?

Husain's artworks are not the first in which Hindu gods and goddesses are portrayed in sexually explicit postures. The Ellora Caves and the Konarak and Khajuraho temples are full of statues, carvings and paintings, depicting gods and goddesses and ordinary mortals in every imaginable sexual activity and posture. Such depictions did not prevent UNESCO from elevating those places to the status of World Heritage Sites. Tourists from around the world flock to those places because of the intrinsic artistic value in them. But when Husain produced artworks similar to the ones that existed in Hindu temples and World Heritage Sites for centuries, they became offensive to Hindu prudes. Is there anything more hypocritical than that?

In 1988, one Hindu-extremist group, the Bajrang Dal, attacked Husain's house and destroyed his artworks. In February 2006, he was arrested and charged with "hurting sentiments of people." One Hindu group even offered a reward of $11.5 million to anyone who would murder him.

In 2007, a suit was filed against him in a court in Gujarat State. The 'crime' Husain committed this time pertained to a painting in which he portrayed a nude woman and made her look like the map of India. He also scribbled the names of Indian states on various parts of the woman's body. The painting was captioned "Bharat Mata [Mother Bharat]."

"Bharat Mata [Mother Bharat]," one of M.F. Husain's paintings that Hindu extremists found offensive.

•

As anyone with an iota of artistic sense can tell (see the picture of the painting on top of this page), the painting is a marvel of creativity. But the fanatical Hindu group that sued Husain for creating it had a different take on it. To the astonishment of most artists around the world, even the judge who presided over the case went along with the group's twisted interpretation of the painting. He ordered that Husain's house in Mumbai be confiscated as punishment for his non-appearance in court on the day of the hearing. Husain responded that he was not aware of any summons requiring his court appearance. The laughable thing about the judge's order was that the house in question was no longer in Husain's name.

Cases like this, against Husain, piled up in various Indian courts. At one point, there were 900 of them. It was constant harassment from the 'Hindu Taliban' and a legal system that willingly cooperated with them that forced Husain to go into exile. An editorial in the May 8, 2007, edition of *The Hindu*, one of the oldest and most prestigious English dailies published from India, said, "There is something terribly amiss about a social order that coerces a law-abiding 91-year-old artist – India's most celebrated painter – into leaving the country because of harassment by rank communalists and moral vigilantes. There is also something lopsided about the priorities of a criminal justice system that orders the attachment of his properties when cases against hardened criminals drag on interminably."

The editorial ended with this profound observation: "There is little doubt that the criminal cases against Mr. Husain will fail. But the mischief-makers may have already succeeded – because the process has become the punishment, especially for a nonagenarian free spirit."

Mr. Husain spent the last six years of his life in exile – in Dubai, England and, in the past one year, in Qatar. In Qatar, he was engaged in works devoted to the history of Arab civilization, commissioned by the emirate's first lady – Sheikha Mozah bint Nasser al Missned – and the works were to be housed in a separate museum in Doha, the emirate's capital. Last year, moved by this world-famous artist's sorry plight as an exile, the emirate's ruler, Sheikh Hamad bin Khalifa Al Than, bestowed Qatari citizenship on him. Husain reluctantly accepted it.

During his years in exile, he had repeatedly told reporters who met him that he was feeling "extremely homesick" and that "I am missing my country." But the government of his country did nothing to bring him back. That's the story behind the Picasso of India's dying in exile as a non-Indian.

India Offers to Fly Back Husain's Body

Was it out of remorse that the Indian government, which did nothing to facilitate his return to India when he was alive, offered to fly his body back to India? That was the question that arose in my mind when I read about the offer. Not surprisingly, Husain's children – four sons and two daughters – rejected the offer. They buried their father at

Brookwood Cemetery, in Surrey, London, on Friday, June 10, 2011.

I read about the burial in *The Times of India*'s online version, on June 11. It appeared under the title "M F Husain buried in Surrey, govt offer rejected." More than the story, it was the comments on the story from *Times* readers that I found saddening. I was saddened to see that most of the 552 comments on the story were a continuation of the vilification campaign the 'Hindu Taliban' ran against Husain while alive. However, at least a few of them did take the Indian government to task for offering to pay for flying his body to India. I also criticized the Indian government's offer, but for a reason entirely different from that of other critics. Here is what I said:

"Offering to fly Husain's body back to India? Where was the government when he repeatedly said, when alive, that he missed his motherland badly and was dying to get back as soon as he could? I can suggest a way in which the Indian government can expiate the sin and honor his memory: Throw into the Arabian Sea all the cases that are pending against him in various courts in India. By my last count, there were 900 of them. Also, it should reprimand the Hindu fanatics who filed those cases and the judges who failed to see their vexatious and frivolous nature. They all should be ashamed of themselves for having caused so much agony to this proud son of India, in the waning years of his life."

My criticism generated five countercriticisms, all of them railing against Husain, and against me for admiring his work. One Oliver from Hyderabad suggested that I become a Muslim. One Madhukar from the U.K. said that I must get my "brain and DNA checked." Kona Sam wrote from Delhi: "If I paint their holy ladies in nude, will they tolerate? If he slaps me and if I did not slap, but complain, I am fanatic. What a convoluted mentality."

I found Kona Sam's comment worth responding to. My response said: "Dear Kona, the beauty of Hinduism is that it gives you the total freedom to laugh at, and with, all gods and goddesses in it. You can worship them in any form you like. You can also reject them all and still be a Hindu. No other religion gives its followers this much freedom. Another important thing: Husain never identified himself with any religion. In fact, there was more Hindu in him than Islam." I was happy to see a kind of corroboration of what I said in the last sentence above in an article by Shobhaa De, in *The Times of India* of June 10.

M.F. Husain, in his London studio, October 25, 2009.

The picture was taken by N. Ram, editor-in-chief of *The Hindu*, a prestigious English daily in India. Mr. Ram was one of Husain's close friends. His heart-warming tribute to Husain appeared in the June 11, 2011, edition of the paper. (*The picture is reproduced courtesy* The Hindu.)

•

This well-known socialite writer from Mumbai was a friend of Husain's for 40 years. In her article, which she wrote after visiting Husain in his hospital bed in London two days before his death, Shobhaa De said, "It is both an irony and a tragedy that his last and most ambitious painting was based on the Hindu epic, the *Ramayana*. He spoke about it with enthusiasm and passion, almost as if another lifetime stretched ahead of him, even as he was breathing with difficulty." Two days later, he breathed his last.

Touching Tribute from Editor of *The Hindu*

The most touching tribute to Husain came from his close friend, N. Ram, editor-in-chief of *The Hindu*. The tribute, titled "Requiem for M.F. Husain," which appeared in the June 11 edition of the paper, says toward its end:

"His quiet and dignified passing in a London hospital brings to a close one of the sorriest chapters in independent India's secular history. I know no one more genuinely and deeply committed to the composite, multi-religious, and secular values of Indian civilization than M.F. Husain. He breathed the spirit of modernity, progress, and tolerance. The whole narrative of what forced him into exile, including the failure of the executive and the legal system to enable his safe return, revolves round the issues of freedom of expression and creativity and what secular nationhood is all about... ."

I cannot think of a more fitting tribute to M.F. Husain.

21

U.S. Congressmen Bought Over by Pakistan's Military?

July 22, 2011

U.S. House Representatives Joe Pitts
of Pennsylvania (left) and Dan Burton of Indiana.

•

Those who have been wondering why some U.S. lawmakers have been vehemently criticizing India and supporting Pakistan, in the dispute between these two South Asian neighbors over Kashmir, can stop wondering now. The supporters have been receiving campaign contributions from the Pakistani military. This stunning revelation was made in two articles that appeared in *The New York Times* on July 20 and 21, 2011.

According to the July 20 article – "Pakistan's Military Plotted to Tilt U.S. Policy, F.B.I. Says," by Charlie Savage and Eric Schmitt – "Pakistan's military, including its powerful spy agency, has spent $4 million over two decades in a covert attempt to tilt American policy against India's control of much of Kashmir – including funneling campaign donations to members of Congress and presidential candidates."

The F.B.I. made the allegations, the article goes on to say, "in a 43-page affidavit filed in connection with the indictment of two United

States citizens on charges that they failed to register with the Justice Department as agents of Pakistan, as required by law. One of the men, Zaheer Ahmad, is in Pakistan, but the other, Syed Fai, lives in Virginia and was arrested on Tuesday [July 19]."

Syed Fai (his full name is Syed Ghulam Nabi Fai) is a person of Indian-Kashmiri origin. He is the director of the Kashmiri American Council, a Washington-based group that lobbies and organizes conferences and media events in the U.S. to promote the Pakistani side of the Kashmir dispute. "According to the affidavit," the *Times* article says, "the activities by the group, also called the Kashmiri Center, are largely financed by Pakistan's spy agency, the Directorate for Inter-Services Intelligence, or ISI, along with as much as $100,000 a year in related donations to political campaigns in the United States. Foreign governments are prohibited from making donations to American political candidates."

The article quotes Neil MacBride, the United States Attorney in the Eastern district of Virginia who is handling the case, as saying: "Mr. Fai is accused of a decades-long scheme with one purpose – to hide Pakistan's involvement behind his efforts to influence the U.S. government's position on Kashmir. His handlers in Pakistan allegedly funneled millions through the Kashmiri Center to contribute to U.S. elected officials, fund high-profile conferences and pay for other efforts that promoted the Kashmiri cause to decision-makers in Washington." In other words, Mr. Fai, who has been masquerading in the U.S. all these years as a champion of Kashmiris, is a stooge of Pakistan.

Network of Straw Contributors

The modus operandi of Mr. Ahmad, a Pakistani American, was slightly different. According to court papers unsealed on July 19, he helped organize "a network of at least 10 unnamed straw contributors" who would make "campaign contributions and donate the bulk of the Kashmiri Center's annual operating budget," the *Times* article says. "The ISI would reimburse them – or their families in Pakistan."

Most of the straw donors were identified only by code in the court document. The investigation was continuing, the article says. As of July 19, "eight F.B.I. field offices executed 17 or 18 search warrants related to other suspected donors."

Citing internal documents of the Kashmiri American Council, the F.B.I. says that the goal of the council "was to persuade the United States government that it was in its interest to push India to allow a vote in Kashmir to decide its future." The two agents of Pakistan knew full well that with ISI-trained terrorists roaming the Kashmir valley, the outcome of the vote would be in Pakistan's favor. That is, all of Kashmir would become part of Pakistan.

Paid Pakistani agents promoting the cause of Pakistan in the U.S. doesn't surprise anyone. What is surprising is that some U.S. lawmakers allowed themselves to be bought over without an iota of suspicion about the motive of the buyers. It's quite possible that the lawmakers didn't know that the campaign funds they received came from Pakistan. But when the favors they were asked to do in return were blatantly pro-Pakistan and anti-India, shouldn't it have rung an alarm bell? At least in the case of some of the lawmakers mentioned in the article, what they received was not an insignificant, one-time campaign contribution. It formed a pattern.

The *Times* article says that "a search in Federal Elections Commission databases for contributions by Mr. Fai showed that he has made more than $20,000 in campaign contributions over the past two decades. The bulk of his donations went to two recipients: the National Republican Senatorial Committee and Representative Dan Burton, a Republican from Indiana. ... Mr. Ahmad also donated to Mr. Burton, records show." That explains why, of all the India critics on the Kashmir issue, Mr. Burton has been the nastiest.

Legislative Effort to Punish India

One is reminded of the time when Mr. Fai testified at a House subcommittee hearing presided over by Mr. Burton. Mr. Fai was working as an ISI agent at the time. It will be worth the House ethics committee's while to investigate whether Mr. Burton was aware of it. After all, he was acting in those days as an unofficial spokesman in Congress for the Kashmiri American Council. He even introduced legislation calling for termination of all humanitarian aid to India unless it repealed laws which, according to him, permitted widespread human rights abuse in Kashmir. Fortunately for India, his legislative effort fell through. But his anti-India vitriol continued. As recently as last September, he criticized the Obama administration for its decision to leave the Kashmir issue for India and Pakistan to resolve through bilateral negotiations.

Mr. Burton, who has been buddy-buddy with Mr. Fai for 20 years, now says that he "had no inkling of his [Mr. Fai's] involvement with any foreign intelligence operation. ..." That's hard to digest. During their 20-year association, Mr. Fai was the principal host of Kashmiri separatist politicians whenever they visited the U.S. Mr. Burton was a 'distinguished' guest at most events held to promote the cause the separatists espoused.

He now says that he would donate all the contributions he received from Mr. Fai to Boy Scouts of America. I can suggest a better idea: Donate them to the victims of ISI-sponsored terrorism in Kashmir.

Apart from Dan Burton, another Republican name that prominently figures in *Times* articles as a recipient of campaign contributions is Representative Joe Pitts of Pennsylvania. He visited Kashmir in 2001 and 2004, and met with Pakistani and Indian leaders. Were his trips paid for by the Kashmiri American Council? The question is very pertinent. He also introduced a resolution in 2004 calling for President George W. Bush to appoint a special envoy to help negotiate peace. Now we know that the driving force behind his excessive interest in the Kashmir question was money he received from Messrs. Fai and Ahmad.

Of course, now he regrets his association with them. "I don't like to be used by anybody," he has been quoted as saying in *The Times*'s July 21 article, by Eric Lipton. "It is very upsetting." A spokesman for Pitts told Lipton that he has donated the money he received – $4,000 – to local charities in Pennsylvania. My suggestion to Mr. Pitts is similar to what I made in respect of Mr. Burton: Donate some money to the Kashmiri victims of Pakistan-sponsored terrorism as well.

Other lawmakers who received contributions from the Kashmiri American Council also have been coming forward with altruistic explanations and looking for ways of expiating their sin. There are also Democrats among them. Democratic Congressmen listed in the July 20 *Times* article as recipients of contributions, "though smaller," from Mr. Fai are Representatives James P. Moran of Virginia, Dennis J. Kucinich of Ohio and Gregory W. Meeks of New York. The article also mentions $250 donations to the 2000 and 2008 presidential campaigns, respectively, of Al Gore and Barack Obama.

All these politicians could have saved the embarrassment they are facing now if they had not repeated verbatim the script on the Kashmir dispute provided to them by two stooges of Pakistan. As revealed in the July 21 article, they "took steps sought by the [Kashmiri American] council, introducing resolutions on the House floor, taking trips to the region and speaking up at hearings or news conferences to pressure the White House to take a more aggressive role.

"What they did not know, though, is that the Capitol Hill gathering, and others they participated in over the years, had secretly been financed by Pakistan's military – including ... ISI. The lawmakers have been caught up in what the Justice Department now says is a scheme over two decades to influence Congress and the White House, with the goal of forcing India to give up control of parts of Kashmir."

They wouldn't be in this pitiable state if they had spent a little time, before taking the money, to get familiarized with both sides of the Kashmir dispute. The dispute over Kashmir between India and Pakistan is not as simplistic as U.S. Congressmen were led to believe by two self-serving, illegally operating agents of Pakistan.

22
An Open Letter to *NYT* Columnist Thomas Friedman on Iraq War

December 23, 2011

Dear Mr. Friedman,
 I have great respect for your analysis of world events. Most of the time, I find myself in total agreement with your analysis. But I clearly remember the one occasion when you made me sick to my stomach. That was when you called those who opposed the Iraq war "knee-jerk liberals."

And now you admit – in "The End, for Now," your December 21, 2011, op-ed column in *The New York Times* – that "Iraq was always a war of choice." The question that you are asking now – whether it was a wise choice – should have been asked before you decided to support the war. If you "never bought the argument that Saddam had nukes that had to be taken out," which was the reason President George W. Bush gave for going to war, why didn't you say so then? Unlike you, "knee-jerk liberals" were bold enough to ask, "Is [not was] it a wise choice?" And they were prescient enough to answer the question with a thunderous no.

Your support for the war was said to have stemmed from the need to "address the root causes of Arab state dysfunction and Islamist terrorism – which were identified in the 2002 Arab Human Development Report as a deficit of freedom, a deficit of knowledge and a deficit of women's empowerment." But not once did President Bush refer to any of those root causes when he declared war on Iraq. In fact, he had decided to go to war before the Arab Human Development Report came out. He did not even mention the actual reason for going to war. Getting rid of Saddam Hussein's weapons of mass destruction, for which he never had any proof, was his proclaimed reason. The actual reason was getting rid of Saddam Hussein himself.

And Mr. Friedman, even now – even after watching the country struggle to come out of the quagmire it finds itself in because of the war – you are not sure whether your decision to support the war, in the beginning at least, was a wise one. You equivocate: "No" and "Maybe, sort of, we'll see."

Please don't be so stupid as to bring in the Al Qaeda factor into the reason for your support. You know very well that there were no Al Qaeda activities in Iraq before the U.S. invasion. The late Osama bin Laden, the founder of Al Qaeda, and Iraqi dictator Saddam Hussein detested each other. Yes, the Arab oil money did finance some suicide bombers. But their number increased rapidly after the Iraq invasion. Most Muslims in the world took it as an attack on their religion.

Again, don't be so stupid as to portray, even indirectly, the democratic awakenings that we are witnessing in Syria, Yemen, Egypt, Libya and Bahrain as a positive outcome of the Iraq war. The Bushies have been shamelessly doing that also. I am sure you don't want to be bracketed with that stupid bunch. If anything, these awakenings are attributable to modern technology, more specifically the internet and social media. Thanks to the facilities provided by social media, people of those countries were able to spread their messages rapidly and share with one another their burning desire for democratic change. Collectively, that desire took the form of mass movements. Those movements have nothing to do with George Bush's ill-conceived Iraq war.

Democracy Movements Must Be Homegrown

Mr. Friedman, the lessons we learn from what is happening in Tunisia, Egypt, Yemen, Libya and Syria are different from what you do. The most important lesson is that movements for democratic transformation of any society should not be initiated from outside. And should never be initiated through military invasion.

People accept the movements as legitimate and support them when they are homegrown.

You may have a point when you say that America "helped to midwife" a social contract in Iraq: "the first ever voluntary social contract between Sunnis, Kurds and Shiites for how to share power and resources in an Arab country and to govern themselves in a democratic fashion." But you must also ask, "At what cost?" According to a recent reliable estimate, nearly 4,500 American soldiers have been killed in the just-ended nine-year war; over 32,000 American soldiers have been severely wounded; and over $1 trillion of American taxpayers' money has been squandered. Of course, the deaths of over 110,000 Iraqis, most of them civilians, are seldom mentioned by American officials and journalists.

Also, you are not being truthful when you say that the contract was voluntary. For the American midwife to bring forth that contract, it took a good deal of goading, cajoling and even browbeating of the three main Iraqi factions. The contract would have been accepted as more legitimate if the midwifing was done by Iraqis. Hardly had the foreign midwife left the scene when the Shiite faction began to settle its old scores with the Sunnis and the Kurds, endangering the survival of the baby.

At this writing, a warrant has gone out from Prime Minister Nuri Kamal al-Maliki, a member of the Shiite majority in the coalition government, for the arrest of Vice President Tariq al-Hashimi, who is a leading Sunni politician. The charge against Mr. Hashimi is that he ran a death squad. He has denied the charge. The Sunnis see the move as an attempt on the part of Prime Minister Maliki to consolidate the Shiite-majority power, at the expense of Sunni and Kurdish minorities. The coalition government in Iraq is on the brink of collapse.

As a well-wisher of Iraqis, I hope and pray that it doesn't happen. I hope, as you do, that Iraq proves to be a harbinger, in the Arab world, of "pluralistic, consensual politics, with regular rotations in power, where people can live as citizens and not feel that their tribe, sect or party has to rule or die." At the same time, I can't help joining you in raising the doubt you did toward the end of your op-ed piece: "I don't know if Iraq will make it."

Even if Iraq makes it, you do owe your readers an apology for supporting the Iraq war in the beginning. Please admit that you were wrong. Hemming and hawing – like "Maybe, sort of, we'll see" – ill-behooves a journalist of your stature.

23

NYT Columnist's Republican Brother Insults Her Readers' Intelligence

January 2, 2012

This is the second time, as far as I can tell, that op-ed columnist Maureen Dowd of *The New York Times* allowed her conservative Republican brother Kevin to trash her column and insult her readers' intelligence. The "political plum pudding," which she served on December 28, 2011, under the title "Kevin Warns Republicans," is nothing but rubbish.

The first time she did it was on December 24, 2005, when she decided to take a break from criticizing then-President George W. Bush and his misguided Iraq war and, in the true Christmas spirit, be nice to him. She invited her Republican brother Kevin, who was also one of the cheerleaders of the Iraq war, to fill her column space (see Chapter 5). He filled it with rubbish, just like this time.

Throughout the 2005 piece, Kevin poured paeans of praise for President Bush and his religiously correct (R.C.), right-wing supporters. He also poured scorns for the politically correct (P.C.) crowd on the left. The context was the controversy raging in the country at the time between the R.C. and P.C. zealots over what wording the White House should choose in the season's greetings – "Merry Christmas" or "Happy Holidays"?

President Bush, a born-again Christian, was at the forefront of the R.C. crowd. Unfortunately, in his enthusiasm to please Bush and his right-wing cronies, Kevin disgraced his sister who detested both crowds. He also made himself a laughingstock when he appealed to the president to "Stay the Course" in Iraq, when the president himself was looking for some face-saving way to get out of it. Kevin should have known that Bush had already announced his decision to reduce the number of U.S. troops in Iraq. Even complete troop withdrawal, a taboo subject until then among Iraq warmongers, was being discussed by them. The weapons of mass destruction in Iraq, in search of which he had invaded that country, had proved to be weapons of mass deception he deployed on Americans to win their support.

Ms. Dowd says that her brother has "some critical things to say about Republicans" in his present piece. She should have known better. He said those critical things in the hope of getting some credibility for his piece. The piece is nothing but a diatribe against Democrats and Democratic President Barack Obama.

Of the possible Republican contenders for presidency in the coming election, Kevin finds Mitt Romney as the "only one who can beat Barack Obama." His reason? "Romney was a governor and a businessman, and we will need that kind of expertise to pull us out of the president's famous ditch."

Doesn't Kevin know that the "famous ditch," into which President Obama fell, was dug by George Bush? And that Bush, too, had been a governor and a businessman before he became president? And that what made the digging faster and the ditch deeper was the disastrous Iraq war, of which Kevin had been an ardent supporter?

Ms. Dowd can tell her brother that none in the country think they are "better off now than" they "were four years ago." The reason is that the ditch George Bush dug during the eight years of his presidency is too deep to get out of in four years. If there is one thing which President Obama can take credit for, it is this: He has prevented the ditch from getting deeper.

Kevin is right, though, to suggest that his fellow Republicans adopt the credo conveyed by the movie "Patton," rather than "Braveheart." But the "Patton" credo must be modified as: "Now I want you to remember that no politician ever won an election by taking responsibility for the mistake he made. He won it by making the other poor dumb bastard [read political opponent] pay for his mistake."

24

Cardinal Dolan Attacks Obamacare Using Jihadist Language

March 14, 2012

Cardinal Timothy Dolan.
(*The picture is reproduced courtesy* Daily News, *New York.*)

•

Dear Cardinal Dolan,

First of all, please accept my congratulations on your recent elevation to cardinal. I am a great admirer of you and have always been fascinated by your energy and sense of humor.

However, my admiration for you doesn't prevent me from conveying to you my disappointment over something you did recently. I am totally disappointed by the letter you sent to your fellow bishops, on March 2, 2012. It doesn't read like an epistle written by a priest. It reads like a political pamphlet. The Republican Party presidential aspirants, who are currently campaigning to unseat President Barack Obama, will find it heartwarming. You can bet they are going to cite it to back up the vow, which they have been repeating at every campaign stop, to repeal the health care law the Obama administration passed two years ago. That being the ultimate goal of your letter, you will find their action heartwarming, too.

After reading your letter, I couldn't help wondering whether you are preparing your flock for another crusade. Of course, this one won't be to liberate any holy place from Muslim 'heathens,' but, as you say, "to protect our religious freedom from unprecedented intrusion from a government bureau, the Department of Health and Human Services (HHS)." I know it's the Obama administration's HHS you were referring to.

Ever since the Obama administration passed the landmark health care law, it has been at loggerheads with the Catholic Church, extreme-right Republicans and the right-wing media in America. You should know, however, that the vast majority in the country, especially the 40-plus million people who have been living without any health care coverage, did heartily welcome it. They applauded their president for achieving a legislative victory, the likes of which the country has not seen in half a century.

Let me now turn to what made you write this letter two years after the passage of the law. It is, in your words, the "restrictive HHS Rule," announced on January 20. You find the rule an "unprecedented intrusion from a government bureau." You also say that it made you "certain of two things: religious freedom is under attack, and we will not cease our struggle to protect it."

You have repeated "religious freedom" ad nauseam in your letter. The repetition may have a shock value. And Catholics, who have not been closely following the health care law controversy, may believe when a cardinal of their church says that their religious freedom is being undermined by a secular administration. Do you know that this is the kind of tactic jihadists resort to whenever they want to incite their co-religionists to act? "Islam is in danger" is their favorite slogan.

Let's examine what the HHS Rule of January 20 says that made you stoop to the level of jihadists. It says that "the final rule on preventive health services will ensure that women with health insurance coverage will have access to the full range of the Institute of Medicine's recommended preventive services, including all FDA-approved forms of contraception. Women will not have to forgo these services because of expensive co-pays or deductibles, or because an insurance plan doesn't include contraceptive services... ."

HHS Secretary Kathleen Sebelius, who issued the new rule, did address the concerns of those who get upset at the very mention of the word contraception. "The administration remains fully committed to its partnerships with faith-based organizations, which promote healthy communities and serve the common good," her January 20 statement, announcing the new rule, says. "And this final rule will have no impact on the protections that existing conscience laws and regulations give to health care providers."

In terms of the protection given to those "conscience laws and regulations," churches had already been exempted from paying for birth-control-related medical services for their employees. The Catholic Church and right-wing conservatives demanded that the exemption be extended to church-run institutions like universities and hospitals. The Obama administration obliged. On February 10, it worked out a compromise with church representatives, under which those institutions would be allowed to shift the cost of birth control coverage to their insurance companies.

Medieval Mind-Set of Catholic Church

I can think of only one reason why you still aren't satisfied: You and many in the Catholic Church have a medieval mind-set. Under your scheme of things, any sexual act that doesn't aim at procreation is sin. So paying for contraceptives is a sinful act. Even insurance companies shouldn't pay for it.

Don't you know, Cardinal, that 98 percent of Catholic women in America are not with you on this? According to a study conducted by the Guttmacher Institute, they have used some form of contraceptives sometime in their lives. Those among them who are sexually active and don't want to become pregnant regularly rely on contraceptive methods that are prohibited by the Catholic Church. Most of them, the same study says, are regular church-goers.

Doesn't a democratically elected government have a responsibility to tailor its law, which relates to women's sexual activities, to reflect the prevalent sexual practice among them? Or should it disregard the interests and rights of those women because a bunch of bachelors like you, to whom sex is supposed to be taboo, consider such tailoring an encroachment on their religious freedom? Most of these contraceptive-using women, to repeat what I said above, consider themselves religious.

You say in your letter: "We have made it clear in no uncertain terms to the government that we are not at peace with its invasive attempt to curtail the religious freedom we cherish as Catholics and Americans. We did not ask for this fight, but we will not run from it."

This is not the kind of language one expects from a Christian priest. And this is not the kind of language that Jesus, whose name you have invoked in your letter at least once, would have approved of. You don't have to go to the extent of showing the other cheek a la Jesus. But you should be catholic enough to give the other party a chance to prove that it means what it says. It says that the new "rule will have no impact on the protections that existing conscience laws and regulations give to health care providers."

In a democracy, adversaries resolve their differences through negotiations. Also in a democracy, every effort should be made to accommodate minority viewpoints. But when a minority tries to impose its antiquated views on the majority, who should be the final arbiter? That's the question you must ask yourself before you pooh-pooh the directive issued by the HHS. The problem with all organized religions is that each claims to be the final arbiter of the truth. Each claims to speak in the name of God.

The belligerent tone in the sentence – "We did not ask for this fight, but we will not run from it" – is followed by a civilized one in the next sentence, thank you. "As pastors and shepherds," you say in the next sentence, "each of us would prefer to spend our energy engaged in and promoting the works of mercy to which the Church is dedicated: healing the sick, teaching our youth, and helping the poor." It conveys the laudable mission of your vocation. Stick to that mission, Cardinal. Don't politicize your noble calling. Also, please show some mercy for the less fortunate in society, whose health issues are at stake here.

Is It a Sin to Prevent Unwanted Pregnancy?

It is unfair to characterize a legal provision aimed at helping women meet their health needs as an "intrusion into the internal life of the church." And nobody is jeopardizing "the ministries entrusted to [you] by Jesus."

Why are you turning your wrath on the Obama administration when you know full well that the 98 percent Catholic women who admit to having used contraceptives did it before the HHS Rule in question was issued? Some of them have been using them since before Obama was born. And what punishment are you going to prescribe for these women? Excommunication or stoning to death?

There is nothing sinful about preventing unwanted pregnancies unless you want to define 'sin' in medieval terms. The Obama administration did not ask women to go and buy contraceptives. It only decided to lessen the financial burden of those who have already been using them. In doing so, it was also implementing a recommendation made by the Institute of Medicine. Do you know that there are insurance companies which pay for performance-enhancing drugs that men use? You know what kind of performance I am talking about. Oh, I get it: The use of such drugs doesn't prevent procreation, and that's the reason why you are not opposed to it.

The second-last paragraph of your letter says: "Brothers, we know so very well that religious freedom is our heritage, our legacy and our firm belief, both as loyal Catholics and Americans. There have been many threats to religious freedom over the decades and years, but these often came from without. This one sadly comes from within. As our ancestors did with previous threats, we will tirelessly defend the timeless and enduring truth of religious freedom."

Which prompts me to ask: Was it while enjoying "religious freedom" that some "pastors and shepherds" engaged themselves in criminal activities? What is the remedy when the victims of those activities are innocent little children? Yes, I am talking about the crimes committed by pedophile priests that rocked the Catholic Church a few years ago. But for the "intrusion" from secular authorities, the rest of the world would never have known about those crimes. And the church hierarchy would have continued to hush them up. Barring an admirable few, all priests, all the way up to the pope, were involved in the hush-up.

Where were you, Cardinal Dolan, when your fellow priests, some of whom you might have known, were engaged in such despicable, sinful acts? I wish you had fought those pedophiles with half the fighting spirit you are demonstrating now to take on the Obama administration. Even now it is not too late. The church is still scandal-ridden, and the issue still hasn't been resolved to the satisfaction of all victims and their families. Why don't you divert your energy and spirit to fighting pedophilia instead of contraception?

In conclusion, I have to say what you already know but won't say: No freedom in this world is, and should be, absolute. If the Catholic Church had been allowed to enjoy unfettered "religious freedom," autos-da-fé would still be prevalent in many countries.

25
Shah Rukh Khan and I Have Names that Arouse Suspicion. Why Blame Others?

May 3, 2012

Shah Rukh Khan.
(*The picture is reproduced courtesy* The Hollywood Reporter.)

•

Shah Rukh Khan is a Bollywood megastar. There is no disputing of that. And he is a superhero to millions of movie-goers in India and many other countries. But to the immigration officials who detained and interrogated him at a New York airport, on April 13, 2012, he was just another passenger who arrived from abroad. They had to follow established procedures just as they would in the case of any other passenger.

Facts: Shah Rukh Khan arrived at the White Plains, New York, airport on April 13, 2012. He was on his way to Yale University, where he was to receive the university's Chubb Fellowship and address a group of people who had gathered there to see him and celebrate the event with him. The celebration was planned by Isha Ambani, daughter of India's billionaire industrialist Mukesh Ambani. Isha is a student at Yale and also the president of the university's South Asian Society. It may be added that Mr. Khan was flown to the U.S. on a private plane owned by Mukesh Ambani. Among those who accompanied him all the way from Mumbai was Mukesh's wife, Isha's mother, Nita Ambani.

The Chubb Fellowship is a rare honor Yale bestows on individuals distinguished in various fields like politics, business, science, and the arts. The only other Indian who received it, before Shah Rukh Khan, was the late Tamil Nadu Chief Minister C.N. Annadurai. Annadurai, apart from being one of the most popular chief ministers Tamil Nadu ever had, was also a powerful writer and orator in Tamil.

Mr. Khan's selection for the fellowship and of his impending visit to Yale was widely publicized both in India and in the U.S. This is how Suman Guha Mozumder, associate managing editor of *India Abroad*, reported it in the weekly newspaper: "Come April 12, Shah Rukh Khan will join the likes of former Presidents George W. Bush, Ronald Reagan and Jimmy Carter; writers Octavio Paz, Carlos Fuentes and Toni Morrison; filmmaker Sofia Coppola; architect Frank Gehry; and choreographer Mikhail Baryshnikov." *India Abroad*, published from New York, is the leading Indian-American newspaper.

Mozumder's report also says: "A measure of SRK's popularity among the Yale community is that all tickets for the event were sold out within 48 hours of its announcement." The question is: What does all this have to do with the immigration procedures everyone arriving in the U.S. has to go through? True, the procedures became too strict and a little too invasive after the terrorist attacks the U.S. suffered on September 11, 2001. Can anyone blame U.S. authorities for making it so, given that it was laxity in immigration procedures that enabled 19 terrorists responsible for 9/11 to enter the country in the first place and execute their plot later?

So the media frenzy, especially in India, over what happened to

Shah Rukh Khan on his arrival at a New York airport is uncalled for. In detaining and interrogating him, the immigration officials were only doing their job. It is to their credit that, once they realized their blunder, they apologized and let him go.

More surprising is the fact that even high-placed Indian officials who should know better joined the frenzy. I am particularly amused by External Affairs Minister S.M. Krishna's reaction to the incident. "It has become a habit these days to first detain and then apologize. This can't continue," he said, according to a report in *The Hindustan Times* of New Delhi. He also reportedly asked Nirupama Rao, India's ambassador to the U.S., to take up the matter with the U.S. authorities. He did it even after the authorities, including the U.S. embassy in New Delhi, tendered their apologies – which they did not have to do. In the absence of prior information from Indian authorities or Shah Rukh Khan himself, they had no way of knowing who he was and what the purpose of his visit was.

Indian Ambassador's Reaction

Ambassador Rao's reaction to the incident was much more mature and thoughtful. As reported in the April 27 issue of *India Abroad*, by Aziz Haniffa, editor of the paper, she did acknowledge that "Khan is an iconic figure not just in India, but across the word." But, unlike her boss back in India, she was gracious enough to give the U.S. authorities the benefit of the doubt. "I believe what happened is that his name figures in what you call 'the system,'" Haniffa quotes her as saying. While she wished that the incident had not happened, "because I don't believe Mr. Shah Rukh Khan deserved to be detained at all," she said she understood why it did: "I think post-9/11, you've had heightened levels of checks and we know you are super-careful."

Shah Rukh Khan, though upset over the incident, decided to laugh it away and even turn it into a positive experience. As reported in *India Abroad*, again, he told the Yale University audience: "Whenever I start feeling too arrogant about myself, I always take a trip to America. The immigration guys kick the star out of stardom." Laughing at himself is characteristic of Shah Rukh Khan.

One may recall the famous movie "My name is Khan and I am not a terrorist," in which he played the lead role. It came out of similar experiences those bearing the name Khan had at U.S. airports. Shah

Rukh Khan himself experienced it at New Jersey's international airport, in 2009. Let's hope that another movie comes out of this incident, too.

Ambassador Rao has the right answer to why it keeps happening to him: Mr. Khan's name "conjures up different images." Thousands of people with suspicion-arousing names have had experiences similar to his at various airports in the world. I am one of them.

'Are You Related to Velupillai Prabhakaran?'

When the late Sri Lankan terrorist Velupillai Prabhakaran was in the news, I was working as an adjunct professor of political science at the City University of New York. At the beginning of every semester, soon after I introduced myself to the new batch of students, I would hear from some of them the embarrassing question: "Are you related to Velupillai Prabhakaran?"

I knew that a mere "no" from me wouldn't satisfy their intellectual curiosity. So I would give them a brief history of how the Sri Lankan terrorist and I, a native son of the southern Indian state of Kerala, got the same name. "Prabhakaran is a common name in Kerala and the neighboring state of Tamil Nadu," I would tell them. "Velupillai Prabhakaran's ancestors emigrated from Tamil Nadu – formerly Madras – to Sri Lanka, when both India and Sri Lanka – formerly Ceylon – were British colonies." The students always found my historical tidbit delightful.

A few years later, I started traveling extensively around the world. The United States and many other countries, including India, had declared Velupillai Prabhakaran as one of the most wanted terrorists in the world. That was when my experience at various international airports became not just embarrassing, but humiliating. After checking my documents against what Ambassador Rao referred to as "the system," the immigration officials would throw a suspicious look at me. Once they were convinced that I was not the terrorist they had in their system, they would ask whether I was related to Velupillai Prabhakaran.

I always disarmed them with a laugh. And then I would add: "I want you to know that I am not at all offended by your question. If my name arouses suspicion, you are not to blame."

Some of them thanked me for my "understanding." A few of them, who had the kind of intellectual curiosity my students had, also wanted to know more about the commonality between me and the Sri Lankan terrorist. I would repeat my "brief lesson in history," as one immigration official put it while thanking me. And my initial embarrassment and humiliation would turn into elation.

The procedures, which those who arrive at U.S. airports have to go through, may have flaws. But let's not forget: If there have been no major terrorist attacks in the U.S. since 9/11, the credit for it goes to those procedures. I hope Shah Rukh Khan, like me, wouldn't mind putting up with a little inconvenience and embarrassment. And let Indian officials and the adoring fans of the Bollywood megastar not be overly critical of U.S. authorities.

26

The 2008 Terrorist Attack in Mumbai Was Sponsored by Pak Spy Agency

July 13, 2012

Pakistanis are as much hurt by Islamist terrorism as people of any other country. What are the authorities in Pakistan doing about it? Of course, when it comes to seeking American aid to fight terrorism, they do a very good job of playing victims. But when it comes to terrorism bred on its soil and directed at India, they are in total denial. The latest denial came at the end of the recent two-day talks in New Delhi between the foreign secretaries of India and Pakistan.

For several days leading to the July 4-5 talks, between foreign secretary Jalil Abbas Jilani of Pakistan and Ranjan Mathai, his Indian counterpart, media in India had been replete with reports of the arrest and confession of another terrorist, an 11th one, involved in the 2008 attack in Mumbai that killed 166 people. The terrorist, Syed Zabiuddin Ansari, disclosed during his confession that the Mumbai attack was planned and directed by the Pakistani army's infamous intelligence wing, the Inter-Services Intelligence (ISI). All 11 terrorists were trained by Lashkar-e-Taiba (LeT), the militant group created by the ISI. Destruction of India has been LeT's avowed goal since its very inception.

Mr. Ansari's disclosure about the ISI role in the Mumbai attack did not come as a surprise to anyone. He was only reconfirming what the world already knew. What did come as a surprise was the Pakistani foreign secretary's feigning of surprise on hearing about it from India's External Affairs Minister S.M. Krishna, whom he had met after the secretaries-level talks. He pretended as though he was hearing about it for the first time. As reported in the media, he even went to the extent of telling Mr. Krishna that if India had any evidence of the ISI role in the Mumbai attack, it should have been first presented to Pakistani authorities and not journalists. Mr. Krishna, as befits a seasoned diplomat, did not laugh away Mr. Jilani's stupid remark. He even dignified it with a response: that it was not possible for a democracy like India to gag the media.

For the Pakistani official's information, India is one of the few countries in the world that can boast of a vibrant, free press. Very often, especially in the case of terror-related stories, enterprising reporters come out with the stories first, and government action follows later. In the present case, it was neither the Indian press nor the Indian government that first disclosed the ISI's despicable plot against India. It was the man whom the spy agency had employed to do the initial dirty work for it. He was David Coleman Headley, who is now in U.S. custody.

To repeat what is discussed in Chapter 18, "India's War on Terror: Troubling Questions on U.S. Cooperation," Mr. Headley was a key player in the 2008 terrorist attack in Mumbai. Son of a Pakistani diplomat by his American wife, he was a criminal who did his time for drug trafficking. He later became a paid informant for the U.S. Drug Enforcement Administration, in Pakistan. His dual citizenship and roots in both Pakistan and the U.S. came in handy for the job. He was the one whom the ISI sent to Mumbai to do reconnaissance work and pick targets for the attack. One of the targets he picked was Mumbai's storied Taj Mahal Hotel, a marvelous piece of architecture, where he had stayed during his reconnaissance trips. He admitted to India's National Investigation Agency, which had questioned him in New York in connection with the attack, that his stay at the Taj was financed by the ISI.

According to a front-page story in the October 17, 2010, edition of *The New York Times*, U.S. authorities had known about Mr. Headley's terrorism link as early as 2005. The story, by the paper's three enterprising reporters, Jane Perlez, Eric Schmitt and Ginger Thompson, says that the authorities first heard about it from Headley's American wife – one of his three wives. She had informed federal investigators in New York that her husband was a member of Lashkar-e-Taiba. He used to shamelessly boast that he was working as an American informant while also training with the terrorist outfit, she had told them, according to the *Times* story.

Two years later, the same *Times* story says, Headley's Moroccan wife, Faiza Outalha, had alerted the authorities on her husband's link to terrorism. Twice in 2007, she approached American officials at the United States Embassy in Islamabad, Pakistan's capital, and told them that Headley had many friends who were known members of Lashkar-e-Taiba. Isn't it reasonable to conclude that the U.S. had shared with Pakistan the information it had about Mr. Headley's terrorist connections? After all, the two countries were allies in the war against terrorism.

LeT, the Most Dangerous Terror Group

Now that Al Qaeda's leadership is decimated, LeT has emerged as the most dangerous terror group in the world. It attained the elevated lethal status mainly because of the consistent support it received from its creator, the ISI. It has been reported that the security of the LeT supremo, Hafiz Muhammad Saeed, is handled by the ISI. It doesn't matter that he heads a terrorist outfit outlawed by the U.S. The protection provided by the ISI enables him to move freely within Pakistan and give lectures to jihadists. And this, despite the fact that the U.S. has announced a $10 million reward for information leading to his arrest. One wonders what prevents Pakistan from arresting him.

Laskar-e-Taiba is a creature of the ISI. The ISI is an integral part of the Pakistani army. How can Pakistan disown responsibility for the Mumbai carnage which was sponsored by the ISI and executed by LeT? What more information do Pakistani authorities need to bring the guilty to justice than the evidence provided by three men who were intimately involved in the attack?

We already discussed the role played by one of them, Mr. Headley. The other two are Ajmal Amir Kasab, the sole survivor among the ten terrorists who carried out the attack and who is now awaiting his sentence in a Mumbai prison cell; and Syed Zabiuddin Ansari, whose arrest and confession last month exposed the dubious double game Pakistan has been playing in the war on terror: taking money from the U.S. to fight terrorism, or at least to make a show of fighting it, while training terrorists and sending them on destroy-India missions.

Terrorists struck Mumbai on November 26, 2008. The bloodbath that followed lasted 60 hours. On November 29, 2008, the Mumbai police learned from Mr. Kasab that he and his fellow terrorists were trained by LeT and sent to Mumbai with instructions to kill as many people as they could. It was from him that Indian authorities heard, for the first time, about the involvement of an eleventh terrorist, an Indian. On May 21, 2009, while giving evidence to Justice M.L. Tahaliyani, at Mumbai's Arthur Road prison, Mr. Kasab said that the man who guided the 60-hour Mumbai operation, from a command-and-control center in Karachi, Pakistan, was one Abu Jundal.

The Indian authorities also learned that it was Abu Jundal who tutored the terrorists on how to conduct themselves as local Hindus while in Mumbai and speak in colloquial Hindi used in that city. He also instructed them to greet people with the Hindu 'Namaste,' not the Muslim 'Asalaamu Alaikum,' and wear the Hindu-holy red threads, says *India Today*, a prestigious Indian fortnightly magazine, in the cover story in its July 16, 2012, issue.

The cover story, entitled "The Secret Plot to Blame India," and written by its senior editor Sandeep Unnithan, adds that it was David Headley who bought the sacred threads. He bought them, for 20 rupees each, at Mumbai's Siddhivinayak Temple, during one of his scouting trips to the city. The *India Today* story also says that all "10 terrorists carried fake identity cards of Arunodaya College, located in Hyderabad. They also took Hindu names. Ajmal Kasab became Sameer Choudhary and Ismail Khan was Naraish Verma. An LeT operative pretended to be 'Kharak Singh from India' and purchased Internet calling services from a US-based firm for $250 (Rs. 10,000). The terrorists were told to communicate with their Karachi-based handlers using phones with Indian SIM cards."

All these details came out during the interrogation of Ajmal Kasab and Abu Jundal, the Indian terrorist. The latter's services came in handy for LeT in its efforts to make the Mumbai attack look like something launched by Indians.

Abu Jundal is not the Indian terrorist's actual name. It is one of the aliases he used to hide his identity. His actual name is Syed Zabiuddin Ansari. Born and brought up in Gevrai village in Maharashtra State's Beed district, he "became an anti-India radical after the 2002 Gujarat riots and went into the shadows of terrorism, first joining the Students Islamic Movement (SIMI), then the LeT," according to the *India Today* story.

Already involved in a couple of terror-related cases in India, he escaped to Pakistan with help from LeT. The *India Today* story goes on to say: "His name entered the public domain when the Indian government handed over a list of 50 Most Wanted Fugitives to the Pakistani authorities in March 2007."

Saudis Deport Abu Jundal to India

Instead of returning the fugitive to India, Pakistan issued him a fake passport and sent him to Saudi Arabia to recruit potential jihadists from Indian laborers, on behalf of LeT. The passport was issued in the name of Riyasat Ali, another alias used by Mr. Ansari. He arrived in Damman, an oil-rich port city in Saudi Arabia, in early 2011. Posing as a Pakistani national, he ran a taxi rental business for cover.

Since his arrival in Saudi Arabia last year, India had been pressuring the Saudis to deport him to India. The U.S. intelligence also put pressure on the Saudis, providing proof of his terrorist connections. Once the Saudis were convinced that he was indeed an LeT operative and an Indian national, not Pakistani as Islamabad claimed, they decided to abide by international law and deport him to India. On his arrival at New Delhi's Indira Gandhi International Airport, on June 21, 2012, the police promptly arrested him.

Apart from his own confession to the Delhi police, Indian authorities had another valuable piece of evidence to prove his being present in the LeT control room in Karachi, handling the Mumbai operation. He was one of the four handlers. The evidence is the record of a cell phone conversation between him and one of the two terrorists assigned to attack the Jewish target in Mumbai, Chabad House. Also known as Nariman House, Chabad House is a synagogue and a Jewish outreach center. Terrorists killed six of its occupants, including Rabbi Gavriel Noach Holtzberg and his wife, Rivka, who was five months pregnant. Their two-year-old son Moshe survived the attack after being rescued by his Indian nanny, Sandra Samuel. Following is the transcript of the conversation between the terrorist and his handler in Karachi, as reproduced in the June 26, 2012, edition of *The Times of India*:

Handler (H): Remember that every one person you kill there is killing 50 other... .
H: Listen.
Terrorist (T): Yes, yes.
H: Get rid of these people. Kill them.
T: By Allah's wish it is all quiet. There is no movement.
H: No, no, wait. Shoot. If firing starts, you won't know the timing, direction and intensity.
T: I've run out of grenades.

H: Do it.
T: What? Shoot them?
H: Yes. Make them sit up and shoot them in the backs of their heads.
(Later)
H: Have you done the job or not?
T: No, I will do it front of you. I was waiting for you.
H: Do it in the name of Allah.
(Woman screams: Please don't kill me!)
H: You killed one?
T: Both together.
T: Allah willing, today is Friday. Today will be the final fight.
H: Use all of your might. Do it. Shoot them. Get them.
T: Intense fire has started. Firing has started in our room.
H: Take cover.
(A little later)
H: Yes, what happened?
T: I've been hit.
H: Where?
T: In my side and on my leg.
H: May Allah protect you.
T: Pray for me, so that I attain martyrdom.

Indian authorities have concluded that the Karachi handler is Mr. Ansari. He has told the Delhi police that ISI personnel were present in the control room when the attack was being monitored and directed.

Conspiracy Theory Floated by Pakistan

What was Pakistani authorities' reaction when all this was brought to their attention?

"Our information is that there were at least 40 Indian nationals who helped the attackers. We want India to come clean on this," an unnamed official of Pakistan's Foreign Office reportedly said to the media. One can bet: The purpose is not to get to the root of the problem and punish the guilty in the ISI. It is to strengthen the conspiracy theory Pakistan has been floating since the attack: That Hindu militants were behind it. Remember the conspiracy theory which apologists for 9/11 terrorists bandied about in the U.S.? That 9/11 was carefully planned and executed by Zionists with a view to defaming Islam?

Pakistan's conspiracy theorists did get some help from a section of the Urdu press in India and some Indian politicians. They blamed Hindu extremists for the carnage. Aziz Burney, the group editor of *Roznama Rashtriya Sahara*, an Urdu daily, had said that "CIA, Mossad, Narendra Modi [the BJP Chief Minister of Gujarat] and RSS [Rashtriya Swayam Sevak Sangh, a Hindu-sectarian organization] are responsible for the attack."

All those conspiracy theorists have been silenced now. Irrefutable evidence provided by the key plotters and perpetrators of the carnage has proved that it was masterminded by the ISI and its terrorist offspring, Lashkare-e-Taiba.

Pakistan is left with only one option: Punish the guilty and cleanse the country of the scourge of terrorism or be prepared to be treated as an international pariah. Playing the victim of terrorism on one hand and aiding and abetting it on the other won't work any longer.

Most Pakistanis that I know want to live in peace with India. And most Indians, I can vouch, want to live in peace with Pakistan, too. What stands in the way is the notorious spy wing of the Pakistani army. Can the civilian authorities in Pakistan do something about it?

Mumbai's famed Taj Mahal Hotel, as it looked after the 2008 terrorist attack (left); and as it looks after being restored to its original grandeur (right).

27
Chetan Bhagat's Stupid Advice to Salman Rushdie

July 23, 2012

Chetan Bhagat is a hugely successful – commercially successful, I mean – Indian novelist. I admire him for that. Not for a moment had I thought that he was capable of coming out with a stupid statement like this one:

"Salman Rushdie was coming to India [for the Jaipur Literature Festival]. The fundamentalists tried to stop it. But I felt he could have reached out to them instead of saying provocative things which he knows can incite tension."

It is hard to imagine that these are the words of the same Chetan Bhagat who had chastised government authorities, on January 17, 2012, with the following tweet: "If you have to appease and pander, at least appease the modern thinking Muslims. A govt with a PhD PM [a reference to the Indian Prime Minister Manmohan Singh who has a doctorate in economics from the London School of Economics] is listening to fundamentalists. Sad."

Now he is chastising Rushdie for not having reached out to those fundamentalists. Will the real Chetan Bhagat please stand up?

The investment banker turned best-selling author made the statement, faulting Rushdie for not having reached out to religious fundamentalists, in an interview with Jason Chow, a Hong Kong-based correspondent of *The Wall Street Journal*. The interview appeared in the paper's July 20, 2012, edition. Mr. Bhagat was visiting Hong Kong to attend the city's annual book fair.

Here is my question to him: When did religious fundamentalists ever listen to reason? And we are not talking about just any religious fundamentalists, but Islamist-religious fundamentalists. In their scheme of things, those who oppose them are infidels killing whom is not only sanctified; it guarantees them a place in Paradise.

Chetan Bhagat goes on to say in the same interview: "As an artist, we should have full freedom. Tomorrow, I can write something that can spark a riot. Should I do it? I have the right to do it, no question, but if I take an extreme stance, never shall the twain meet."

As an artist, you also have a responsibility to speak the truth, Mr. Bhagat. Fundamentalists will twist and turn your words to advance their agenda. No matter what you meant when you used those words, they can see "extreme stance" in it, if they want to. A true artist doesn't play to the gallery. Maybe that's what makes Salman Rushdie different from you. Do what your conscience dictates. But don't be under any illusion that you are in a position to give advice to Rushdie.

For the benefit of those who are not familiar with the background of Mr. Bhagat's advice to Mr. Rushdie, let me briefly narrate it:

The Jaipur Literature Festival, an annual gathering of litterateurs and literature lovers, which started in 2006 with a mere 18 writers and 100 attendees, has by now grown into the largest annual literary gathering in the Asia-Pacific region. The festival takes its name from the capital city of the Indian state of Rajasthan, where it is held. Jaipur is also known as the Pink City for the pink coating given to most of its buildings.

The 2012 festival, held from January 20 to 24, got mired in controversy even before it began. The reason? The festival organizers had touted the world-famous author Salman Rushdie as one of this year's major attractions, along with American TV talk show queen Oprah Winfrey. Rushdie, who had attended the festival in 2007, had been enthusiastically looking forward to doing it this year too. Alas, that was not to be. Islamist fundamentalists in India and a few politicians cowed down by them successfully campaigned to keep him out of it.

The Satanic Verses

Mr. Bhagat may please note that it was not any "provocative things" Mr. Rushdie said recently that instigated the fanatics to act. Their ire against him goes all the way back to 1988, the year in which his famous novel *The Satanic Verses* was published. No sooner had the novel been published, on September 26, 1988, than the fanatical fringe among Muslims got outraged. They found it blasphemous to Islam, because of the allegorical allusions in it to the Prophet Muhammad and a few other characters in the Koran.

Barely a month after the book's publication, India banned it. That is, India banned *The Satanic Verses* even before most Muslim countries did it. Iran not only banned the book, but also issued a fatwa to kill its author. The fatwa was issued, on February 14, 1989, by the late Ayatollah Ruhollah Khomeini who was the Supreme Leader of Iran at the time. The British government swung into action to protect its celebrity citizen. It moved him from safe house to safe house and made sure that no crony of Khomeini's would touch him.

The persecuted author got a respite in 1998, when the new government of Iran, under its reformist president Mohammad Khatami, announced that it no longer had any intention of enforcing, or of helping anyone to enforce, the fatwa. Since then, Rushdie has been relishing his new-found freedom of movement, though the fanatics' threat on his life always lurked in a corner of his mind all the time.

Getting back to India's banning of *The Satanic Verses*, it did it at the instance of the late Rajiv Gandhi who was the prime minister of the country, and in control of the Congress Party, at the time. And he did it with a view to currying favor with the large Muslim followers of the Congress Party. Disgustingly, the ban is still in force in democratic India, while in many authoritarian countries, which had once banned the book, it is freely available now. It has been translated into over 50 languages around the world.

It deserves special mention here that in Turkey, which is 98 percent Muslim, the book is available. Not in India, whose population is only 16 percent Muslim. Such is the power of the Muslim vote bank in India. That power, it is said, was what kept Rushdie out of the Jaipur Literature Festival this year.

As soon as it was announced that he would participate in the festival, the clerics of the Darul Uloom Deoband, an Islamic seminary based in Deoband, in the northern Indian state of Uttar Pradesh, and of other Islamic institutions called on their followers to organize protests to block his arrival. It is reasonable to assume that hardly any of these protesters had read *The Satanic Verses*, let alone appreciate its literary merit. Thanks to its literary merit, the book won, barely two months after its publication, the Whitbread Book Award (now known as the Costa Book Award) for the novel of the year. Mr. Rushdie had won the prestigious Booker Prize in 1981 for *Midnight's Children*, a historical novel set in the context of India's transition from colonial rule to independence.

Congress Party Appeases Fanatics

The moment a few Muslim fanatics declared that the man who "insulted Islam" would not be allowed to come to the Jaipur festival, the Congress party-controlled government of Rajasthan State, headed by Chief Minister Ashok Gehlot, decided to appease them. Mr. Gehlot expressed concern over the possible disturbance to peace Rushdie's visit might cause. The state authorities, with the tacit approval of the central government under Prime Minister Manmohan Singh, let it be known to festival organizers, and even to Rushdie, that his safety could not be guaranteed. A distressed Rushdie issued the flowing statement from abroad:

"For the last several days I have made no public comment about my proposed trip to the Jaipur Literary Festival, at the request of the local authorities in Rajasthan, hoping that they would put in place such precautions as might be necessary to allow me to come and address the Festival audience in circumstances that were comfortable and safe for all.

"I have now been informed by intelligence sources in Maharashtra and Rajasthan that paid assassins from the Mumbai underworld may be on their way to Jaipur to 'eliminate' me. While I have some doubts about the accuracy of this intelligence, it would be irresponsible of me to come to the Festival in such circumstances; irresponsible to my family, to the festival audience, and to my fellow writers. I will therefore not travel to Jaipur as planned."

Many in India had thought until then that only a bunch of Muslim fanatics was opposed to Rushdie's participation in the festival. The government agencies' warning to Rushdie, if true, made it clear to them that the fanatics were in collusion with the Mumbai underworld. Which meant that the fanatics knew the whereabouts of the underworld goons who wanted to "eliminate" Rushdie if he showed up at the festival. Why didn't the authorities arrest them?

Manufactured Threat

All this adds credibility to Rushdie's suspicion, which a section of the Indian media confirmed at the time, that the threat was manufactured by the Congress Party so it could portray itself as the "caretaker of Muslim interests." It was also reported at the time that the party was prompted to do it because of the soon-to-be-held election in Uttar Pradesh. The Congress Party calculated that the large Muslim population of Uttar Pradesh, which is the most populous Indian state, could sway the outcome of the election.

The prestigious Indian daily *The Hindu* hit the nail on the head when it wrote in its January 23, 2012, editorial entitled "A national shame": "Occupying centre stage in the hall of shame is Rajasthan Chief Minister Ashok Gehlot, who ought to have ensured his administration defended Indian law by securing Mr. Rushdie. ... The Rajasthan Police, for their part, must come clean on precisely who in their ranks fabricated the plot against Mr. Rushdie. ... The police officers concerned not just broke the law but have brought about the humiliation of the country. ... Self-styled Muslim leaders, as well as political groups who have opportunistically allied themselves with these forces over the years, should also be held to account for the real damage they have caused to democracy and secularism in India – and, thus, to the interests of the religious community they claim to speak for. Mr. Rushdie is entitled to a full apology for this shameful episode and to an unconditional assurance that he is welcome in India at any time and place. Prime Minister Singh must ensure he receives both."

The editorial is required reading for Chetan Bhagat.

28

An Appeal to Civilized Nations in the World:
Can One of You Come Forward to Try Iraq War Criminals?

March 24, 2013

The architects of the Iraq war in the George W. Bush administration (clockwise from top left): President George W. Bush; Vice President Dick Cheney; Deputy Defense Secretary Paul Wolfowitz; and Defense Secretary Donald Rumsfeld.

•

The United States began invasion of Iraq on March 19, 2003. It gave two reasons for the invasion: one, Iraq possessed weapons of mass destruction (WMD) which posed an imminent threat to the U.S.; and two, it had ties to Osama bin Laden's Al Qaeda, which was responsible for the September 11, 2001, terrorist attacks on the U.S. Both reasons turned out to be lies fabricated by the Bush administration.

It was easy for the administration to make the lies believable because the country was still reeling from the 9/11 attacks, which had claimed more than 3,000 lives and destroyed property worth billions of dollars. However, within months of the invasion, it became clear that Iraq did not have any weapons of mass destruction. It also became clear that, long before the Bush administration ordered the invasion, it had known that the Iraqi dictator Saddam Hussein and Al Qaeda founder Osama bin Laden detested each other. More astonishingly, evidence began to emerge that the Bush administration had slanted and hyped intelligence data on the so-called Iraqi threat to justify the invasion, which it had been planning from day one in office. The ultimate goal of the plan was to get rid of Saddam Hussein at any cost.

No normal human being in the world is sorry that Saddam Hussein is gone. The question is: At what cost? To quote from *The New York Times*'s March 20, 2013, editorial, "Ten years after it began, the Iraq war still haunts the United States in the nearly 4,500 troops who died there; the more than 30,000 Americans wounded who have come home; the more than $2 trillion spent on combat operations and reconstruction, which inflated the deficit; and in the lessons learned about the limits of American leadership and power.

"It haunts Iraq too, where the total number of casualties is believed to have surpassed 100,000 but has never been officially determined; and where one strongman was traded for another, albeit under a more pluralistic system with a democratic veneer."

The popularity of the present "strongman" (read Prime Minister Nuri Kamal al-Maliki) and his "pluralistic system" of government can be gauged from the way many Iraqis observed the tenth anniversary of the invasion. They did it by setting off a dozen bombs that killed 65 people and wounded nearly 200.

There were no anti-American terrorist groups in Iraq during Saddam's rule. The American invasion has given birth to quite a few. One of them calls itself Al Qaeda in Iraq and it has claimed responsibility for the tenth anniversary carnage.

As a report from Baghdad, in *The Huffington Post*, says, "The symbolism of Tuesday's attacks was strong, coming 10 years to the day, Washington time, that President George W. Bush announced the start of hostilities against Iraq." The report also says that most of the attacks targeted Shiite areas in Baghdad. The post-Saddam Hussein Iraq is continually racked by sectarian violence, mainly between Shiites, who constitute 60 percent of the population and who play the lead role in the present government, and Sunnis, who make up only 20 percent of the population. It may be noted that the Sunnis were part of the ruling elite under Saddam Hussein, who was a Sunni himself.

It was at the behest of the U.S. that the Iraqi government, which came to power with U.S. blessings, initiated legal proceedings against Saddam Hussein and his henchmen for the atrocities they committed during their tyrannical rule. They were made to pay a heavy price for what they did. Saddam Hussein paid for it with his life.

The Biggest Culprits in Iraq War

But what about the biggest culprits, in pursuance of whose lies the U.S. went to war in Iraq? I am referring to the architects of the Iraq war in the Bush administration: President George W. Bush himself; Vice President Dick Cheney; Defense Secretary Donald Rumsfeld; and Deputy Defense Secretary Paul Wolfowitz. They haven't uttered even a word of regret for what they did. Bush is hiding somewhere in his Texas ranch. And Rumsfeld has not been heard from lately. Surprisingly, Wolfowitz and Cheney, continue to justify their action, though the former doesn't do it in as sickening a form as the latter.

Though, theoretically, President Bush must take ultimate responsibility for whatever was done in the name of his administration, the whole world knows that the Torquemada of the Bush campaign in Iraq was Vice President Dick Cheney. In a recently released documentary entitled *The World According to Dick Cheney,* he says, shamelessly, "If I have to do it over again, I will do it in a minute."

That makes us wonder whether this man, who has somebody else's heart beating in him, is of stable mind. One shudders to think that, for long eight years, he was only a heartbeat away from presidency. If the Iraq invasion has made the rest of the world ridicule America as an international bully, Vice President Dick Cheney is largely to blame. Americans owe it to their Constitution that he and his cohorts in crime be brought to book. The crime is violation international law, which in turn is a violation of the U.S. Constitution.

There was a move in Congress to impeach President Bush. It did not go far enough because the Democratic members of Congress, with some notable exceptions, proved to be a spineless lot. The same can be said about most members of the media in the country, too. They were easily sold on Bush lies about WMD. And when the impeachment move was on, most of them did not give it the importance it deserved. The few in the print media that cared to report it buried it in inside pages. The broadcast media – the ones that deigned to air it at all, I mean – gave it a passing reference. In fact, foreign media gave the impeachment drive against Bush a wider coverage.

Here is how it fizzled out: On June 9, 2008, Democratic Congressman from Ohio, Dennis Kucinich (now retired), introduced a resolution in the House of Representatives, listing 35 cases of "high crimes and misdemeanors" against President Bush, and demanded his impeachment. Article II, Section 4 of the U.S. Constitution says: "The President, Vice President and all Civil Officers of the United States, shall be removed from Office on Impeachment for, and Conviction of, Treason, Bribery, or other high Crimes and Misdemeanors."

Though the Democrats were in majority in the House at the time, they were lackadaisical toward the Kucinich resolution. By a 251-to-166 vote, the House decided to send the articles of impeachment to a committee for further consideration. It is a strategy often used to kill a resolution. The reason given by Nancy Pelosi, Speaker of the House at the time, and other members of the Democratic leadership in the House, was that such a resolution would be too divisive. So they decided to take it "off the table" and allowed to languish in a committee. But what about the vow they took to "support and defend the Constitution"?

Impeachment of Bill Clinton

It may be recalled that when Republicans were in majority in Congress and when they decided to impeach President Bill Clinton, they did it with a vengeance. What was the crime Mr. Clinton committed? He lied about an affair he had with a White House intern. The affair might have caused some stain on the intern's dress. But not a single human being was killed as a result of Clinton's lies about it. What Bush did in pursuance of his lies has not only caused the deaths of thousands of people but also permanently stained the reputation of America as a law-abiding country. And the Democratic-controlled Congress had no guts to go after the man who did it!

Now that President Bush, Vice President Cheney and the others involved in the crime are out of office, talking about a failed move to impeach them may be a waste of time. But we owe it to posterity that they be held accountable for what they did. It is not enough that we preach to rogue nations like North Korea and Iran to respect international law and order. We have to set an example by respecting them ourselves.

President Bush and the other architects of the Iraq war in his administration are guilty of war crimes. Let them not be under any illusion that they are absolved of their culpability simply because they are out of office; and simply because no court in the U.S. acted against them until now. They should know that the International Criminal Court and the courts of law in all countries that are parties to the U.N. Charter are vested with the authority to try war criminals. The authority is derived from what is known in international law as universal jurisdiction.

It is no secret that Bush and Cheney have utter contempt for international laws and international organizations. But let them be on notice that the arms of international law will reach them one day. I am sure they are aware that there are a few countries in Europe waiting for a chance to apprehend and put on trial former Secretary of State Henry Kissinger for the crimes he committed while in office. He has been running away from the legal jurisdictions of those countries. His crimes have been well documented in the late Christopher Hitchens's *The Trial of Henry Kissinger*.

The war crimes the architects of the Iraq war committed are far graver than those of Kissinger. Can one of the civilized nations in the world come forward to try them?

29
Triumph of Capitalism Under Lenin's Very Nose

October 1, 2013

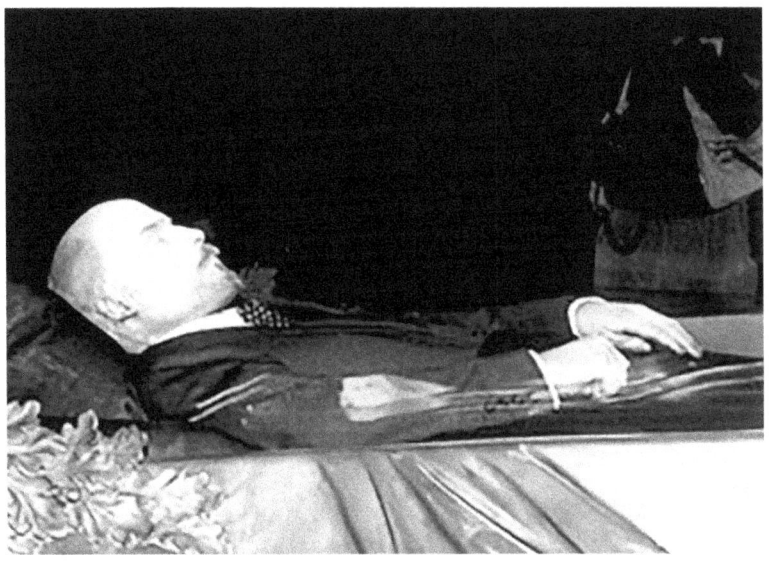

Vladimir Lenin's embalmed body preserved inside the Lenin Mausoleum, in Moscow's Red Square.

•

Last month, I took a river cruise from Moscow to St. Petersburg. Other than Moscow and St. Petersburg, the largest and the second-largest cities in Russia, the cruise was entirely through its countryside. Given the size of the country, the largest in the world, straddling two continents and stretching over six and a half million square miles, the area a 10-day river cruise can cover is insignificant. The experience I had, however, was memorable. My first appraisal at the end of the cruise was: Czars might have come, ruled and gone. Communists might have come, ruled and gone. But the beauty of Russia's countryside and the simplicity of life in its villages have remained untarnished.

Though some of the czars were tyrannical, the monuments and

icons representing the country's czarist past are zealously preserved and have become great tourist attractions. Now, they are rich sources of revenue for both government and tour companies. That's not the case with the remnants of the country's communist past that are still lying around, though. If anything, those remnants reinforce the widely held view that the communists, who were the unchallenged rulers of Russia for over seven decades, have become an endangered species now. Among the few exceptions I noticed were the cruise ship, which was my home for 10 days, and a tomb in Moscow's Red Square. Both memorialize Vladimir Lenin, the man who led the Bolshevik Revolution in 1917, which ushered in the era of communism in Russia in 1918.

As we entered the ship, the *MS Lenin*, we were welcomed aboard by two young women at the reception desk. Though they were young and attractive, deserving of prolonged gaze, my gaze soon fell on a picture that was hanging on the wall behind the desk. It was that of Lenin. I couldn't help contrasting the exalted position Lenin occupied on the ship – maybe because the ship was named after him – with the contemptuous level he has been relegated to in all former communist countries. In Budapest, the capital of Hungary, which I had visited three years earlier, the statues of Lenin, Stalin and other oracles of communism have been removed from all public squares and dumped in a place called the Statue Park.

It struck me as odd that a cruise company that is a capitalist enterprise should name one of its ships after a person who worked for the destruction of capitalism all his life. I came up with my own explanation: The American-based travel agency that sold me the cruise package did not choose the ship and did not care whom the ship was named after. It settled for the best deal it could get for the money it collected from me and others who bought the package. The best deal was offered by Vodohod, a Nizhny Novgorod-based cruise company.

Vodohod, the largest cruise company in Russia, owns many ships, one of which is the *MS Lenin*. When the 272-passenger-capacity ship was built, in 1987, the Soviet Union, of which Russia was a constituent republic, was still a communist country. And Lenin was revered as the father of the nation. The collapse of communism in the Soviet Union, which led to its eventual disintegration into several independent nations, occurred only in 1991. The ship which Vodohod put on the Volga River cruise, in the time slot we chose, happened to be the *MS Lenin*.

It will be interesting to watch whether the company is going to change the ship's name sometime in the future, given the present de-Leninization and de-Stalinization trend in all former communist countries. Until then, we will have to live with the dichotomy of a ship named after a man who was the embodiment of communism engaging in capitalist activity.

Proletarian Meal

Though the ship was engaged in bourgeois activity, the very first meal we were served on board was very proletarian: a small quantity of baked potatoes and meat, with no second helping. We were disappointed. But the beauty and friendliness of the Ukrainian waitress who served us more than made up for it. The quantity and quality of meals improved somewhat in subsequent days, though they never reached the level one is used to on oceanic cruises. Maybe that's the difference between a river cruise and an oceanic cruise.

Other than the ship, there was another important reminder of Russia's communist past during the ten days we spent in the country: Lenin's tomb, also known as Lenin's Mausoleum, in Red Square. We were given a tour of Moscow on the first two days, before the cruise began,. There is hardly any conducted tour of the city that doesn't include visits to the Kremlin and Red Square. In 1990, the UNESCO elevated them to the status of World Heritage Sites. Lenin's Mausoleum is on the wall that separates the Kremlin from Red Square.

Admission to the mausoleum was free. Surprisingly, despite free admission, the number of people that we saw lining up to get in was small, compared with the long lines in front of other landmark structures in Red Square, especially St. Basil's Cathedral and the State History Museum. Only a few people from our tour group decided to join me when I announced my decision to visit the mausoleum.

There were also other reasons for my decision: On the day I was in Red Square four years earlier, the mausoleum was closed, and I was disappointed. During that visit, standing in front of the mausoleum, a woman from Siberia who had been in my tour group had whispered into my ears that what was lying inside was not Lenin's embalmed body, but his look-alike in wax. "His actual body was shipped away long ago and buried elsewhere," she had said, following it with a chuckle. I took the chuckle to mean that I was not supposed to take what she said seriously.

Lately, rumors have been rife that the body could any day be removed from the mausoleum and buried somewhere else. "I should visit the mausoleum before that happens," I said to myself while heading toward it.

Once inside, I had the same eerie feeling as when I was inside the Ho Chi Minh Mausoleum in Hanoi, three years earlier. Maybe the Ho Chi Minh Mausoleum, including the darkness of its chambers, was modeled on this one. At both places, the guards were as motionless as the bodies they were guarding. The only time they showed some signs of life was when visitors lingered in front of the bodies longer than a few seconds. Using their index fingers, the guards gestured to them to move on.

At the Ho Chi Minh Mausoleum, I had been the target of the guard's finger-wagging, but for a different reason. After watching Ho Chi Minh's body for a few seconds, I wanted to jot down the immediate thoughts that crossed my mind. When I reached into my trousers' pocket for my notebook and pen, a guard standing nearby stared at me and wagged his index finger. He meant that my intended action was forbidden. Did he think that I was reaching for a weapon?

GUM Department Store

The mausoleum visit took only a few minutes. It was not part of the conducted tour. As we came out of the mausoleum, I reminded my friends what our tour guide had said while leaving us on our own to do whatever we felt like doing before we headed back to the ship. If time permitted, she had said, it wouldn't be a bad idea to do some window-shopping at GUM. We had one more hour left. GUM, the largest shopping mall in Moscow, was staring at us from the opposite side of Red Square. We decided to go in.

GUM is acronym for *Glavnyi Universalnyi Magazin* in Russian. It literally means the main universal store. In Soviet times, when it was state-owned, it was called *Gosudarstvennyi* (state) *Universalnyi Magazin*. The partial change in the name was made in 2005, when the store became 50 percent privatized. It is now fully privatized.

GUM has a storied past. The site on which it stands now has been used for trading throughout Russia's history. The first building, a large stone arcade, came up in 1520. Later, during the reign of Catherine the Great (1762-1796), a huge trade center was built in its place. The

The GUM Department Store in Moscow, as seen from the main entrance in Red Square. The sprawling store, stocked with imported goods produced by multinational corporations in the West, symbolizes the triumph of capitalism in what was once the center of the Communist World. It offers a striking contrast to the Lenin Mausoleum, situated right across from it in the same Red Square, which memorializes the era of communism in the Soviet Union.

•

trade center was commissioned by the empress and designed by the famous Italian neoclassical architect of the period Giacomo Quarenghi. Unfortunately, the building burned down in 1812, during Napoleon's attack on Moscow.

Another impressive structure came up in its place. It was designed by Joseph Bove, another famous architect with Italian roots. But in the 1880s, it was demolished to make way for what came to be called the Upper Trading Rows. The new structure was a collaborative venture undertaken by architect Aleksander Pomerantsev and engineer Vladimir Shukov. It was completed in 1893. Its steel framework and glass roof were, at the time, on the cutting edge of technology. At the end of the 19th century, it was the largest shopping center in Europe.

After the Bolshevik Revolution, the shopping center was nationalized and renamed GUM. In 1928, Stalin closed GUM and decided to use the building as the headquarters for officials working on the country's first Five Year Plan. In 1953, after the dictator's death, it was reopened. When re-opened, GUM became one of the few stores in the Soviet Union that did not have shortages of consumer goods. It is said that the shoppers who lined up to get in often extended all the way to the other end of Red Square.

There were no such long lines when we visited the place. Most of the people we saw were window-shoppers like us. A quick glance at the products displayed at all storefronts told us why they refused to be actual shoppers: The products, almost all of them manufactured by Western multinational corporations, were priced too high. Too high, even for tourists from the United States. Having just come out of the Lenin Mausoleum, one couldn't help thinking that malls like this one would make Lenin's embalmed body squirm. Wasn't it Lenin who said that capitalism would break at its strongest link? Well, what broke at its strongest link was not capitalism, but communism.

GUM, the mammoth department store in Moscow's Red Square, symbolizes the triumph of capitalism under Lenin's very nose.

30

Nixon and Kissinger Were Complicit in the 1971 Genocide in Bangladesh

May 2, 2014

President Richard Nixon and National Security Adviser Henry Kissinger, aboard Air Force One as it heads toward Brussels, Belgium, for a NATO meeting. Mr. Nixon is seen resting his legs on a pillow atop a table to ease the pain caused by phlebitis. (*The picture and the caption, as edited, are reproduced courtesy* Getty Images.)

•

(*The main source for this article is* THE BLOOD TELEGRAM: Nixon, Kissinger, and a Forgotten Genocide, *by Gary J. Bass, published in 2013 by Alfred A. Knopf.*)

The first thought that came to mind after I finished reading *THE BLOOD TELEGRAM* was: If Nazi criminals are still being hunted down and punished for the crime of genocide against Jews committed over 70 years ago, how come there has never been any such move against the perpetrators of genocide against Bengalis, committed over 40 years ago? Let's thank Gary J. Bass, a professor of politics and international affairs at Princeton University, for not letting the world forget the 1971 genocide in Bangladesh and the culprits responsible for it.

First, a quick survey of the events that led to the heinous crime, which in turn led to the breakup of Pakistan and creation of a new nation called Bangladesh:

When the British decided to grant independence to the Indian Subcontinent, in 1947, they also decided to partition it into two independent states: India and Pakistan. Pakistan was carved out of the Muslim-majority areas in the eastern and western wings of the Subcontinent. The carnage that preceded and followed its creation had claimed a million lives. Because of that carnage, and because of a few yet-to-be-settled issues associated with the partition, relations between India and Pakistan have never been cordial. Since their independence from Britain, they have fought three wars and engaged in numerous armed conflicts on their borders.

The viability of Pakistan as one political entity had been in doubt at its very birth, mainly because it existed in two wings separated by a thousand miles of India. When author Gary Bass calls it a "cartographic oddity," he is only rephrasing the term used by the late Louis Mountbatten. As the last British viceroy in India, Lord Mountbatten had the unpleasant task of presiding over its partition. He called the newly created Pakistan a "geographic aberration." It had also been mocked as "a bird with two wings, but no body." The people of the two wings had nothing in common except their religion, Islam.

Though the Bengalis of the eastern wing, called East Pakistan, were in a majority, they felt neglected and exploited by the Punjabis of the western wing, called West Pakistan. All prominent institutions of government, especially the military, were controlled by the Punjabis. "Bengali nationalists," as Mr. Bass says, "grumbled that they had replaced British colonialism with West Pakistani colonialism." The country somehow survived as one political entity for 23 years.

Except for brief periods of civilian rule, Pakistan had been under military dictatorship since its birth, until its breakup in 1971. Though demands to end the military rule were frequently raised by democracy enthusiasts in both wings, the generals were able to stifle those demands – by banning political parties, imprisoning their leaders, suspending civil rights and such other measures. The demands were louder in East Pakistan. The Bengali-speaking people of that region "hoped to turn their numbers into political clout," as the author puts it. Their number was 75 million, as opposed to West Pakistan's 61 million.

In March 1969, it was Gen. Agha Muhammad Yahya Khan's turn to usurp power. He declared himself president, foreign minister, defense minister and martial law administrator of Pakistan. To his credit, soon after grabbing power, he promised to hold elections and hand over power to an elected civilian government. He regretted it later, though.

In the elections, held on December 7, 1970, the Awami League of East Pakistan, led by Sheik Mujib-ur-Rahman, emerged victorious by a wide margin. As was expected, the victory upset the West Pakistanis. The thought of being ruled by Bengalis, whom they considered ethnically inferior, bothered them. The person most upset was the late Zulfiqar Ali Bhutto, whose Pakistan People's Party (PPP) had finished second in the election.

There was one more reason for West Pakistanis' nervousness. Autonomy for East Pakistan was the Awami League's main campaign platform. Gen. Yahya Khan and political leaders of the west feared that autonomy was only a step away from total independence. They were determined to prevent Mujib-ur-Rahman from forming the government.

The simmering grievances of Bengalis now came to the boil. They took to the streets in protest demonstrations. Yahya Khan banned the Awami League. On March 25, 1971, he sent 30,000 troops (later increased to 70,000), consisting mostly of Punjabis, to crush the protest. Mujib-ur-Rahman was arrested, brought to West Pakistan and tried for treason. He was sentenced to death. Fortunately for Mujib, the sentence was not carried out right away.

The military crackdown only strengthened the Bengalis' resolve to continue their campaign. By then, they had put together a guerrilla force, known as Mukti Bahini, meaning the liberation force. What started as a peaceful demonstration, demanding that Yahya Khan respect the outcome of the election, turned into a civil. The Bengalis' goal was no longer autonomy within Pakistan, but total independence from it. The seed of an independent Bangladesh was sown. What followed was a bloodbath, caused by the Pakistani military, mostly with American-supplied weapons.

To digress a little, Pakistan had been receiving weapons from the U.S. ever since it became a member of the U.S.-sponsored military alliances, the now-moribund Central Treaty Organization (CENTO) and Southeast Asia Treaty Organization (SEATO). But those weapons were meant to be used in their supposedly joint fight against communism. That not a single shot was fired toward that goal is a different matter. What matters here is that not a murmur of protest was heard from the powers that be in Washington when those weapons were used by Pakistan to massacre its own people.

Butchering of Bengalis

At the time, Washington's actual power, especially in the foreign policy area, was wielded by two individuals, President Richard Nixon and his national security adviser, Henry Kissinger. Though, in terms of hierarchy, next to Mr. Nixon, Secretary of State William P. Rogers should have been the one who wielded power in the foreign policy area, he was overshadowed by Mr. Kissinger. (To get slightly ahead of our narration, Mr. Rogers quit the job in disgust on September 3, 1973, and since then, until the Watergate scandal forced President Nixon to resign on August 9, 1974, Mr. Kissinger doubled his role as national security adviser and secretary of state.)

Nixon and Kissinger were culpably silent when Yahya Khan, a friend of both, who was also an alcoholic and womanizer, kept butchering his people, using American weapons. Yahya took their silence for tacit approval of what he was doing. That's why Nixon and Kissinger were accused of being complicit in the crime. *The Blood Telegram* makes a convincing case of their complicity.

It gives a chilling account of the atrocities committed by Yahya Khan's troops. The atrocities soon assumed genocidal proportions. Washington was apprised of those atrocities, and of the use of American weapons to commit them, by no less a person than its own chief diplomat in the area, Archer Blood. At the time, he was consul general of the United States in Dacca, the capital of East Pakistan. He sent cable after cable on what he and his colleagues witnessed: Transporting of soldiers from West Pakistan to East Pakistan on American-supplied C-130 airplanes; the Pakistani Air Force using American weapons – F-86 Saber jet fighters, M-24 Chaffee tanks and jeeps equipped with machine guns – to bomb and strafe rebel-held areas; and so on. Several villages were strafed and burned, killing tens of thousands of innocent civilians.

In one of the telegrams, Mr. Blood reported the slaughter of professors and students at Dhaka University. It was part of the troops' revenge killings against the intellectual community for the role it played in publicizing Bengali grievances. The troops also raped tens of thousands of women.

Neither Kissinger nor Nixon was bothered by the use of American weapons. Nixon was even prepared to condone such use, as was evident from the advice he once gave to "another brutal anticommunist strongman, Suharto of Indonesia." The advice was: "sufficient military strength is essential also for internal security."

One of Blood's cables had "Selective Genocide" as its subject line. In that cable, as Bass puts it, "Mr. Blood held nothing back: 'Here in Dacca we are mute and horrified witnesses to a reign of terror by the Pak military.' ... He warned of evidence that the military authorities were 'systematically eliminating' Awami League supporters 'by seeking them out in their homes and shooting them down.' ... This assault, he wrote, could not be justified by military necessity: 'There is no rpt no resistance being offered in Dacca to military.'"

After witnessing the slaughter for two weeks and frustrated by Washington's inaction, some of Blood's subordinates at the consulate sent a "dissent telegram." They knew full well that in sending a telegram that was nothing less than an indictment of Nixon and Kissinger's policy, they were risking their jobs. (To get slightly ahead of our story, Mr. Blood did pay a heavy price: he was recalled to Washington and put on desk duty, thereby denying him the chance to become an ambassador, which had been his dream.)

The explosive dissent telegram was signed by 20 consulate staffers "who are among the finest US officials in East Pakistan," in the words of Blood who added a note fully subscribing to their views. (Being the head of the consulate, Mr. Blood had found it inappropriate to add his signature to the telegram.) Sent on April 6, 1971, with "Dissent from U.S. policy toward East Pakistan" as its subject line, it came to be known as "the Blood telegram" – a double entendre alluding to the name of the person who authorized it and to the ongoing blood-letting that necessitated it. Gary Bass fittingly used it as the title of his book. The telegram, among other things, said:

"Our government has failed to denounce the suppression of democracy. Our government has failed to denounce atrocities. Our government has failed to take forceful measures to protect its citizens while at the same time bending over backwards to placate the West Pak dominated government and to lessen likely and deservedly negative international public relations impact against them. Our government has evidenced what many will consider moral bankruptcy, ironically at a time when the USSR sent President Yahya a message defending democracy, condemning arrest of leader of democratically elected majority party (incidentally pro-West) and calling for end to repressive measures and bloodshed. … [W]e have chosen not to intervene, even morally, on the grounds that the Awami conflict, in which unfortunately the overworked term genocide is applicable, is purely [an] internal matter of a sovereign state. Private Americans have expressed disgust. …" The telegram ends with an appeal to redirect U.S. policies "in order to salvage our nation's position as a moral leader of the free world."

"The telegram," in author Bass's words, "detonated in all directions, to diplomats in Washington, Islamabad, Karachi, and Lahore. ... The confidential cable ... was probably the most blistering denunciation of U.S. foreign policy ever sent by its own diplomats."

It did nothing to get the policy changed, though. The secretary of state, Roger Williams, was "livid" when he read it. Henry Kissinger was "furious." He was afraid that "it will probably get to Ted Kennedy." It did. The late Senator Kennedy became one of the fiercest critics of the Nixon administration's complicity in the slaughter in East Pakistan.

It is important to note that both Mr. Blood, in his own separate telegrams, and his subordinates, in the one they sent, had used the word "genocide." They did not use it loosely as politicians do. They had positive proof that those who suffered the most in the troop crackdown were Hindus. About 11 million of East Pakistan's 75-million population were Hindus. The troops singled them out for elimination because they were suspected to be sympathetic to India. Whether they were Hindus or not was determined by lifting their *lungi* (sarong) and examining the foreskin of their penises.

Estimates vary on how many people died. "A senior Indian official put the Bengali death toll at three hundred thousand," Mr. Bass says, "while Sidney Schanberg, who had excellent sources, noted in the *New York Times* that diplomats in Dacca thought that hundreds of thousands of Bengalis – maybe even a million or more – had been killed since the crackdown started on March 25." Mr. Schanberg was *The Times*'s New Delhi bureau chief at the time. Based on figures provided by nongovernment agencies, it seems reasonable to set the number at 500,000. Bass settles for 200,000.

India Saddled with 10 Million Refugees

Those who survived the troops' bullets fled the country and sought refuge in neighboring India. At the height of the civil war, India was saddled with 10 million refugees. Again, an overwhelming majority of them – about 80 percent, according to Senator Kennedy who had visited the refugee camps in India – were Hindus.

It was the influx of refugees that got India involved in what it had treated until then as an internal matter of Pakistan. The responsibility of sheltering and feeding 10 million refugees put a heavy burden on India. As it was, the country had difficulty feeding its own people, over 600 million at the time. India desperately looked for ways of sending the refugees back. But it wouldn't send them back only to be butchered by Yahya Khan's troops.

In the beginning, India relied on Mukti Bahini guerrillas to drive the West Pakistani troops out. It provided them with weapons and weapons training. When the guerrilla war was found going nowhere, India started making preparations for military action. It also beefed up its position by signing a treaty of friendship and cooperation – a euphemism for military pact – with the Soviet Union. The news of the treaty reached Kissinger as a "bombshell." He feared that it would destroy "everything we have done with China [described below]." The treaty also sent a clear message to Pakistan that India was getting ready for war.

What did Nixon and Kissinger do when they realized that an India-Pakistan war was imminent? Instead of using the influence they had on the Pakistani dictator to prevent it, they encouraged him to take on India boldly. And when the war did break out, they reinforced Pakistan's arsenal.

Direct supply of weapons to Pakistan had been banned since 1965, the year in which it fought its second war against India. Nixon and Kissinger found a way of getting around that ban. They persuaded Jordan and Iran to transfer some of their American-supplied F-104 Starfighter jet interceptors to Pakistan. (Iran, under the rule of Shah Mohammad Reza Pahlavi, was an ally of the U.S. at the time.) In doing so, they knew they were clearly violating U.S. law. Kissinger was a little apprehensive. But Nixon couldn't care less. Breaking the law was second nature with him, as the world would learn three years later. Remember the Watergate scandal that cost him his presidency? The illegal transfer of weapons to Pakistan to massacre the ethnic and religious minority in that country proved Nixon and Kissinger's complicity in the Bengali genocide.

Contempt for Indians and Indira Gandhi

Thanks to *The Blood Telegram* we now learn that the decision Nixon and Kissinger made to support Yahya Khan were influenced by two extraneous factors: their need to enlist his help in befriending China and their contempt and hatred for Prime Minister Indira Gandhi in particular and Indians in general.

It was realpolitik considerations that prompted them to open up to China. China, they thought, could help the U.S. get out of the losing war in Vietnam without losing face. More importantly, by having China as a friend, the U.S. would be strengthening its position in the ongoing Cold War with the Soviet Union. Nixon and Kissinger knew that Pakistan had friendly relations with China and that Chinese premier Zhou Enlai and Yahya Khan were friends.

Yahya was more than willing to be used as a secret channel of communication to China. It was he, it may be added, who facilitated Kissinger's clandestine trip to China, in July 1971. Remember Kissinger's feigning stomachache while on a visit to Pakistan and disappearing from public view, only to resurface in Beijing later?

In April 1971, the same month "the Blood telegram" arrived in Washington, Nixon had received his invitation to visit China. An excited Nixon boasted to Kissinger that it was going to be a "great watershed in history, clearly the greatest since WWII." Kissinger was even more excited. According to him, it was going to be "the greatest since the Civil War."

The purpose of Kissinger's secret July 1971 trip to China was to pave the way for the eventual Nixon visit, which would materialize in February 1972. All this was accomplished courtesy Yahya Khan. No wonder Kissinger and Nixon ignored all the telegrams on his atrocities.

Moreover, Nixon had a special affection for Yahya. "I understand the anguish you must have felt in making the difficult decisions you have faced," Bass quotes him as saying.

Let's now turn to the other factor that was instrumental in Nixon's and Kissinger's adopting the butchery-condoning foreign policy: their contempt for Indians and India's prime minister at the time, Indira Gandhi. The words they used to describe Indians and Indira Gandhi, during their numerous conversations which Bass has reproduced after listening to the Nixon White House's secret tapes, would shock even ruffians and thugs. To Nixon, Indira Gandhi was an "old bitch," "a witch," etc. The Indians were "a slippery, treacherous people." On one occasion he says, "I don't know why the hell anybody would reproduce in that damn country but they do."

On another occasion he starts a sentence, saying, "The Indians need – what they really need is a," when Kissinger interrupts him to say, "They're such bastards." Nixon completes his thought: "a mass famine." The Indians were "insufferably arrogant," with "convoluted minds," Kissinger says on one of the tapes.

Nixon's and Kissinger's hatred for Indira Gandhi is understandable. She had treated them with utter contempt, and deservedly so, in my opinion. But what made them hate India and Indians so much? India was not Indira Gandhi, as Nixon and Kissinger were not America. Indians were the first to criticize some of the deplorable things Indira Gandhi did, the same way Americans expressed their disgust when Nixon and Kissinger proved to be crooks. But there was one thing all Indians, and all right-minded people in the rest of the world, applauded Indira Gandhi for: her decision to host 10 million refugees who escaped Yahya Khan's tyranny; and her decision to go to war with Pakistan to enable the refugees' safe return to their homes. If for that reason Nixon and Kissinger hated her, and Indians as a whole, their sick minds are to blame. The White House tapes, which are among the main sources of Mr. Bass's book, are quite revelatory of that sickness.

India-Pakistan War

The whole world knew that Mrs. Gandhi decided to go to war with Pakistan only as a last resort. The only way she could stop the refugees from pouring into India and to enable those who were already in India to return safely was to stop the carnage going on in East Pakistan.

Two men who could have done something to prevent the war, and to stop it once it started, were Nixon and Kissinger. To the disappointment of most people in the world, they behaved like warmongers, not statesmen.

When the war was going on, with India steadily winning, they dispatched nuclear-armed ships from the U.S.'s Seventh Fleet into the Bay of Bengal. With a view to intimidating India further, they encouraged China to move troops to its border with India. That was also their way of warning the Soviet Union not to come to India's aid. But China and the Soviet Union knew better. The leaders of the two countries behaved more maturely throughout the 13-day war between India and Pakistan than the two men in the White House. The latter behaved like bullies.

It is important to note that though India had been ready to go to war, the first shot was fired by Pakistan, on December 3, 1971. It happened in the form of simultaneous attacks on six Indian airfields. The war ended on December 16, with Lieutenant General A.A.K. Niazi, commander of the Pakistani troops, unconditionally surrendering to Lieutenant General Jacob-Farji-Rafael Jacob, the chief of staff of the Indian army's Eastern Command.

Soon after the surrender, Mrs. Gandhi declared: "India has no territorial ambitions. Now that the Pakistani Armed Forces have surrendered in Bangla Desh and Bangla Desh is free, it is pointless in our view to continue the present conflict." She also unilaterally ordered cease-fire on the western front, effective the next day.

In ordering the cease-fire, Mrs. Gandhi was also giving the lie to Nixon and Kissinger who had repeatedly said that India's ultimate goal in the war was to destroy Pakistan. How did the two react to the cease-fire declaration? Shamelessly, they took credit for it. Bass has reproduced a conversation the two had soon after the cease-fire declaration.

Kissinger phoned up Nixon and said: "Congratulations, Mr. President. You saved W[est] Pakistan."

Nixon: "She [Indira Gandhi] shouldn't get credit for starting the fire and then calling in the fire department. It's back to Hitler."

Was it a slip of the tongue that made Nixon utter the name of Hitler? Or was it the fault of his mind? Either way the survivors of the crime he and Kissinger committed should be grateful. They should take it as a reminder that the crime was no different from what Hitler and his fellow Nazis committed prior to and during World War Two. The name of the crime is genocide.

The next of kin of the Bengali victims of the genocide are entitled to sue Kissinger in any court anywhere in the world. But they would be better off doing it in a U.S. court. They are also entitled to go after Nixon's estate, now that he is no more. They can take a cue from what the Jewish victims of Nazi crimes are still doing.

Bengalis in the countryside of East Pakistan fleeing their burning homes in the wake of the Pakistani troops' crackdown on them. The devastating crackdown began on March 25, 1971. (*The picture is reproduced courtesy* The Blood Telegram.)

31

'The Emir of NYU' Builds Abu Dhabi Campus with Petrodollars and Exploited South Asian Labor

June 2, 2014

New York University's newly built Abu Dhabi Campus (left) and some of the 6,000 migrant workers who built it (right). Migrant workers were put up in tiny rooms, as many as 15 men to a room, by contractors who hired them. One of New York University's labor values states that contractors should not house more than four people in a bedroom. These workers earn as little as $272 a month. (*Pictures, by Sergey Ponomarev, are reproduced courtesy* The New York Times.)

•

New York University's recently completed Abu Dhabi campus is a product of petrodollars and exploited South Asian labor. The inhuman condition in which workers from Pakistan, India and Bangladesh lived, while building a state-of-the-art campus for NYU, has been the subject of many an exposé in the media. The latest one appeared in the May 19, 2014, edition of *The New York Times*, under the title "Workers at N.Y.U.'s Abu Dhabi Site Faced Harsh Conditions."

The *Times* story, by Ariel Kaminer and Sean O'Driscoll, is based on interviews with dozens of workers who endured the "harsh conditions" detailed in it. It is also based on what the two reporters witnessed themselves at some of the labor camps in which the workers lived. At one such camp – "squalid quarters," they call it – "the bedrooms are so crowded that the men must sleep three to a stack – one on the upper bunk, one on the lower bunk and one below the lower bunk, separated from the floor by only a thin pad for a mattress. In the space between the beds, the men pile cauliflower, onions and 75-pound sacks of Basmati rice to cook after working all day and washing the construction dirt from their clothes. Tangles of exposed wiring hang down from the ceiling, and cockroaches climb the walls."

In some apartments, the *Times* report says, there were 15 men to a room. According to the university's labor values, "there should be no more than four."

Over 6,000 men working at various construction sites for NYU Abu Dhabi, like millions of other South Asian laborers in the Middle East, are there just to make enough money to support their families back home. *The Times* spoke to one who "is helping support five brothers. Another supports four children, ages 6 to 14. Others have toddlers they have never met."

For the May 19 story, *The Times* had also reached some workers who had already been deported back to their home countries by the Abu Dhabi government. Why were they deported? Because they had gone on a strike when their living and working conditions became unbearable. In Abu Dhabi and most Middle Eastern countries, it is illegal for workers to strike. The *Times* report goes on to say:

"Virtually everyone said he had to pay recruitment fees of up to a year's wages to get his job and had never been reimbursed. N.Y.U.'s list of labor values [issued by the university in 2009] says that contractors are supposed to pay back all such fees. Most of the men described having to work 11 or 12 hours a day, six or seven days a week, just to earn close to what they had originally been promised, despite a provision in the labor statement that overtime should be voluntary.

"The men said they were not allowed to hold onto their passports, in spite of promises to the contrary... ."

This is what happened, according to the *Times* story, to those who struck work: "The strike had entered its second day when construction workers at Labor Camp 42 got word that their bosses from the BK Gulf [the firm which had hired the workers living at this camp] had come to negotiate. Mohammed Amir Waheed Sirkar, an electrician from Bangladesh, scrambled down the stairs to meet them. But when he got to the courtyard, he saw the truth: It wasn't the bosses who had come. It was the police.

"They pounded on doors, breaking some down, and hauled dozens of men to prison. Mr. Sirkar was taken to a Dubai police station, where officers interrogated him. After a while, new officers arrived. That's when things got rough.

"'They beat me up,' he said through an Urdu interpreter, 'asking me to confess I was involved in starting the strike.' Others were slapped, kicked, or beaten with shoes, a special indignity in Arab culture.

"After nine days in jail, Mr. Sirkar was deported, as were hundreds of other workers."

The *Times* story did shake up the higher-ups at NYU, in New York. Hours after it was published, they got to work on damage control, says another story in *The Times*, this one by Andrew Ross Sorkin, published on May 27, 2014. According to this story, Martin Lipton, the chairman of NYU's board of trustees, sent an email to some members of the board, saying that he was unaware of the labor abuses on the Abu Dhabi site. The email also said that an independent investigation would soon be undertaken, according to Mr. Sorkin's story, based on what he heard from the "people who were briefed on the message." Most members of NYU's board of trustees, like its chairman, are among the movers and shakers of Wall Street. So, the caption to Sorkin's story, "N.Y.U. Crisis in Abu Dhabi Stretches to Wall Street," is very appropriate.

There is another important reason why *The Times* gave that caption. The authorities at NYU have been trying to distance themselves from the scandal, saying that the workers who were abused were not employed by the university but by private contractors who built the campus. Mr. Sorkin exposed the hollowness of that argument. The overall contractor of the Abu Dhabi project, the Sorkin story says, was Mubadala Development Company. All subcontractors who built the various units of the campus were answerable to this company. The CEO and managing director of Mubadala is Khaldoon Khalifa Al Mubarak. And Al Mubarak is a member of the board of trustees of NYU. He had also played a key role in persuading the university to start a full-fledged campus in Abu Dhabi.

When the chairman of NYU's board of trustees says that he was unaware of the abuse of workers who built the Abu Dhabi campus, we may give him the benefit of the doubt. Not when John Sexton, the president of NYU, does it. As all supporters and opponents of the Abu Dhabi project know, no one was more adamant about going ahead with the project than Mr. Sexton. In fact, they all say, NYU Abu Dhabi is Sexton's "brainchild." Right from the time the idea for it was conceived, he has followed its progress every step of the way. That's why the statement he issued, in response to *The Times*'s revelations of the ill-treatment of workers at his pet project came as a surprise even to those who were remotely connected with the project. The statement, among other things, said that the ill-treatment, "if true as reported, [is] troubling and unacceptable."

The "if true" qualification to what was meant to be an apology gives the impression that Mr. Sexton doesn't find the *Times* story all that convincing. His statement also gives the impression that he came to know about the harsh conditions the workers endured only after *The Times* reported them. On which planet has "the Emir of NYU" been living?

Criticism from NYU Faculty

"The Emir of NYU" is the title of a feature that appeared in the April 13, 2008, issue of *New York* magazine. The feature, by Zvika Krieger, did warn that the Abu Dhabi campus, which by then had become an obsession with Mr. Sexton, was going to be built on the sweat and tears of migrant workers. It pointed out that Abu Dhabi had "come under fierce criticism from groups like Human Rights Watch for its mistreatment of foreign laborers, mostly Pakistani and Indian, who have shouldered much of the country's breakneck development. With few labor laws in place, there is little NYU can do to assure that its new campus will not be built by this workforce."

Several senior faculty members of NYU criticized the plan right from its incipient stage. Some did it openly, but most of them anonymously for fear of retribution from their boss.

According to the faculty critics, the *New York* article says, "the Abu Dhabi project embodies the worst of John Sexton's indulgences and the short-sightedness of his glory-seeking ambitions. Mary Nolan,

NYU president John Sexton with Khaldoon Al Mubarak, the CEO of the Mubadala Development Company that built NYU's Abu Dhabi campus. (*The picture is reproduced courtesy* New York/ NYU photo bureau.)

•

a history professor who has been teaching at the university for almost 30 years, describes the Abu Dhabi project as 'a quintessentially Sexton operation. He thinks he has some sort of a missionary calling, but he operates in a very autocratic manner. ....'"

Sexton's 'Spiritual Experience'

Prof. Nolan's charge – that Sexton "thinks he has some sort of a missionary calling" – is not an ill-founded one. Mr. Sexton himself boasted to *New York* that the four thirteen-hour flights he took to Abu Dhabi, over two years, to personally broker the deal with the crown prince of the emirate were a "spiritual experience."

The *New York* article goes on to say: "He believes he connected to the prince metaphysically: 'The crown prince told me that he felt it in my handshake, in my eyes, in my aura at that first meeting.' And perhaps most significant to Sexton, when they prepared to part ways, the prince said, 'What, no hug?' (Sexton is famous for hugging most everyone in sight.) 'I knew right then and there,' Sexton remembers fondly, 'that we had found our partner.'"

The partner, in terms of the deal, would finance the entire NYU Abu Dhabi and a good deal of NYU New York. Toward the latter, a $50 million "gift" would be given right away, to be followed by several similar gifts. "We will go through an annual budgeting process," the *New York* article quotes Sexton as saying, "but the crown prince is committed to helping NYU Abu Dhabi and NYU in Washington Square to become one of the world's ten great universities by 2020."

Many of Sexton's faculty colleagues had a different take on the deal. "NYU is behaving exactly like a corporation that is entering its mergers-and-acquisitions phase," *New York* quotes Andrew Ross, who specializes in labor and globalization, as saying. "To a lot of the faculty, it just feels cheap, like we're just another brand being bought in a worldwide shopping spree, like Gucci."

No criticisms and no warnings would dissuade Mr. Sexton from pursuing his plan, whose ultimate goal, according to him, was to convert NYU into "the world's first global university in the world's first truly global city."

Vulgar Ostentation

Abu Dhabi is awash in petrodollars. Thanks to its wealth, this richest city-state in the world has been able to buy technology from the West and cheap labor from the East. The opulence which its citizens enjoy and the vulgar ostentation in which some of them live are attributable entirely to these two factors. By the way, its citizens make up only 20 percent of its population of 2.5 million.

Yes, Abu Dhabi has everything money can buy. But when it comes to culture, all that money can buy are its trappings. Nouveaux riches try to present themselves as cultured by collecting trappings of culture. Abu Dhabi's latter-day efforts to clone Western cultural icons, like the Louvre Museum of Paris and the Guggenheim Museum of New York, stem from its desire to get accepted as a cultured nation.

But the real culture is something that cannot be bought with money. It has to evolve from within. What makes a society cultured is the cultivation of the minds of its members. Admittedly, it doesn't happen overnight. The deplorable way Abu Dhabi has been treating the workers who built its prosperity, which in turn has enabled it to build at least some trappings of culture, shows that it has a long way to go before it gets accepted as cultured.

Abu Dhabi behaving like a nouveau riche is understandable. What is not understandable is that the president of a prestigious American University got carried away by an upstart nation's display of wealth. Read the very first paragraph of *New York* magazine's article referred to above:

"John Sexton's office, which sits on the top floor of NYU's Bobst Library and boasts an impressive view north to Washington Square Park, has recently begun to resemble a shrine to Abu Dhabi. The university president has installed a massive Oriental rug, a gift from the crown prince, on one entire wall. On another hangs a framed portrait of the sunglasses-clad founder of the United Arab Emirates, Sheikh Zayed bin Sultan Al Nahyan. In the center of the room is a large framed photograph of an Emirati woman, hand covered in a henna tattoo, gazing provocatively from behind a sequined veil."

Was the NYU president taken in by the Emirati woman's provocative gaze, too?

32

U.N. Pooh-Poohs Trump's Threats and Rebukes His Stance on Jerusalem

December 24, 2017

Riyad Mansour, center, the Palestinian representative at the U.N., walking past Nikki R. Haley, the U.S. ambassador to the U.N., on December 21, 2017. *(Picture, by Justin Lane of European Pressphoto Agency, is reproduced courtesy* The New York Times.*)*

•

It all started with the arrogant, arbitrary decision made by U.S. President Donald Trump on the status of Jerusalem. The decision, which he declared on December 6, 2017, says: "I have determined that it is time to officially recognize Jerusalem as the capital of Israel. While previous presidents have made this a major campaign promise, they failed to deliver. Today, I am delivering."

The president left out an important part from his declaration: that he was delivering on the promise he made to wealthy campaign contributors and the powerful Jewish lobby in America. Making Jerusalem the capital of Israel is a matter that is dear to the hearts of most Jews in the country.

Mr. Trump was, in effect, repudiating all U.N. resolutions on the final status of Jerusalem and discarding the position of all previous U.S. administrations on the issue. The U.S. position – and this one was mediated by the U.S. itself – has been that the final status of Jerusalem should be determined by Israelis and Palestinians through negotiations. The final status of Jerusalem is the most sensitive of all issues that divide the two groups. All previous negotiators thoughtfully put off tackling it to the end, so it wouldn't stand in the way of resolving other issues involved in the 70-year-old dispute.

The hope of resolving the Jerusalem issue was predicated on East Jerusalem being recognized as the capital of Palestine that would eventually be created. Israel has been in illegal occupation of many territories, including East Jerusalem, which it grabbed during the 1967 Arab-Israeli war. Those territories are parts of Palestine envisaged in the U.N. resolution of 1948. No two-state solution, which the world community has been hoping for, is possible as long as Israel is in illegal occupation of them.

Negotiations have been stalled ever since Israel started constructing new settlements on the illegally occupied land. President Trump's December 6 declaration condones the occupation and emboldens Israel to continue its construction activities. The Palestinians are now left with no incentive to go back to the negotiating table. The shortsighted, ill-timed Trump decision has destroyed the United States' reputation as an impartial mediator in this dispute.

As was expected, most countries in the world condemned the decision. The 15-member U.N. Security Council met on December 18, hoping to adopt a resolution demanding that the decision be rescinded. A Security Council resolution, as we know, has the status and validity of international law. Fourteen members of the council, including five close allies of the U.S. – France, Britain, Germany, Sweden and Italy – vehemently criticized the Trump decision. But to no avail. The resolution failed to pass because of the U.S. veto.

Security Council Move Infuriates Trump

The move at the Security Council infuriated President Trump and his obeisant ambassador to the U.N., Nikki R. Haley. A similar move had already been underway at the General Assembly. A resolution identical to the one defeated by the U.S. at the Security Council had been scheduled to be put to vote on December 21, 2017. Hoping to thwart the move at the General Assembly, Mr. Trump issued the following threat:

"All of these nations that take our money and then they vote against us at the Security Council or they vote against us, potentially, at the Assembly, they take hundreds of millions of dollars and even billions of dollars and then they vote against us.

"Well, we're watching those votes. Let them vote against us; we'll save a lot. We don't care."

Pardon the president's affront to the English language, which is his mother tongue. But there is no mistaking of whom his threat was directed at. It was directed at the poor nations in the world that receive U.S. foreign aid.

As if acting on cue from her boss, and using the same blackmail tactic, Nikki Haley issued a threat of her own: "We will remember it when we are called upon once again to make the world's largest contribution to the United Nations. And we will remember when so many countries come calling on us, as they so often do, to pay even more and to use our influence for their benefit."

I wish the American ambassador had been half as mature and decent as the Palestinian foreign minister Riad Malki, who responded to her threat thus:

"History records names, it remembers names – the names of those who stand by what is right and the names of those who speak falsehood." He added that Palestinians "will not be threatened" and that the United States had been "ignoring the dangerous repercussions of its decision."

Pooh-poohing the threats from the U.S. president and his loyal ambassador, an overwhelming majority of the General Assembly – including U.S. aid-recipients like Egypt, Jordan, Afghanistan, Iraq and Pakistan – voted for the resolution that rebuked Mr. Trump's decision on Jerusalem. It's a shame that in the 193-member world body, other than Israel, the only countries that supported the U.S. were seven tiny, insignificant ones: Guatemala, Honduras, Togo, the Marshall Islands, the Federated States of Micronesia, Nauru and Palau. Trump and Haley can derive some satisfaction from the fact that their threats were not a total waste. All seven countries are heavily dependent on American aid.

33

Trump's Solution to Gun Violence in Schools: Arm Teachers with Guns

March 1, 2018

Students staged a "lie-in" outside the White House on February 19, 2018. This is part of the protest demonstrations they have been conducting around the U.S. since the February 14 shooting at Marjory Stoneman Douglas High School in Parkland, Florida, that claimed 17 lives. Their goal is to promote gun control reform. According to the National Rifles Association and other gun rights advocates, the students are being manipulated by liberals to exploit the Parkland tragedy and take away their constitutional right to bear arms. (*The picture, by Zach Gibson/Getty Images, is reproduced courtesy* The New York Times.)

•

President Donald Trump's genius for saying stupid things, even in the face of great tragedies, is by now known to all. Maybe he has begun to realize it himself. That could be the reason why he decided to carry a cue card – no, it was a piece of paper with empathetic messages scribbled on it – while interacting with survivors, and relatives of victims, of the recent shooting at Marjory Stoneman Douglas High School in Parkland, Florida. The shooting by a deranged student at the school, which occurred on February 14, 2018, claimed the lives of 14 students and three adults.

It was so gracious of Mr. Trump that he invited those affected by the Parkland shooting, and by school shootings before that, to the White House and listened to their woes and angry outbursts. And guided by the scribbled notes, he also uttered words that were appropriate for the occasion – words like: "I know you've been through a lot"; "All I can say is that we're fighting hard for you, and we will not stop"; "I grieve for you"; and so on.

Regrettably, the February 21 White House event is remembered not for those empathetic words he uttered. It is remembered for the controversy he stirred by using the event to pitch his own idea of how to prevent gun violence in schools. His idea is to allow teachers and other educators to carry concealed weapons.

In fact, the idea is not his. He has only been recycling and repeating what was enunciated and popularized by Wayne LaPierre, the obnoxious executive vice president of the National Rifles Association (N.R.A.). According to LaPierre, "The only way to stop a bad guy with a gun is with a good guy with a gun."

The first time he articulated this laughable theory was in the wake of another campus shooting, by another deranged person: the 2012 shooting at Sandy Hook Elementary School in Newtown, Connecticut, which claimed the lives of 20 children and six adults. Since then, he has been repeating it at every opportunity he gets. The idea to arm teachers stemmed from that theory and he made it a campaign theme for the N.R.A.

Trump Is Peddling the N.R.A. Line

Mr. Trump, who owes his election as president partly to the support he received from the N.R.A., has been enthusiastically peddling the theme ever since. None is surprised by it. What has surprised most people is that he did the latest peddling at a gathering of those who were mourning the loss of lives of their dear ones to Parkland, Sandy Hook and other shootings; and those who were still reeling from the trauma they suffered witnessing the carnage at Parkland.

Despicably, he continued the peddling the next day, both at a second White House meeting and via Twitter, the medium he is the most comfortable with. The second White House meeting was of central, state and local law enforcement officials, which he convened to explore various ways of preventing school shootings. In Mr. Trump's twisted thinking, "a 'gun free' school is a magnet for bad people."

His stupidity hit a new low when he tweeted that the knowledge that teachers have guns of their own would deter "the sicko" from heading to a school in the first place. He did it even as it was being reported that a sheriff's deputy who had been the only armed guard present at the scene of the Parkland shooting resigned after surveillance video showed him looking for cover to save himself when students were being mowed down.

Even a person with minimal education and average intelligence knows that a "sicko" is one who doesn't think rationally. He is a deranged person who doesn't think of the consequences of his action. So, when the president of the United States, who never tires of boasting of his superior intelligence and education, says that the mere awareness that teachers are carrying guns would scare a "sicko" away, it does evoke derisive chuckle.

The same day Mr. Trump tweeted that stupid idea, the N.R.A. vice president repeated his "shibboleth" (courtesy *The New York Times*) with a slight variation. "To stop a bad guy with a gun, it takes a good guy with a gun," Wayne LaPierre said at a gathering of conservative activists. "Actually, it's hard to tell who was parroting whom," *The Times* says in its February 22 editorial.

Here is something Mr. Trump may want to ponder over: No country in the world possesses more deadly weapons than the U.S. Has the awareness of that fact stopped terrorists from around the world from attacking the U.S. and U.S. interests? Terrorists are in the category of "the sicko" Mr. Trump tweeted about. They are prepared to die for what their sick minds think is right.

In carrying a weapon to the class, a teacher is indirectly conveying to his students that he is afraid of them, that he views them as his enemies. Is that the kind of teacher-student relationship Mr. Trump wants to build in the country he presides over?

The only consolation here is that Mr. Trump's (read N.R.A.'s) idea of arming teachers has been rejected by an overwhelming majority in the country. At the forefront of those who did it are teachers and other educators themselves. "Even in gun-friendly locales like rural Indiana, teachers reacted with alarm to Mr. Trump's plan," says a report in *The New York Times*. Opposition also came from the leaders of large school districts. "The mere thought that teachers should be armed in order to ward off violence is utterly illogical and will only result in making our students and teachers less safe," *The Times* quotes Tommy Chang, the superintendent of Boston Public Schools, as saying. "The real issue at hand continues to be access to guns."

The Times report on the February 21 White House event also quotes 18-year-old Samuel Zeif, one of the survivors of the Parkland shooting who attended the event, as saying: "I don't understand why I can still go in a store and buy a weapon of war, an A-R." I wish Trump and N.R.A. had half the maturity and commonsense of this teenager.

When *The Times* says that the "best way to prevent the threat of a bad guy with a gun is to keep him from getting the sort of battle-field weapon the Parkland killer used, by banning assault weapons and high-capacity magazines, and by tightening background checks" ("Let the Teachers Teach," editorial, February 22, 2018), it is echoing the sentiments expressed by the 18-year-old Parkland student. The student did not read it from a cue card or scribbled notes. He spoke from his heart.

34

Dinesh D'Souza, Once Ousted from Job for Adultery, Now Pardoned by President Trump

June 14, 2018

First, a clarification: The pardon President Trump issued on May 31, 2018, has nothing to do with the adultery Dinesh D'Souza committed a few years ago. The adultery did cost this Indian American his job as president of an evangelical college in New York. But adultery is no big deal for Donald Trump, himself an adulterer and philanderer. More about his adultery, in a little bit.

Of the many things Trump and D'Souza have in common, the most despicable one is their hatred for former President Barack Obama. Each has been engaged in his own character assassination campaign against Obama for nearly a decade now. Since Obama left the presidency and Trump entered it, the latter added one more goal to his campaign: to erase all traces of Obama's achievements during his eight years in office. The pardon he issued last month, absolving D'Souza of the crime he committed during the 2012 election, is Trump's way of rewarding him for the stupendous work he did in spreading anti-Obama venom. It is also aimed at enabling D'Souza to continue that work. More about the pardon, in a little bit.

Trump started his destroy-Obama campaign soon after Obama became the Democratic Party nominee for president. He started it with the lie that Obama was born in Kenya. Under the U.S. Constitution, only a native-born American is eligible to be president. As such, the Trump lie was aimed at getting the Obama candidacy invalidated. The only basis for the lie was that Obama, though born to an American mother, had a Kenyan father.

D'Souza Questions Obama's Patriotism

Once that lie was exposed, with documents proving that Obama was a native-born American, and Obama became president, D'Souza's character assassination campaign against him took another form: building a conspiracy theory questioning President Obama's patriotism. That Obama was born to a Kenyan father gave him ample material to build the theory on. Building conspiracy theories based on figments of imagination has been a favorite pastime of both Trump and D'Souza, and is another trait they have in common.

It's on the basis of such theories that D'Souza made outlandish claims like: Obama is against business because of the anticolonialist trait in his character which he inherited from his Kenyan father; the 9/11 terrorist attacks happened because of "America's moral decadence" caused by liberals; the scandalous incident at the Abu Ghraib, Iraq, prison was the fault of liberals, because the soldiers who did those sickening things, Lynddie England and Charles Graner, were divorced, sex-crazed partiers acting out "the fantasies of blue [Democratic] America"; the liberal billionaire-financier-philanthropist George Soros, a Jew born in Nazi-occupied Hungary, was actually a Nazi collaborator; and so on.

When D'Souza, a native of India who became a naturalized citizen of America, questioned the patriotism of a native-born American, he may have evoked derisive laughs in many quarters. But he had no qualms about doing it because he knew full well that playing the patriotism card was the surest way of getting accepted in the ultra-right wing of the Republican Party.

According to D'Souza, all economic policies Obama adopted, and actions he took in pursuance thereof, could be traced to his anticolonialist mind-set. He dwelt at length on this theorizing in a cover story he wrote for *Forbes* magazine. The story, titled "Obama's Problem With Business," was published in the September 27, 2010, issue of the magazine. It portrays anticolonialism as evil and elaborates on his bizarre idea that President Obama was executing in the U.S. the anticolonial agenda of his Kenyan father.

D'Souza's *Forbes* story ends thus: "Incredibly, the U.S. is being ruled according to the dreams of a Luo tribesman of the 1950s. This philandering, inebriated African socialist, who raged against the world for denying him the realization of his anticolonial ambitions, is now setting the nation's agenda through the reincarnation of his dreams in his son. The son makes it happen, but he candidly admits he is only living out his father's dream. The invisible father provides the inspiration, and the son dutifully gets the job done. America today is governed by a ghost." (Read my response to the *Forbes* article in Chapter 16.)

D'Souza dwelt at length on the same idea in his book, *The Roots of Obama's Rage*, published in 2010, and a documentary based on the book, released in 2012. Though many in the U.S. found the idea stupid and sickening, the book sold very well. The documentary, titled *2016: Obama's America* and produced with financial help from another Obama-hating conservative, billionaire Joe Ricketts, "was one of the highest-grossing political documentaries of all time, behind only Michael Moore's *Fahrenheit 9/11*," according to *The New York Times*. D'Souza must have been very happy that spreading anti-Obama venom pays.

The ideas he promoted through his numerous articles; nearly a dozen books; two documentaries (the second documentary, *Hillary's America: The Secret History of the Democratic Party*, was released on July 22, 2016); and appearances on radio and television talk shows won him a large following among conservatives in the Republican Party. With the publication, in 2007, of the book, *What's So Great About Christianity*, he also became the darling of the evangelical wing of the party, making him a much-sought-after speaker at mega-churches in the country. His new-found status among evangelicals also won him the top-most position at The King's College, an evangelical institution in New York. The presidentship of the college came with a seven-figure salary.

Extramarital Affair

But the fame and prestige, which the presidentship of an evangelical college brought him, lasted only two years – from August 2010 to October 2012. On September 28, 2012, the man who masqueraded as a holier-than-thou-Christian was spotted in an un-Christian-like act: He was seen sharing a room with a woman at a hotel in South Carolina. His explanation that he had already been divorced from Dixie Brubaker, his wife since 1992, and that Denise Odie Joseph II, the woman he was with, was his fiancée turned out to be only half-true. Nor did anyone believe him when he said that "nothing happened" in the hotel room between him and Denise.

The story on D' Souza's illicit affair first appeared in the October 16, 2012, issue of *World*, a bi-weekly Christian news magazine published by God's World Publications. Reporter Warren Cole Smith who broke the story later discovered that D'Souza filed for divorce from Dixie only on the day his story appeared in *World*. In the wake of the controversy the scandal stirred, The Smith's College forced D'Souza to resign.

I had published an article on the controversy, and on D'Souza's fall from grace, in the online monthly, *The East-West Inquirer*, under the title "Obama-Baiting Indian American Eased Out of His Job for Adultery." The article, among other things, said: "A man losing his job for an extra-marital affair may come as a surprise to many, especially in this day and age. But we are not talking about just any man and just any job. The adulterer we are talking about is one who steadily ad-vanced his career by extolling Christian values and kissing up to the extreme right wing of the Republican Party. And the job he has been eased out of is the presidentship of an evangelical college whose mission statement emphasizes a "commitment to the truths of Christianity and a biblical worldview."

That the immoral act took place at the conclusion of an event at which 2,000-odd people had gathered "to hear high-profile Christians speak on defending the faith and applying a Christian worldview to their lives," as the Smith story in *World* puts it, made it all the more appalling. Dinesh D'Souza was the keynote speaker at the event and Smith's story exposed his hypocrisy.

Illegal Campaign Contribution

It seems 2012 was the cruelest year thus far in D'Souza's career. While the immoral act mentioned above cost him his job and the prestige he enjoyed among evangelicals, an illegal act he committed the same year made him a liability to the Republican Party. Until President Trump came to his rescue, that is. Let's briefly go through what happened:

In the 2012 election in the U.S., the Republican candidate for Senate from New York was Wendy Long, a friend of D'Souza's since his Dartmouth College days. Ms. Long had requested him to help her raise campaign funds by appealing to wealthy Indian doctors in West-chester. D'Souza knew that he was the last person whom even Republicans among Indians would lift a finger to help. So, he found another way of helping his friend. He persuaded the woman he was having an affair with (the same Denise Odie Joseph II, married and 22 years his junior, who shared a hotel room with him in South Carolina) and her husband; and another couple (a young employee working under him and her husband) to contribute to Long's campaign fund. The total contribution came to $20,000. Strictly speaking, there was nothing illegal about it, the legal limit of individual contribution being $5,000. But the $20,000 which the four individuals contributed was reimbursed by D'Souza, as per his prior arrangement with them. In other words, he used the four people as straw donors, a practice prohibited under campaign finance laws.

Sometime in 2013, when the F.B.I., while going through the campaign records of Wendy Long, spotted large sums appearing in the middle of small contributions, it raised a red flag. On further investigation, the Justice Department was able to trace the source of the $20,000 donation to D'Souza. He was charged with breaking campaign finance laws, "willfully and knowingly," and with causing a false statement to be made to the Federal Election Commission. The fact that his friend lost the election to her opponent, the incumbent Democratic Senator Kirsten Gillibrand, did not make his illegal contribution less of a crime.

For four months D'Souza refused to plead guilty, arguing that he was a victim of "selective prosecution." He was being targeted, he said, because he was a "sharp critic of the Obama presidency who has incurred the president's wrath."

Richard M. Berman, the judge who presided over the case, dismissed D'Souza's arguments as "all hat and no cattle." On September 23, 2014, he issued his verdict. D'Souza was fined $30,000 and sentenced to five years' probation, including eight months in a supervised "community confinement center."

He was languishing in infamy, at least in the eyes of many, when he received the heart-warming news about his being pardoned by President Trump. The first thing D'Souza did, after he heard of the pardon, on May 31, 2018, was to send out tweets thanking Trump and railing at Obama. His tweet on Trump said: "Obama & his stooges tried to extinguish my American dream & destroy my faith in America. Thank you @ realDonaldTrump for fully restoring both."

The next tweet, sent out on the same day, was directed at Preet Bharara, the federal attorney who prosecuted the case, who happened to be Indian American. It read: "KARMA IS A BITCH DEPT: @ PreetBharara wanted to destroy a fellow Indian American to advance his career. Then he got fired & I got pardoned."

Preet Bharara was the U.S. attorney in New York and the investigation of D'Souza's wrong-doing was undertaken by his office. Both D'Souza and Donald Trump despised him. As was expected, Bharara became one of the early casualties of Trump's erase-the-Obama-legacy campaign. No reason was given for his abrupt dismissal. It's true that presidents don't have to give any reason for dismissing anyone in the executive branch. However, it was widely believed that Bharara's dismissal had a lot to do with his involvement in the investigation into the Trump campaign's alleged collusion with the Russian meddling in the 2016 election and with his being a protégé of Senator Chuck Schumer. It may be added that Schumer, Democrat from New York and the minority leader in the U.S. Senate, is another bete noire of Donald Trump's. Since his dismissal, Bharara has been a vehement critic of Trump.

He defended his prosecution of D'Souza via a tweet of his own, which said: "The President has the right to pardon but the facts are these: D'Souza intentionally broke the law, voluntarily pled guilty, apologized for his conduct & the judge found no unfairness."

The Real Reason Behind the Pardon

Yes, the president has the right to pardon anyone. But impartial observers can never stop wondering what made him pick D'Souza for this preferential treatment, ignoring all established procedures for granting pardons and disregarding more than 10,000 cases that are pending. The reason could be, many of them say, that the character assassination campaign against Barack Obama, which D'Souza has been conducting, resonates well with the one Trump has been engaged in. He doesn't care that his action could be criticized as a clear abuse of president's pardoning power.

The New York Times has come up with another explanation: "Maybe the president is sending a signal of loyalty and reassurance to friends and family members who may soon find themselves facing similar criminal charges in connection with the special counsel's Russia inquiry" ("Dinesh D'Souza? Really?" – editorial, *nytimes.com*, May 31, 2018). It is pertinent to note here that one of the crimes that Trump's lawyer Michael Cohen is now being investigated for is the same as the one D'Souza was convicted of.

Here is my take on the D'Souza pardon: Trump wants him out there continuing his favorite job of spewing anti-Obama venom.

35

Trump Should Be Impeached. Are There Republicans with Spine Who Will Do It?

August 2, 2018

U.S. President Donald Trump (left) and Russian President Vladimir Putin at a press conference in Helsinki, Finland, on July 16, 2018. At the end of the press conference, Putin surprised Trump with a gift – a football, in commemoration of the 2018 World Cup which was hosted by Russia. Presenting the gift, Putin said (as translated by CBS News): "Speaking of football, Mr. President, I give this ball to you and now the ball is in your court," an allusion to the fact that the 2026 World Cup will be hosted by the United States. It was reported that Mr. Trump tossed the ball to the first lady, Melania, who was sitting in the audience.
(*The picture is reproduced courtesy* bing.com/images)

•

President Donald Trump has already committed crimes that are impeachable under the U.S. Constitution. Apolitical Americans are demanding that he be impeached right away. Are there Republicans with spine in U.S. Congress who will initiate the process without wasting any more time? They don't have to wait until special counsel Robert S. Mueller III completes his investigation into Russia's meddling in the

2016 presidential election and into the alleged collusion between the Trump campaign and Russia during that election.

Demands for Trump's impeachment became louder in the wake of his disgraceful performance at the press conference he held jointly with Russian President Vladimir V. Putin, in Helsinki, Finland, on July 16, 2018. Most Americans were appalled to see the president of their country fawning before the Russian dictator, who is also a murderous thug. They bowed their heads in shame when they heard the president challenge the findings of the intelligence community of his own country, in the presence of the man who has been implicated in those findings. Nothing comparable to that has ever happened in the history of their country, they all say.

The press conference followed a secret one-on-one meeting of the two leaders, with only two translators present. Except for some stooges of Trump, all Americans had expected him to cancel the hastily arranged meeting, because, only a week earlier, the Mueller investigation referred to above had taken a critical turn: It had indicted 12 officers of the GRU, Russia's military intelligence service, for their role in their country's attack on America's electoral system. The 29-page indictment detailed how these officers, at the behest of their president, hacked into the computers of over 300 people working for Democratic Party presidential candidate Hillary Clinton and of the Democratic Party itself; stole thousands of emails and other documents; and used them to prepare anti-Clinton propaganda material. They opened fake social-media accounts to release the material to the public. (At this writing, Facebook, the social-media site that has the widest reach in the U.S., has announced the closing of 32 fake accounts and their respective web pages, on suspicion of being linked to the Russian meddlers in the U.S. election. The fake accounts were opened to disrupt the midterm election that is only three months away.) President Trump, who has been ridiculing the Mueller investigation as a "witch hunt" and the allegations of Russian interference in the 2016 election as a "hoax," paid no heed to the indictment and went ahead with the planned summit with his favorite Russian dictator.

Putin could not have asked for a better warm-up to the summit than the Twitter message Trump issued on the morning of the summit. In that message, he blamed the years of tension with Russia on the "foolishness and stupidity" of his own country, as well as the "Rigged

Witch Hunt," meaning the Mueller investigation. Americans are anxious to know what the two leaders discussed at their one-on-one secret meeting. What little they have known so far came to them in dribs and drabs from the government-controlled Russian press, not from the free press of their own country. The free press of the U.S., which is the envy of the rest of the world, is being lambasted by Trump as "the enemy of the people." It puts out only "fake news," he keeps saying, to the delight of Putin and his cronies.

Does Mr. Trump know that an attack on the free press is an attack on the First Amendment to the U.S. Constitution, which he has sworn to "preserve, protect and defend"? The time will come when he will be made to pay a heavy price for this deplorable behavior. But the words he uttered at the press conference, and the way he conducted himself in the presence of the man who ordered the attack on the very democratic foundation of his country; annexed Crimea; is supporting rebels in Ukraine; is defending the murderous Assad regime in Syria; and has poisoned his political opponents both at home and abroad call for action right now.

Standing next to that man, Trump challenged the findings of the Justice Department, the intelligence community and both chambers of the legislature of his own country. All of them had concluded that Russia had attacked the United States during the 2016 presidential election. The attack, which took the form of hacking into the digital devices used in the election, was called cyberattack. It was an attack on the very democratic foundation on which the country is built. As such, it was an attack on the country itself. Despite the irrefutable evidence of the attack that the Mueller investigation produced, Trump repeated his ridicule that the investigation was a "witch hunt." This time he did it in the presence of the man who necessitated the investigation.

Putin, as was expected, denied that his country had anything to do with the hacking. But he did admit, in his answer to a reporter's question, that he wanted Trump, and not his Democratic opponent Hillary Clinton, to win the election. The reason for his preference, he added, was that Trump had "talked about bringing the U.S.-Russia relationship back to normal." To a follow-up question, put to Trump, whether he trusted Putin more than his own intelligence community, Trump gave this reply: "I have confidence in both parties. I have great confidence in my intelligence people, but I will tell you that President Putin was extremely strong and powerful in his denial today."

That response, and his responses to many other questions, drew strong protests not only from Democrats, but from some Republicans too. Some even characterized some of his words "treasonous" and called for his impeachment. Let's examine whether those words rise to the level of treason.

'Treason' Under the U.S. Constitution

Under the U.S. Constitution, "Treason against the United States shall consist only in levying War against them, or in adhering to their Enemies, giving them Aid or Comfort."

Russia is an enemy, and it has been waging war against the U.S. for some time now. As stated above, it is a new kind of war, something unheard of at the time the U.S. adopted its Constitution. The term used to refer to it is "cyberwar." If it can be established that cyberwar falls within the purview of war as defined in the Constitution, President Trump's performance in Helsinki was treasonous, and the demand for his impeachment is justified. He called Putin's denial of the cyberwar "extremely strong and powerful;" praised him as a "good competitor," hastening to add that "the word competitor is a compliment;" and denigrated his own country as "foolish" for allowing its relationship with Russia to deteriorate. If words like these don't give comfort to the enemy we are confronting in the present war, the cyberwar, what will? The charge of treason leveled against Trump is a valid one.

There was also a moment when Trump uttered something which even his lackeys back home found loathsome. He did it when Putin offered, while responding to a reporter's question, to allow special counsel Mueller to interview the 12 Russians indicted by him in exchange for allowing Russian investigators to interview Bill Browder and those close to him. Mr. Browder, a billionaire, born in the U.S. but now a British citizen (which fact Putin didn't seem to know), has been at the top of the list of Putin's foreign enemies for 10 years. Trump welcomed what Putin said as "an incredible offer."

How did Bill Browder make the list of Putin's enemies? Browder himself has answered the question. His answer, published in an article, titled "Viewpoint: The View from the Top of Putin's Enemies List," in the July 30, 2018, issue of *TIME* magazine, is: "Putin almost never utters the names of his enemies – except for mine, which lately seems to be very much on his mind. Why? Because I am the person responsible for lobbying the Obama Administration to pass the Magnitsky Act in 2012. The law allows the U.S. to freeze the assets and withhold the visas of people who are violating human rights in Russia. The act was named for my lawyer Sergei Magnitsky, who was murdered in a Moscow jail in 2009 after uncovering a massive $230 million Russian government corruption scheme – one we have since traced to Putin's cronies."

Since the passage of the Magnitsky Act, Russia has been reeling from the punishing sanctions imposed on it by the Obama administration, and re-imposed by the Trump administration after a great deal of arm-twisting by both Democrats and Republicans. Several European allies of the U.S. have expressed solidarity with it by passing their own versions of the Magnitsky Act and imposing sanctions on Russia. Many other countries around the world are also in the process of taking similar steps. No wonder Putin detests Bill Browder. Browder's *TIME* magazine article also gives a clue to why Trump did not have a word of criticism for Putin and was obsequious toward him throughout the Helsinki news conference.

Trump's Links to Russian Oligarchs

Rumors have been rife that Donald Trump's business activities in Russia were bankrolled by Russian oligarchs. Some of them could as well be "Putin's cronies" that Browder referred to in his article. The fear of his questionable dealings with those cronies being exposed may be the reason behind Trump's persistent refusal to release his tax returns. The same fear may be what stands in the way of his confronting Putin for the election meddling. That also explains his tirade against the Mueller investigation which, among other things, has been looking into Trump's business activities in Russia.

We will know more about those activities and about Trump's links to Russian oligarchs as the trial of his former campaign chairman, Paul Manafort, progresses. The trial is going on in a federal court in Alexandria, Virginia, as I write this. This is the first trial stemming from Mueller's Russia probe, though the crimes Manafort is charged with have nothing to do with the Russian meddling in the U.S. election. He is charged with tax evasion and bank fraud. The 32 charges he is facing arose largely from his work as a political consultant in Ukraine.

Manafort's main client in Ukraine was Viktor F. Yanukovych, the pro-Russian politician whom he helped become president of Ukraine in 2010. Since his removal from power in February 2014, Yanukovych has been living in exile in Russia. Manafort also worked for some pro-Russian, pro-Yanukovych Ukrainian oligarchs. Payments for his work came through bank accounts in Cypress, which he did not show in his tax returns. Manafort's defense team says that those accounts were opened by the Ukrainian oligarchs who were his clients. Ukrainian oligarchs' links to Russian oligarchs are well-documented. The possibility that some of them are linked to Donald Trump, too, cannot be ruled out.

The star prosecution witness in the Manafort case is Rick Gates, his longtime partner in the political consultancy work, who had also worked as number two person in Trump's presidential campaign, when Manafort was its chairman. He stayed on with the campaign even after Manafort was removed from it when controversy over his work in Ukraine erupted. While Manafort decided to fight the charges against him, Gates pleaded guilty and offered to cooperate with the prosecution. He is now one of the 35 prosecution witnesses.

Since the Manafort trial began, Trump has been going berserk. He and his attorney, Rudolph Giuliani, have intensified their tirade against the Mueller investigation. Trump has even asked Attorney General Jeff Sessions to fire Mueller and call off the investigation. People are surprised that the man who pilloried Sessions for his recusal from the Russia probe is now asking him to end the probe.

Russia's Offer of 'Dirt' on Hillary Clinton

The media was abuzz throughout last week with a new revelation on the controversial meeting Donald Trump Jr. had with a Russian lawyer, in June 2016, at Trump Tower, New York. The lawyer, Natalia Veselnitskaya, reportedly has strong ties to the Kremlin. The meeting was held in pursuance of an email Trump Jr. received from Veselnitskaya, offering some "dirt" on Hillary Clinton. The dirt was supposedly gathered by Russian intelligence. The meeting was attended by high-ranking officials of the Trump campaign, including chairman Manafort.

Donald Trump had said all along that he knew nothing about the meeting, held at his own New York residence, which was also his campaign headquarters at the time. Michael Cohen, his longtime personal lawyer, confidant and fixer, who fell out with him recently, threw a bombshell last week, saying that Trump was lying. If Cohen has concrete evidence to prove that Trump had prior knowledge of the meeting, that will take the Mueller team a step closer to concluding that the Trump campaign did collude with Russia.

Among the numerous documents confiscated during the FBI raid on Cohen's apartment in Manhattan, in April, when Cohen was Trump's attorney, were dozens of tapes containing recorded conversations between the two. It was through the airing of one such tape, leaked to CNN, that another lie of Trump's got exposed. The lie related to an affair Trump had with Karen McDougal, a former Playboy model, and to the payment to her of $150,000 as hush money to buy her silence about the affair. Until the tape containing Trump's conversation with Cohen about how to pay the money was aired, Trump had kept denying that he had any affair with Ms. McDougal.

The McDougal story broke out in the wake of the controversy stirred by another Trump lie about another affair of his. The woman involved in that affair is a pornographic film actress known as Stormy Daniels. The hush money paid to her was $130,000. Here again, the middleman was Michael Cohen. How Cohen raised the money to pay the porn star and what made her break the silence about the affair and expose another Trumpian lie were juicy topics of gossip in the media, as well as in political circles, for several months. Though the controversy has not derailed his presidency, Trump is not out of the woods yet. Stormy Daniels has taken the matter to court. Michael Avenatti, the attorney representing her in the case, also represents three other women who claim that they had affairs with Trump, too. All three, Avenatti disclosed to the media, were paid "hush money" before the 2016 election. We will hear more juicy stories when those cases go on trial.

Trump has expressed shock that his own personal attorney had been secretly taping his conversations with him. He is also afraid that having been a longtime associate, Cohen may spill the beans on many more of his personal, business and political activities during his testimony. Investigators are examining Cohen's role in the payment of hush money to women during the 2016 campaign and whether such payments violated campaign finance laws. More than anyone else, Cohen knows that he could be implicated in many questionable activities Trump was involved in as a real estate tycoon. So, his offer to cooperate with the investigators is understandable.

A panic-stricken Trump has launched a Twitter tirade against the Mueller investigation. He is very much aware of the disastrous consequences of what Cohen may reveal to the authorities. His tirade against the Mueller investigation has now taken the form of a character assassination campaign against Mueller himself. His personal attorney now is Rudolf Giuliani, a former New York mayor and himself a federal prosecutor once. Giuliani has been making himself a laughingstock by saying stupid and contradictory things in defense of his client. The latest stupid thing he said was that even if there was collusion between the Trump campaign and Russia, "collusion is not a crime." I leave it to legal experts to tutor him on that. What he and his client don't seem to realize is that their attacks on the special counsel could be construed as obstruction of justice, which is a solid ground for impeachment.

Conclusion

I can go and on to stress the point that the demand for impeachment of President Trump is a well-founded one. Apart from treason, which we discussed above, "bribery and other high crimes and misdemeanors" are also grounds for impeachment under the Constitution. We already discussed some of the activities and utterances of Trump that fall within that area. By the time the Mueller team completes its work, we will surely learn about many more that reach the level of impeachability. Remember, we are talking about a man who, according to *The Washington Post*, utters 6.5 lies a day, on average. He doesn't know when he lies that some of them could be perjurious, which is another ground for impeachment.

If Congress is serious about impeaching Trump, it doesn't have to wait until the Russia probe is completed. It already has ample material to initiate the process. Alas, it won't happen as long as the composition of the present Congress is what it is. It is Republican-controlled, and most Republicans are too timid to stand up to Trump. His modus operandi is such that even a mafia don would want to learn a lesson or two from him. He has been running the country as though it is part of his sprawling business empire.

Will some Republicans in Congress prove that they have spine by coming forward to initiate the process of impeachment? Any effort by Democrats will get nowhere because they are in a minority in both the House of Representatives and the Senate. The initiative should come from Republicans. They owe it to their country to act before it is too late. And they owe it to the Constitution which they have sworn to "support and defend ... against all enemies, foreign and domestic."

36

Hypocrisy, Thy Name Is Donald Trump!

April 14, 2019

Donald Trump and Joe Biden at their first debate before the 2020 presidential election. (*The picture is reproduced courtesy* bing.com.)

•

When President Donald Trump mocked at the way former Vice President Joseph Biden Jr. greeted and interacted with both women and men in his social and political circles, it evoked contemptuous laughs all around the world. Trump has no moral authority to do it if the question is of a man's alleged trespassing on, and lack of respect for, a woman's space. We'll come to how Trump did the mocking in a minute. Let's first put the story in context.

Over the years, we have seen the touchy-feely way Biden greeted and showed his affection for people whom he felt close to. We have seen him hug, kiss and caress people at political and social functions and on campaign trails. My friends and I were often amused by it. We laughed it away as "teenagerish."

Never had we thought that it was invasive of the privacy of the person at the receiving end of his affection. Not once did we think that

Biden was behaving like a dirty old man. (He is now 76 years old.)

That's why we were surprised when a few women disclosed the other day that the manner in which Biden showed his affection for them years ago had made them feel uncomfortable. The first woman who did it was Lucy Flores, a former Nevada State legislator. In an essay published in *The Cut*, an online sister publication of *New York* magazine that focuses on women's issues, she says that at a campaign rally in November 2014, Biden "inhaled my hair" and planted "a big slow kiss on the back of my head." Flores was the Democratic nominee for lieutenant governor of Nevada and Biden, vice president of the country at the time, had gone to Nevada to lend a helping hand to perk up her sagging campaign. (That she lost the election despite Biden's help is irrelevant here.) The recipient of the help now says that what he did at the rally had made her feel "uneasy, gross and confused."

Biden issued a statement addressing her accusation. The statement said, "In my many years on the campaign trail and in public life, I have offered countless handshakes, hugs, expressions of affection, support and comfort. And not once – never did I believe I acted inappropriately. If it is suggested I did so, I will listen respectfully. But it was never my intention."

His explanation did not put the controversy to rest. Taking advantage of the trend in the present #MeToo era, a few more women – the number has reached seven at this writing – came forward saying that they too had felt uncomfortable by what Biden did to them. Amy Lappos of Connecticut is one of them. She says in an interview with *The Hartford Courant* that at a fund-raiser in Connecticut in 2009, Biden "put his hand around my neck and pulled me in to rub noses with me." The overture "wasn't sexual," she adds. The reason for her complaint is that there was "a line of respect" which she says Biden crossed. She also says that she "never filed a complaint, to be honest, because he was the vice president. I was a nobody."

It is important to note that none of these women have attributed sexual motive to Biden's behavior. In matters like this, however, how the person at the receiving end feels is all that matters, not the motive of the person showing the "affection." That's the case even with sexual harassment. It is a welcome romantic overture if the other party likes it; sexual harassment if the other party doesn't.

That said, a question that can legitimately be asked is: Why didn't these women disclose their discomfort when it occurred. If only they had done it, say those who know Biden well, he would have apologized to them and found other ways of showing his affection. If it was Biden's position as vice president that made them keep quiet, they could have at least shared their experience with some of his close associates. Or they could have made their friends do it for them. If they had shared their experience with some of their friends, why did those friends keep quiet all these years?

The fact that these women chose to come out of the woodwork and throw this bombshell when Biden became the most likely Democratic candidate in the next presidential election makes their motive suspect. Though 95 percent of the people, two-thirds of them women, questioned in a recent survey don't find the allegations so serious as to disqualify him from entering the race, some of the Democratic contenders for nomination have seized on them and demanded that he account for his behavior.

Biden's Apologetic Video

Biden released a video doing precisely that. The video shows him in a somber mood and saying: "Social norms are changing. I understand that, and I've heard what these women are saying. Politics to me has always been about making connections, but I will be more mindful about respecting personal space in the future. That's my responsibility and I will meet it."

Most women, including most commentators on TV news channels and talk shows, have accepted Biden's explanation and decided to move on. But there is one person who is not willing to do it: President Donald Trump. It seems he has already decided to take advantage of Biden's alleged faux pas and make it an issue in his reelection campaign, which he has already begun.

He tweeted a video of his own mocking at Biden. It's a doctored version of the explanatory, apologetic video Biden had posted a day earlier. The doctored version – with a "WELCOME BACK JOE!" caption – shows Biden speaking to the camera. As he does it, another image of Biden, a cartoonish one, pops up, massaging the shoulders and smelling the back of the head of Biden in the original image. Watching it, one couldn't help thinking: Isn't it how high school bullies settle scores with their adversaries? The Trumpian prank may have warmed the heart of Lucy Flores, whose accusation against Biden it is trying to convey. But most people in the country, and in the whole world, find it hypocritical and shameless.

Here is a man who has been accused by several women – the number is 19, by the latest count – of sexual misconduct and assault. An unwritten rule in the American legal system, which says that a sitting president should not be indicted, stands in the way of their suing him now. They are waiting in the wings for his tenure as president to be over, the womanizer-in-chief may please note.

Hush Money Paid to Trump's Mistresses

The juicy details of his extramarital affairs with two of them, which provided grist to the gossip mill for weeks, had nearly derailed his 2016 campaign. The first one, Stormy Daniels, was a pornographic film actress; and the second, Karen McDougal, a former Playboy model. Trump arranged to buy their silence with bribes. Daniels was paid $130,000 and McDougal $150,000.

Extramarital affairs, though immoral, are not illegal. Even buying silence of the women involved in them is not illegal. But if the payments made to buy their silence are aimed at influencing the outcome of an election, they are illegal. They break campaign finance laws. Trump's campaign survived, eventually leading to his victory, because the sources of the hush money could not be traced directly to him. Those who know what a smooth operator he is were not surprised.

In the case of Daniels, it was paid by Michael Cohen, Trump's former lawyer, also known as his fixer, who at the time said that he used his own money to do it. The fixer has since fallen out with his client and partner in crime and become a prosecution witness. Right now, he is cooperating with federal and New York State prosecutors in return for possible reduced sentences for all the crimes he committed on behalf of Trump.

The payment to Playboy model McDougal was done in an ingenious way. Trump's friend David J. Pecker, who is also the publisher of *National Enquirer*, paid $150,000 to her for exclusive right to publish the salacious story about her affair with Trump and never published it. In the world of yellow journalism, this sleazy method is known as "catch-and-kill." McDougal was very upset. We will know more about the real source of the hush money paid to her and Daniels as the cases now pending in courts against Michael Cohen and the Trump Organization move forward and, more importantly, if and when special counsel Robert Mueller's 400-page report on Trump's 2016 campaign is released in its unredacted form.

To Trump, women are just sex objects. Who can forget the remarks he made about them, which were captured on the by-now-infamous "Access Hollywood" tape? When the tape went viral, he even contemplated withdrawing from the presidential race. On the tape, he was heard bragging about using his fame to grope women without their consent. "When you're a star, they let you do it," he was heard saying. According to him, when one is famous, one can do anything to women, even "Grab 'em by the pussy."

And what about his comments about his own daughter Ivanka – that she was hot and that if she weren't his daughter, he would date her? That must have made many parents throw up.

In Bob Woodward's book, *Fear: Trump in the White House*, he is quoted as saying that his advice to friends who were the targets of sexual-assault accusations was: "You've got to deny, deny, deny and push back on these women." That's what he did in the wake of the controversy that erupted when the "Access Hollywood" tape went viral. Though he first admitted it, saying that it was just "locker room talk," he later denied having said it. He even went to the extent of saying that the voice on the video was not his.

Deny, deny, deny – that's what he has been doing in response to all the charges leveled against him by the victims of his promiscuous behavior. Though former President Bill Clinton is no saint when it comes to making sexual advances toward women, Trump should be the last person saying this about him: "There's never been anyone in the history of politics, in this nation, that's been so abusive to women." He said it at a press conference in October 2016, just before his debate with Hillary Clinton, his Democratic Party opponent in the presidential race. His purpose, obviously, was to humiliate Hillary.

The man with this much baggage is now mocking at Joe Biden because a few women, for reasons they alone know, have said that he had interacted with them in an improper manner, years ago.

Hypocrisy, thy name is Donald Trump! How else can one explain the bizarre behavior of this accidental president of America?

37
Trump Acting as Apologist for Saudi Prince Accused in Journalist's Murder
June 24, 2019

Saudi journalist Jamal Khashoggi. He was murdered at his country's consulate in Istanbul, Turkey, on October 2, 2018 *(The picture is reproduced courtesy* Getty Images*)*

•

On October 2, 2018, Jamal Khashoggi, a Saudi journalist, went into his country's consulate in Istanbul, Turkey, and never came out. When news spread that he was murdered inside the consulate by a hit team that flew in from Saudi Arabia, it caused an international uproar. The uproar prompted Turkish authorities, U.S. intelligence agencies, the United Nations and leading media outlets in the world to investigate the murder. All investigations pointed to the de fact ruler of Saudi Arabia, Crown Prince Mohammed bin Salman, as the person responsible for it. The C.I.A. even said that MBS, as the crown prince is popularly known, ordered the killing. Let's briefly examine how Khashoggi, a one-time friend of MBS and of the Saudi ruling family, later became a bête noire of both.

Born in the holy city of Medina in Saudi Arabia on October 13, 1958, Jamal Khashoggi began his career in journalism as a correspondent at *Saudi Gazette*, an English-language daily, in 1983. He did it after earning a bachelor's degree in business administration from Indiana State University in the U.S. His coverage of the Soviet invasion of Afghanistan and interviews with Osama bin Laden brought him fame and recognition as a journalist quite early in his career. (When Khashoggi interviewed him in the late 1980s and early 1990s, the late bin Laden had not yet become the notorious terrorist that he did, after the September 11, 2001, terrorist attacks in the U.S., which he masterminded.)

Khashoggi rapidly rose in the profession, working for various Arab newspapers and covering major events in the Middle East, including the first Gulf War. The first Gulf War, it may be added, was fought in Kuwait, against Iraq, in 1990-'91, by a 32-nation coalition led by the U.S. In 1999, Khashoggi became the deputy editor-in-chief of *Arab News*, the largest-circulated English-language daily in Saudi Arabia. He left it in 2003 to join *Al Watan*, another daily, as its editor. But he lasted there only two months. What cost the progressive-minded Khashoggi his job at *Al Watan* was his criticism of Saudi Arabia's Wahhabi religious establishment.

From 2003 to 2007, he served as media adviser to Prince Turki al Faisal, Saudi Arabia's ambassador, first to the United Kingdom and then to the United States. His relationship with the Saudi ruling family began to rupture when he became an advocate for women's rights and for freedom of expression in the country. He was also a critic of his country's involvement in the war in Yemen, which killed thousands of innocent civilians.

In 2017, on being told by the authorities to "shut up" and fearing imminent arrest, he fled Saudi Arabia and took up residence in the U.S. Since then, he had been living at McLean, Virginia. He continued his career in journalism with a monthly column in *The Washington Post*. His new status as a columnist in a prestigious newspaper in the West gave more clout to his campaign for reforms in his native Saudi Arabia.

Khashoggi's very first column in *The Post* appeared just days after the crown prince's notorious crackdown on hundreds of leading businessmen and members of the royal family whom he perceived as threats to his claim to the Saudi throne. MBS placed them all under arrest at the Ritz Carlton hotel at Riyadh, the country's capital. "I have left my home, my family and my job, and I am raising my voice," Khashoggi wrote in his first column. "To do otherwise would betray those who languish in prison. I can speak when so many cannot." Titled "Saudi Arabia Wasn't Always This Repressive. Now It's Unbearable," the column was a withering attack on the crown prince's excesses.

Purpose of Consulate Visit

The purpose of Khashoggi's visit to his country's consulate in Istanbul was to collect some documents confirming his divorce from his Saudi wife, so he could marry his Turkish fiancée, Hatice Cengiz. He had been promised the documents when he visited the consulate four days earlier. Ms. Cengiz had accompanied him to the consulate on his October 2, 2018, visit. She was told to wait outside until he finished his work inside. It wouldn't be longer than a few minutes, she was assured.

She waited. And waited. When she did not see her fiancé come out even after 10 long hours of waiting, she began to panic. She called a friend of Khashoggi's and informed him what was happening. Khashoggi had given her the friend's phone number and told her to contact him if anything untoward happened. Dr. Yasin Aktay, the friend, who is a member of Turkey's ruling party, with contacts at the highest levels, immediately called the head of Turkish intelligence and also alerted the office of the country's president, Recep Tayyip Erdogan, on what he heard from "a really worried … lady I didn't know."

Rumors began to swirl that Jamal Khashoggi was murdered inside the consulate. Though Khashoggi's relationship with the Saudi ruling family and its de fact ruler had been strained since 2017, he had never thought that the strain had put his life in danger. If he had, he wouldn't have made the mistake of going in.

Crown Prince's Reaction to the Murder

MBS's initial response to the news of the murder was that he knew nothing about it. He even told Bloomberg News, just two weeks after it happened, that Khashoggi had left the consulate "a few minutes or one hour" after he entered it. "We have nothing to hide," he added.

As if to lend credibility to the crown prince's claim, Saudi officials released a surveillance footage on October 22, 2018, showing a Khashoggi lookalike, dressed in the clothes that the real Khashoggi had worn while entering the consulate, leaving the consulate and moving around Istanbul on the day of the murder. It came to light later that the lookalike was Moustafa al-Madani, an intelligence officer at the Saudi palace. He was one of the 15-member hit team flown all the way from Riyadh to Istanbul to carry out the crown prince's mission. The mission was to bring Khashoggi back to Saudi Arabia – alive, if possible; dead, if not.

Thanks to the investigations conducted by all the entities mentioned above, we now have the identities of all 15 men who took part in the murder mission. Citing Turkish officials and sources with ties to the Saudi royal court, *Al Jazeera* reported that most of them worked in the Saudi military, security or intelligence services, including at the royal court. This gave the lie to the crown prince's claim that he knew nothing about the murder. The two private jets that brought the murder team to Istanbul in the dead of night were chartered from a company owned by the Saudi government, the *Al Jazeera* report says.

The U.N. initiated its investigation when the controversy over the murder continued to rage, with Saudi authorities issuing conflicting narratives on it. The investigation was conducted by Agnes Callamard, a special rapporteur appointed by the U.N. Human Rights Council. She submitted her findings in a 100-page report, released on June 19, 2019. According to the report, Jamal Khashoggi was "the victim of a deliberate, premeditated execution, an extrajudicial killing for which the state of Saudi Arabia is responsible." The report also says that the investigation found "credible evidence" of involvement in the killing by Crown Prince Mohammed and other high-level Saudi officials.

The leader of the hit team was Maher Abdelaziz Mutreb, a senior intelligence officer and MBS's bodyguard. In one of the audio recordings of what happened inside the consulate, which the Turkish authorities had secured and shared with the U.N., the U.S. and other friendly nations, he was heard greeting Khashoggi at the consulate with these words (as translated by *Al Jazeera*): "Please sit. We have to take you back [to Riyadh]." He went on to say: "There is an order from Interpol. Interpol demanded you be returned. We are here to take you." Khashoggi replied that he was not aware of any such order. The conversation turned into confrontation, and we all know what happened after that.

Another member of the hit team was Salah al-Tubaigy, a high-ranking forensics and autopsy expert in the Saudi interior ministry. According to the audio transcripts, the first thing he asked as soon as he entered the consulate was whether "the sacrificial animal" had arrived. He was also heard joking about how he "worked on cadavers"; that he "never worked on a warm body"; and about listening to music, sipping coffee and smoking cigars while cutting "cadavers." The presence of an autopsy expert on the team proves that the hit team had decided from the very beginning that the crown prince's first option, bringing Khashogi back to Saudi Arabia alive, would not materialize.

A *New York Times* report says that, according to Turkish intelligence, about 24 minutes after Khashoggi's arrival at the consulate, a sound of sawing could be heard on the audio recording, followed by the sound of shuffling plastic sheets. It has been said that Khashoggi's body was sawed to pieces and put in a plastic bag and disposed of. After that, according to *The Times*, Mr. Mutreb was heard saying to someone over phone, "Tell your boss" that the "deed was done." The "boss," obviously, was Mohammed bin Salman.

Khashoggi's remains have not been found to this day. The Saudis have said that the remains were handed over to a "local collaborator." They refused to say who the local collaborator was.

Saudi Narrative Keeps Changing

As proof of Khashoggi's murder became irrefutable, the Saudi officials' narrative of what led to it underwent several revisions, each taking special care to absolve the crown prince of any responsibility for it. According to the last revision, issued by the county's deputy public prosecutor Shaalan al-Shaalan, the journalist was murdered after "negotiations" for his return to the kingdom broke down. He died from a lethal injection and his body was dismembered and taken out of the consulate building. The al-Shaalan version also said that the killing was ordered by the head of the negotiating team, meaning the crown prince had nothing to do with it.

Saudi authorities have also implicated two prominent officials in the case, though they were not part of the group that flew to Istanbul for the "rogue operation." They are Saud al-Qahtani, an adviser to the royal court and MBS's right-hand man, and General Ahmed al-Asiri, the country's deputy intelligence chief. American intelligence agencies have identified al-Qahtani as the brutal enforcer of all highhanded operations ordered by the crown prince. Both men have since been fired from their positions.

Al-Asiri has been put on trial. According to the U.N. inquiry, he told the court that he had ordered the team to convince Khashoggi to return home but had never ordered the use of force.

The Saudis have charged 11 more men with murder and put them on trial. Five of them could face death penalty, the U.N. report says. The trial is taking place behind closed doors. The U.N. rapporteur called the trial a sham and has demanded that it be opened to the public and international observers. Though Saudi officials have not disclosed the identities of the defendants, the U.N. rapporteur has been able to do it with help from "various governments' sources."

Not just the U.N. rapporteur, the publisher of *The Washington Post,* Fred Ryan, also has called the trial "a sham." In a powerful op-ed piece, published on April 2, 2019, he says: "The Saudis have adopted a strategy of evasion. They still have not produced Khashoggi's body, preventing his family from holding a proper Islamic funeral. The regime has scapegoated expendable officials, seeking to quell international furor by staging a sham trial. The coordinator of the operation that killed Khashoggi, Saud al-Qahtani, remains free – and is actively advising the crown prince. ..."

President Trump's Reaction

More than the Saudis' conflicting narratives on the gruesome murder and their efforts to protect their de facto ruler from any responsibility for it, it is the reaction of the U.S. president to it that has sickened many people in the world. This is what he said when U.S. intelligence agencies' initial findings held MBS responsible for the murder: "Our intelligence agencies continue to assess all information, but it could very well be that the crown prince had knowledge of this tragic event – maybe he did and maybe he didn't."

But people who are sickened by the remark also know that President Trump wouldn't utter a word against a head of state who is useful to him in furthering his personal interests. It doesn't matter to him that the head of state is a murderous thug. And it doesn't matter to him that, in pursuing his personal interests, he is hurting national interests. Trump's "maybe he did and maybe he didn't" response reminds one of what he said about the Russian meddling in the 2016 U.S. presidential election.

All 17 U.S. intelligence agencies had concluded that Russia did meddle in the election to help candidate Trump win against his Democratic opponent Hillary Clinton. They also had proof that it was done on orders from Russia's president, Vladimir Putin. Putin, of course, had denied it. This is what President Trump said in response to a reporter's question whether he trusted Putin more than his own intelligence community: "I have confidence in both parties. I have great confidence in my intelligence people, but I will tell you that President Putin was extremely strong and powerful in his denial today." He said it, standing next to Putin, at a joint press conference held in Helsinki, on July 16, 2018. The whole world could see the smirk Trump's remark produced on Putin's face.

To get back to Khashoggi's murder. There was no change in Trump's wishy-washy reaction to it, even after the U.N. rapporteur's investigation definitively established the crown prince's culpability. He brushed off the culpability because the Saudis "spend $400 to $450 billion over a period of time, all money, all jobs, buying equipment. I'm not like a fool that says, 'We don't want to do business with them.' And by the way, if they don't do business with us, you know what they do? They'll do business with the Russians or with the Chinese." He made this surprising statement in his interview with Chuck Todd, on NBC's "Meet the Press" program, on June 23, 2019. That's just four days after the U.N. rapporteur released her report.

It was the businessman in Trump that was speaking. He can see the world only through the prism of business and money. But the monetary gains he spoke about were based on unrealistic expectations. They were premised on the promise the Saudis gave. The promise has yet to be fulfilled. Defense analysts have said that, of the "$400 to $450 billion" the Saudis promised to spend on arms purchase, a sale worth only $14.5 billion has been booked so far. They have also said that the Saudis have not concluded any major arms purchase deal since Trump took office.

The surprising thing here is that the president of a country that prides itself in being the champion of human rights is willing to condone the violation of the most sacred of those rights, the right to life, simply because the violator has promised lucrative business deals.

Trump can learn a lesson or two from Germany, Denmark and Finland, the countries that have banned arms sales to Saudi Arabia because of that violation.

All Americans should hang their heads in shame that their president is acting as an apologist for a murderous thug. To quote Fred Ryan, publisher of *The Washington Post*, again, "An innocent man, brutally slain, deserves better, as does the cause of truth and justice and human rights."

The 15-member Saudi hit team that murdered journalist Jamal Khashoggi on October 2, 2018. It is alleged that the murder was carried out on orders from Saudi Arabia's de fact ruler, Crown Prince Mohammed bin Salman. *(The picture is reproduced courtesy* Al Jazeera*)*

38

A Plea to President Trump: Reenter Iran Nuclear Deal and Avoid Another Middle East War

July 2, 2019

On June 20, 2019, President Trump issued an order to bomb three targets in Iran, in retaliation for its downing of an American spy plane. Then, just minutes before the order was to be carried out, he issued another order canceling it. The reason he gave for the abrupt reversal was that he checked with those in the American military who were to carry out his order what the collateral damage of the bombing would be. When he was told that at least 150 civilians would be killed, he changed his mind, he said. Killing 150 civilians, he reasoned, would be too disproportionate a punishment for the downing of an unmanned spy drone.

Many have pointed to the issuance of the first order without giving any thought to its consequences as yet another proof of Donald Trump's unpredictability and impulsive decision-making habit. It has also added to the confusion of America's friends and foes alike about the modus operandi of this president. That said, there is no denying that, in this particular case, his abrupt change of mind has saved the world from another U.S.-initiated war in the Middle East. As we all know, the Iraq war, which President George W. Bush started in 2003 and has caused tens of thousands of deaths and cost American taxpayers trillions of dollars, is still going on.

There is another striking similarity between the Iraq war and a war with Iran that could still happen. President Bush had used fabricated evidence – that Iraq, at the time ruled by dictator Saddam Hussein, had weapons of mass destruction – to justify his decision to go to war. President Trump's decision to pull out of the Iran nuclear deal, which has brought the country to the brink of war now, was premised on unsubstantiated allegation that Iran has been cheating on the deal.

Trump had vowed to pull the U.S. out of the deal even when he was a candidate for president, even before he read it. He had to make good on the promise once he became president. The real reason why he pulled out of the deal was not that Iran had been cheating on it, but that the deal was a major foreign policy achievement of the Obama administration. Eradicating all Obama legacies is a mission Trump has been engaged in from day one of his presidency.

The Iran nuclear deal was the product of prolonged, at times frustrating, efforts made by various individuals and agencies to prevent Iran from acquiring nuclear weapons. The efforts intensified early this century, when the International Atomic Energy Agency (IAEA) discovered uranium-enrichment programs in Iran's underground nuclear facilities. It's public knowledge that these programs could easily expand into ones producing nuclear weapons. Refusing to believe Iran's protestations that the programs were meant for peaceful purposes, the U.N. decided to do whatever it could to stop it.

In 2006, the U.N. Security Council passed a resolution (Resolution 1696) demanding that Iran halt its uranium-enrichment programs. When Iran refused to comply, the Security Council passed another resolution (Resolution 1737), this one spelling out sanctions for noncompliance. The sanctions would continue until Iran met the Security Council demand, the new resolution said. It may be added that these sanctions were on top of what had already been imposed by the U.S. in 1979. (More about the U.S.-imposed sanctions, in a little bit.)

Even as new sanctions were being imposed, talks were held by major Western powers, conveying to Iran that the only way it could save itself from being hurt by the sanctions was to give up its plans to acquire nuclear weapons. Iran kept insisting that its nuclear programs were not weapons-related.

Obama Tries to Repair U.S.-Iranian Relations

That was the situation when Barack Obama came on the scene as president, in January 2009. He saw in it a historic opportunity to repair U.S. ties with Iran, which had been severed since the 1978-79 uprising, later known as the Iranian Revolution. Iran, at the time, had been under the dictatorship of Mohammad Reza Shah, who owed his position and survival in it largely to the help he received from the U.S.

The Iranian revolution led to the overthrow of the Shah, on February 11, 1979, and establishment of an Islamic republic. Students were at the forefront of the revolution. The U.S., because of its long association with the Shah dictatorship, had been a target of their ire from the very beginning of the revolution. On November 4, 1979, a group of them overran the U.S. embassy in Tehran, the Iranian capital, and held 52 American diplomats and citizens hostage. The hostages were released after being held in the embassy for 444 days.

Iran has been reeling from the sanctions imposed on it by the U.S. in the wake of the 1979 embassy takeover and later joined by other Western powers. Whatever the Iranians' grievances against the U.S., most of which very legitimate, the embassy takeover by students had earned them the wrath of all civilized nations around the world. More sanctions were imposed, by President Ronald Reagan, in 1987, and President Bill Clinton, in 1995, for other international law violations and hostile actions toward the U.S..

President Obama took a personal interest in the negotiations that had been going on to get Iran to give up its uranium-enrichment program. As the U.S. had no diplomatic relations with Iran, his administration could not get involved in direct negotiations with Iran. So, his secretary of state, first Hillary Clinton and then John Kerry, worked through back channels and good offices of U.S allies. Such indirect contacts produced a thaw in the relationship between the two countries, setting the scene for a contact between the two heads of state, at least by phone.

The September 2013 phone conversation that President Obama had with the newly elected Iranian president, Hassan Rouhani, was the first of its kind in decades. That phone conversation led Obama to believe that "we can reach a comprehensive solution." His own initiative plus the prodigious work done by others in his administration finally paid off. The result was the Joint Comprehensive Plan of Action (JCPOA), which five permanent members of the U.N. Security Council – China, France, Russia, the United Kingdom and the United States – plus Germany, commonly referred to as P5 + 1, signed with Iran on July 14, 2015.

In return for Iran's compliance with the restrictions placed on it under JCPOA, all the existing sanctions on it were to be lifted in a phased manner. The pace of lifting would depend on the pace of Iran's compliance. The first step toward compliance was the stopping by Iran of all its nuclear-weapons-related activities right away. Many of the other restrictions would last for 10 years, some for 15 years, and some for 25 years. The agreement also made it mandatory for Iran to give U.N. inspectors free access to its nuclear facilities.

The phased lifting of sanctions began on January 16, 2016. Since then, the international Atomic Energy Agency has been closely monitoring Iran's compliance with the deal. All signatories to the deal were fully satisfied with the progress made under the deal, which was reported from time to time by IAEA inspectors. They were happy that a potentially catastrophic military conflict had been averted. Unfortunately, their happy feeling proved to be short-lived.

Trump Pulls U.S. Out of the Deal

Soon after Donald Trump began his term as president, in January 2017, he started working toward fulfilling his campaign promise to pull the U.S. out of the Iran nuclear deal. More than the decision to pull out, it was the reason he gave for doing it that surprised those involved in the implementation of the deal. He kept saying that it was a horrible deal and that Iran had been cheating on it. Finally, on May 8, 2018, he issued an order unilaterally withdrawing from the deal. He also revived all sanctions the U.S. had imposed on Iran in 1979 and had been in place until they were suspended in 2015, in accordance with the terms of JCPOA.

By pulling out of the deal, Trump may, in addition to besmirching the reputation of Obama, have also strengthened his cheek-by-jowl relationship with two leaders of the Middle East: the murderous Mohammed bin Salman who is the de facto ruler of Saudi Arabia; and the megalomaniacal Benjamin Netanyahu who still remains prime minister of Israel despite the corruption scandal he and his wife are involved in. Crown Prince Salman and Prime Minister Netanyahu have been trying to scuttle the Iran deal since its very inception. It was reported that the Netanyahu government even had plans to assassinate Iran's nuclear scientists. Not surprisingly, he was the first foreign head of state to praise Trump for pulling out of the deal.

The Deal Is Not Dead

What Trump and his minions don't realize is that the U.S. exit doesn't mean that the deal is dead. The other signatories to the deal are doing everything they can to keep it alive. And the rest of the world is indebted to them for their efforts. It is also laudable that the leaders of Iran are conducting themselves in a much more mature way than the leader of the free world. Despite provocations from the latter, they have decided not to abandon the deal – at least as of now.

After humiliating Iran at every turn, after dragging that country to the brink of war, Trump now says that he wants to work on a new deal. And he has invited Iran for talks. Iran's response to his invitation: "Talks and threats are mutually exclusive." The response was given by Majid Takht Ravanchi, Iran's ambassador to the U.N., while answering a question put to him by CNN's Fareed Zakaria, on June 30, 2019.

If President Trump is keen on avoiding a war with Iran, which he repeatedly said he is, all that he has to do is reenter the existing deal and spell out his terms for improving it. Any man-made document can be improved upon. But dismissing it as bad even before reading it is an insult to the men and women who spent days and nights and drew on their expertise to prepare it. Does Mr. Trump think that all of them are stupid and that he is the only wise guy around?

•

UPDATE: *On the same day the above article was published, in* The East-West Inquirer, *an online monthly, Iranian news agencies reported, and it was confirmed by the International Atomic Energy Agency, that Iran violated a key provision in the deal. The provision was the one that stipulated how much nuclear fuel Iran can possess and, according to the news report, it exceeded that limit. Even after the Trump administration withdrew from the deal and reimposed U.S. sanctions on Iran 14 months ago, Iran had continued to comply with it, thanks to the persistent efforts made by the other signatories to the deal to keep it alive and to the promise they gave to Iran to find ways to ease the burden caused to its economy by the U.S. sanctions. Though Iran is still far from being able to produce a nuclear bomb, the news of violation unnerved the other signatories.*

President Trump, who pushed Iran into committing this violation, reacted to the news, saying that Iran was "playing with fire." According to a report by David E. Sanger, in the July 2, 2019, issue of The New York Times, *the Trump administration, which repudiated the deal 14 months ago, now insists that Iran abide by its terms. Is there anything more laughable than that? Doesn't it contradict Trump's repeated demand that a new deal be negotiated? According to the same Sanger report, Iran's response to the demand is that the U.S. must first return to the existing deal. That response, plus the fact that the other parties to the deal have not given up on it, gives us hope that it can be salvaged. Will someone in the Trump coterie convince him that it is the best way out of the present dangerous situation?*

39

NY Times Columnist Identifies Racist Bones in Trump's Body

July 23, 2019

Congresswomen Rashida Tlaib, Ayanna Pressley, Ilhan Omar and Alexandria Ocasio-Cortez, at a news conference in Washington, D.C., on July 16, 2019. The news conference was held to respond to President Donald Trump's Twitter fusillade on July 14, 2019, asking them to "go back" to the countries they came from. All the four, nicknamed "the Squad," are women of color and freshmen in the U.S. House of Representatives. *(The picture is reproduced courtesy Alex Woblewski/Getty Images.)*

•

Columnist Nicholas Kristof of *The New York Times* has identified some of the racist bones in President Donald Trump's body. His July 18, 2019, column in the paper, titled "Racist to the Bone," is a repartee to Trump's claim that he doesn't "have a racist bone in his body." Let me put the whole thing in perspective.

On Sunday, July 14, 2019, President Trump issued a string of tweets, asking four Democratic members of the U.S. House of Representatives to "go back" to the countries they came from, rather than "loudly and viciously telling the people of the United States" how to run the government. All of them are freshmen in the House and all are women of color.

"Go back to your country" is a taunt most first-generation Americans, mostly of color, have heard now and then from those, especially whites, who came to the country before them. Almost always, the taunt is hurled by ruffians during arguments at street corners, parking lots, and even in schoolyards. This is the first time we heard it come out of the mouth of the president of the United States, which prides itself in being a country of immigrants.

Another first in this case is that all the four targets of the president's taunt are elected members of the U.S. Congress. What did they do to provoke it? They exercised their constitutional right to dissent during legislative processes. Three of them – Alexandria Ocasio-Cortez of New York, Rashida Tlaib of Michigan and Ayanna S. Pressley of Massachusetts – were born and brought up in the U.S. and, as such, they are as much American as Mr. Trump is. The fourth one, Ilhan Omar of Minnesota, arrived in this country at the age of 12, accompanying her father and grandfather (her mother had died when she was two) who had fled Islamist terrorism and civil war in their home country, Somalia. Arriving in the U.S. in 1992, the family secured asylum in 1995. Ilhan Omar first became an immigrant and then, at the age of 19, became a naturalized U.S. citizen. She is as much American as President Trump's grandfather was. Didn't his grandfather come to America as an immigrant from Germany? And her path to citizenship is more straightforward than that of Mr. Trump's present wife Melania, who came to the U.S. from Slovenia on a visitor visa and then earned money as a model before she was authorized to work.

The four women, nicknamed "the Squad" by fellow lawmakers in the Democratic Party, had some differences with Speaker Nancy Pelosi and other senior members of the party, especially on issues related to immigration. The differences became louder during the recent debates in the House on the funding of President Trump's plans for border security. The Squad was particularly critical of the inhuman way the Trump administration has been treating asylum-seekers at the U.S.-Mexican border. The four women had criticized Speaker Pelosi for not placing enough restrictions on the administration, while passing the emergency border aid package.

The House of Representatives being Democratic-controlled since January 2019, these four idealistic young women had expected their leader in Congress to use their Party's newly gained clout against the Republican president. The purpose of Trump's Twitter fusillade was to exploit the feud within the Democratic Party to his advantage. It didn't work the way he expected, though.

All four women refused to take Trump's bait and reacted to his insulting tweets in a mature way that made fellow Democrats proud. At a press conference jointly held by them, they gave fitting responses to Trump, whose tweets had even questioned their loyalty to the country. The response of Ms. Omar, one of the first two Muslim women in Congress along with Ms. Tlaib, is very poignant. It said: "You are stoking white nationalism… . [Y]ou are angry that people like us are serving in Congress and fighting against your hate-filled agenda."

Speaker Pelosi Acts as a True Leader

Speaker Pelosi rose to the occasion as a true leader and came to the defense of her freshmen colleagues. She joined the millions of Americans who were outraged by the president's racist tweets and issued a couple of tweets of her own, condemning his "xenophobic" remarks. One of her tweets pointed out that when Trump "tells four American Congresswomen to go back to their countries, he reaffirms [that] his plan to 'Make America Great Again' has always been about making America white again. Our diversity is our strength and our unity is our power."

"Make America Great Again," by the way, was the slogan the Trump team coined and popularized during the 2016 election campaign.

Pelosi did not stop at that. She pushed a resolution through the House, which, among other things, criticized Trump's "racist comments that have legitimized increased fear and hatred of new Americans and people of color." The nonbinding resolution was voted against by all Republican members, except four. That is, despite Pelosi's plea that "[e]very single member of this institution, Democratic and Republican, should join us in condemning the president's racist tweets," only four

Republicans had the guts to cross party lines, over to the side of the truth.

The resolution, passed on July 16, may be nonbinding. But it has sent out a powerful message that the country is being torn apart by racism and that it is aided and abetted by no less a person than the president himself. It is laudable that, in voting for the resolution, 240 members of the House put their conscience and courage above the senseless House rule that prevents the president from being called a racist. What else should he be called when there is overwhelming evidence to prove that he is a racist?

Neither the resolution nor the July 17 impeachment initiative in the House that was stalled has had any effect on the president, though. Paying no heed to the fact that it was his tweets on Sunday asking four congresswomen "to go back" to their countries that led to the July 16 House resolution, he doubled down on his attack on them the next day at a Greenville, N.C., rally. He once again smeared Ilhan Omar as trafficking in "vicious anti-Semitic screeds"; and as a left-wing radical who sympathizes with Al Qaeda, hates America and "looks down with contempt on the hard-working Americans."

The crowd at the rally responded with "send her back, send her back" chant. The chanting lasted 12 seconds, with Trump looking around approvingly.

As was expected, Trump was outraged by the House resolution. He issued another tweet, characterizing it as a "con game." The new tweet also said: "This should be a vote on the filthy language, statements and lies told by the Democrat Congresswomen, who I truly believe, based on their actions, hate our Country."

This is another one of the thousands of lies that Trump has uttered since he became president. While not all Americans agree with the four congresswomen's positions on certain issues, none has any problem with the language they use to express them. It has always been decent. It is Mr. Trump who is known around the world as one who habitually uses filthy language while attacking his adversaries. The Republicans who voted against the House resolution refuse to see racism in Trump's tweets, directed at their four female colleagues of color. They would do well to listen to the veteran Democratic Representative John Lewis's words: "I know racism when I see it, I know racism when I feel it... ."

Lewis was a victim of racist lynch mob in his early days as a civil rights activist. Nobody is accusing Trump of physically lynching anyone. But the words he has used in his despicable tweets have the same effect.

Second President in History Rebuked by Congress

With this resolution, Trump has become the second president in U.S. history to be rebuked by Congress on charges of racism. The first one was William Howard Taft, who served from 1909 to 1913. Trump kept denying that his tweets about the four women were racist. "I don't have a Racist bone in my body!" he said in another tweet, issued on July 16, 2019. To which Ocasio-Cortez, the most articulate of the four women, responded: "You're right, Mr. President. You don't have a racist bone in your body. You have a racist mind in your head, and a racist heart in your chest."

It was this exchange that inspired Nicholas Kristof of *The Times* to do some anatomical exploration of Trump's body to identify the racist bones in it. His July 18 column, which I referred to in the beginning of this article, is the outcome of that exploration. Here are some of the racist bones in Trump's body that Kristof identified:

Phalanges and metacarpals These are bones of the fingers and hands that Trump has used to tweet tirades against black and brown people and to retweet Nazi sympathizers, including, twice, an account called @WhiteGenocideTM with a photo of the founder of the American Nazi Party.

Mandible and maxilla These are the jawbones that Trump has used to denounce Mexican immigrants as "criminals, drug dealers, rapists," not to mention to refuse to criticize the Ku Klux Klan.

Femurs, fibulas, tibias, metatarsals These foot and leg bones carried Trump into his casinos, where black staff members would be rushed off the floor so he couldn't see them, according to a former employee, Kip Brown.

Virtually every remaining bone was implicated in Trump's early refusal to rent apartments in his buildings to blacks, leading the Nixon administration Justice Department (not exactly a pillar of liberalism) to sue him for housing discrimination in the 1970s. A former building superintendent working for Trump explained that any rent application from a black person was coded "C," for "colored," apparently so that the office would know to reject it.

To the 187 Republican members of the House who voted against the resolution and others who condemned it, arguing that calling the president a racist violates the rules of decorum, Kristof poses this question: "How can members of the party of Lincoln today protest the *label* of racism, but not the racism itself – in a man who for 45 years has shown himself to be a racist from his mandible to his metatarsals?"

I fully endorse the question.

40

Pakistan's PM Issues Nuclear Threat Over India's Latest Move on Kashmir

September 9, 2019

Kashmiri women, in the Soura area of Srinagar, the state's capital, protesting against the revocation of special status for Kashmir, provided under Article 370 of the Indian Constitution. Soura, near Anchar Lake, is famous for Sher-i-Kashmir Institute of Medical Sciences, home to a prestigious medical college and hospital. (*The picture is reproduced courtesy Abid Bhat/*BBC News.)

•

Prime Minister Imran Khan of Pakistan has issued a warning to the world that India's latest move on Kashmir could spark a nuclear war. The latest move was the withdrawal by the Indian government of the special status Kashmir had been enjoying in the Indian federation. The status was special because the other states did not have it.

It was embodied in Article 370 of the Indian Constitution. On August 5, 2019, the Indian government, under Prime Minister Narendra Modi, made a surprise announcement abrogating the article. As expected, the announcement upset most Kashmiris. The sudden loss of any privilege, which one has been enjoying for seven decades, would upset anyone. But it seems the prime minister of Pakistan is more upset than the Kashmiris. He has raised the possibility of a nuclear war with India over what it did.

In an August 31, 2019, article in *The New York Times*, published under the title "The World Can't Ignore Kashmir. We're All in Danger," Prime Minister Khan says: "If the world does nothing to stop the Indian assault on Kashmir and its people, there will be consequences for the whole world as two nuclear-armed states get ever closer to a direct military confrontation." He justifies his warning by taking out of context a remark, which India's defense minister had made some time ago, that India's "no first use" nuclear weapons policy would "depend on circumstances." The Pakistani prime minister sees in that remark "a not-so-veiled nuclear threat" against his country.

That the use of nuclear weapons in any war will "depend on circumstances" is true of any country that has nuclear weapons, Mr. Khan may please note. If it is confronted with a life-or-death situation, it will use the most powerful weapon it has at its disposal. But a rational leader of any country would use it only as a last resort.

I am not a great fan of Prime Minister Narendra Modi. And I detest some of the things the political party that brought him to power, the Bharatiya Janata Party (BJP), espouses. But ever since he became prime minister, he has not given any indication that he would do anything irrationally. So, Mr. Khan can be sure that, in the unfortunate event of another war breaking out between India and Pakistan, India wouldn't be the first to introduce nuclear weapons in it. It will adhere to its "no first use" policy.

There isn't much worry on the Indian side about Mr. Khan behaving irrationally. After all, he was nurtured in the culture of cricket, which is considered a gentlemen's sport. The laurels he earned for him and his country as a cricket player and the way he conducted himself on the cricket field have won him numerous fans all over India. But in Pakistan, when it comes to war, and even politics, it is not the civilian authority that calls the shots. It is its military that does it. As Shashi Tharoor, an accomplished author and currently a member of the Indian Parliament, is fond of saying: In Pakistan, the military has a state, while in India, the state has a military.

Three of the four wars India and Pakistan fought in the past stemmed from their dispute over Kashmir. Almost all the skirmishes between the two countries have also been over that dispute. The skirmishes were not limited to the countries' armed forces. There have been numerous confrontations between Kashmiri militants and India's security forces. Some militants have been fighting for their state's independence from India and others for its merger with Pakistan. Many of them have taken to terrorism, thanks to the training and financial support they receive from terrorist networks freely operating in Pakistan. Some of these networks operate with the blessings of Pakistani military's notorious intelligence wing, the Inter-Services Intelligence (ISI).

Terrorists May Gain Access to Nuke

It's no secret that in Pakistan, it is the military that controls its nuclear weapons. The possibility of some of those weapons falling into the hands of terrorists, who are fighting against India with the blessings of the ISI, cannot be ruled out. Most of these terrorists call themselves jihadists or holy warriors. They claim to be fighting in the name of Allah, against infidels. Killing infidels guarantees them a place in paradise, they believe. In their war against infidels, jihadists will gladly use nuclear weapons, if they can gain access to them. Mr. Khan's *Times* article, in which he raised the possibility of nuclear weapons being used in future confrontations between India and Pakistan, could be construed by these terrorists as a tacit approval of that use.

None would question the genuineness Mr. Khan's desire "to normalize relations with India through trade and by settling the Kashmir dispute, the foremost impediment to the normalization of relations between us," as he puts it. He is right: the Kashmir dispute is "the foremost impediment" to any attempt at normalization. But the first step toward resolving that dispute is to recognize what caused it. He is distorting historical facts when he says that India annexed Kashmir illegally. For the benefit of those who could be misled by his article, let me briefly state the origins of the dispute.

The Origins of the Kashmir Dispute

India and Pakistan came into being as two independent nations, in 1947, as a result of the partitioning of the Indian Subcontinent done by the British before they granted it independence. Pakistan, it may be added, was carved out from the predominantly Muslim areas in the eastern and western wings of the Subcontinent.

When the British partitioned the Subcontinent, they did it only vis-à-vis the areas directly administered by them. There were 565 princely states lying scattered around the Subcontinent, which were under British suzerainty, but autonomous in all internal matters. The British, who were in a hurry to finish the job and leave, were not all that concerned about what the princes were going to do with their states. Naturally, many of them envisioned total independence, independence not only from Britain but also from India and Pakistan, the two sovereign nations that were being created. They did the envisioning, even though people in those states were very much involved in the Subcontinent-wide freedom struggle against the British. Those people were seeking an end not just to the British Raj, but to the rule of Indian rajas as well.

With coercion and promises of compensation, all but two of the 565 princely states were persuaded to give up their dream of total independence and to choose either India or Pakistan. Two criteria they had to follow in making the choice were their geographical contiguity to one or the other and the religion of the majority community in them, whether Hindu or Muslim. The two princely states that refused to fall in with the rest and continued to toy with the idea of total independence were Hyderabad and Kashmir. In the case of Hyderabad, overwhelmingly Hindu in population and situated deep inside India, it took a military operation to accomplish its merger with India. In the case of Kashmir, the solution of the problem was not that simple.

Wedged between India and Pakistan, the kingdom could join either country, going by the geographical-contiguity criterion. But being 95 percent Muslim, Pakistan considered its claim to Kashmir stronger and more legitimate than that of India. After all, Pakistan's very *raison d'etre* was a homeland for the Muslims of the Subcontinent. However, the Hindu ruler of Kashmir, Maharaja Hari Singh, was not comfortable joining a Muslim country. That's not to say that he was happy to join India. He kept dreaming of total independence.

Once he was convinced that his dream would never come true, he requested both India and Pakistan to allow him some time to make up his mind. The request was granted under an agreement called the Stand-Still Agreement. This was the situation as of August 15, 1947, the day India declared its independence. (Pakistan had declared its independence a day earlier.)

Pak Army Invades Kashmir

The situation changed dramatically in a matter of two weeks, when armed tribesmen from Pakistan, backed by its regular army, invaded Kashmir. Their goal was to end the stalemate and annex Kashmir by force. The ruler of Kashmir panicked. He appealed to India for military help to drive out the marauders. India, under the leadership of the late Prime Minister Jawaharlal Nehru, was more than willing to help. With a view to making its involvement legal, India insisted that it be preceded by the state's formal accession to India. Accordingly, on October 26, 1947, Maharaja Hari Singh signed a document detailing the terms and conditions of the accession. With the signing of the document, called the Instrument of Accession, Jammu and Kashmir, as the state is officially called, became one of the states in the Indian federation.

Though the legality of Kashmir's accession to India was not in question, there is no denying that the Instrument of Accession was signed under extraordinary circumstances. Recognizing this fact, India gave an assurance to the Kashmiri ruler that "as soon as the law and order have been restored in Kashmir and its soil cleared of the invader, the question of the State's accession should be settled by a reference to the people." This was the origin of the offer of plebiscite on Kashmir, which we have heard a lot about ever since. It is important to note that the offer was made by India, and it was made voluntarily and earnestly.

U.N. Resolution on Kashmir

Soon after the signing of the Instrument of Accession, the Indian army went into Kashmir to expel the Pakistani invaders. What followed was a war between India and Pakistan, their first war over the Kashmir dispute, which dragged on for over 14 months. Even as the war was going on, with India steadily winning, India took the dispute, and the plebiscite offer, to the United Nations. On January 4, 1949, the U.N. Security Council passed a resolution, calling upon both countries to cease the fighting, which they did.

By the time the cease-fire resolution was passed, India had expelled the invaders from two-thirds of Kashmir. One-third of the state, which had been under Pakistan's control then, has remained so till now. The line along which the state got virtually divided at the time of the cease-fire came to be called the Line of Control (LoC).

The cease-fire resolution also stipulated certain conditions to be fulfilled by both countries for the conduct of the plebiscite. The first, and the most important, condition was that Pakistan withdraw its troops from the area of Kashmir it had illegally occupied. To this day, it hasn't been fulfilled. And for that reason, to this day, the promised plebiscite has not been conducted.

I wish the Pakistani prime minister had refreshed his memory on the foregoing historical facts and sequence of events before he wrote in his *Times* article about "honoring the right to self-determination the Kashmiris were promised by the Security Council resolutions and India's first prime minister, Jawaharlal Nehru." To reiterate what is said above, the promise of self-determination, also called plebiscite, was first made by India and it was incorporated in the Security Council resolution at India's instance.

India Withdraws Plebiscite Offer

The readers of Mr. Khan's article can now decide who is to blame for not honoring the resolution. I would like to remind Mr. Khan that because of the change in circumstances, India was forced to withdraw the plebiscite offer a few years later. So, there is no point in harping on it now.

In a speech before the Indian Parliament, on March 29, 1956, Prime Minister Nehru gave three reasons for the withdrawal. The first was what is stated above: the failure on the part of Pakistan to fulfill the condition that it pull its troops out of Kashmir. The second reason was that Kashmir's Constituent Assembly had approved the state's merger with India and accepted India's Constitution. The third reason was that Pakistan's membership in the United States-sponsored (now moribund) security alliances – the Southeast Asia Treaty Organization and the Baghdad Pact (later renamed the Central Treaty Organization) – made India suspect that it intended to seek military solutions to its problems involving neighbors.

For Mr. Khan's information, under the *rebus sic stantibus* (Latin for "things standing thus") principle recognized in international law, India's withdrawal of the plebiscite offer was perfectly legal.

Pakistan dragged India into three more wars, two of them stemming from the same Kashmir dispute. It suffered humiliating defeat in all of them. The losses it suffered in men and materiel were far greater than what India did. By the time the third war ended, on December 16, 1971, with 90,000 Pakistani soldiers surrendering to India, it had lost half of its territory, too. What was known as East Pakistan until then, broke away into an independent country called Bangladesh.

Kashmir Becomes Haven for Terrorists

By the end of the last century, Kashmir had become a haven for terrorists. Many of them received their training in the terrorist-training camps operated in the Pakistani-controlled part of Kashmir. Others were Islamist terrorists from neighboring Afghanistan and distant lands, who arrived in Kashmir to fight what they called holy war (jihad). Since the 1990s, Kashmir has been racked by frequent attacks launched by jihadists. Their targets include not just Indian interests, India's security forces and minority Hindus of the state, but also ordinary Kashmiri Muslims who are opposed to them.

By the turn of the 21st century, Pakistan-based terrorist networks started taking their fight deep inside India. The December 2001 terrorist attack on the Indian Parliament in New Delhi was planned and executed by one such network, Jaish-e-Mohammed (the Army of Mohammed). In November 2008, 10 terrorists, trained by Lashkar-e-Taiba (the Army of the Pure), another Pakistan-based terrorist outfit, carried out 12 well-coordinated shooting and bombing attacks in Mumbai, India's commercial capital. The city was under siege for four days. The terrorists' targets were high-profile places like the Chhatrapati Shivaji Terminus railway station, two luxury hotels and a café frequented by Westerners, a Jewish community center that is also home to a synagogue, and the historic Gateway of India. At least 174 people were killed in the attacks. The number included 20 security force personnel, 26 foreign nationals and nine of the 10 terrorists.

Though the attacks in New Delhi and Mumbai earned Pakistan international condemnation, terrorists are still said to be freely roaming in that country and frequently foraying into Kashmir. Their main targets within Kashmir are India's security forces. Attacks on the security forces are too numerous to list here. The one that occurred on February 14, 2019, which Mr. Khan has referred to in his article, proved to be a turning point toward what we are witnessing in Kashmir right now.

On that day, a member of Jaish-e-Mohammed loaded a vehicle with explosives and rammed it into an Indian military convoy of 78 vehicles on a busy highway in Kashmir's Pulwama district, killing 40 soldiers. Prime Minister Khan is surprised that "[t]he Indian government promptly blamed Pakistan" for the attack. He wouldn't believe unless India provided evidence.

He is right that the Modi government didn't waste any time doing it, for it knew that Mr. Khan wouldn't dare act on it. If he had acted, his days would be numbered. Instead of wasting time arguing about who was to blame, "Mr. Modi sent Indian Air Force fighter planes across the border to Pakistan," to quote from the Khan article. What those fighter planes did was something that the Pakistani military should have done long ago: destroying at least a few terrorist-training camps.

If that was all that Indian warplanes did, shooting down one of them is not something that Mr. Khan should be proud of. That said, Indians should appreciate and be grateful that "he made a conscious decision to show that Pakistan had no intent of aggravating the conflict between two nuclear-armed states" and "returned the captured Indian pilot, with no preconditions," as he says in the *Times* piece.

How Islamic Terrorism Helped BJP

Mr. Khan has rightly observed that there has been a rise in Hindu fundamentalism in India, which in turn has helped the BJP. But he either failed to observe or chose not to mention that it is correlated to the rise in Islamic fundamentalism and terrorism in Pakistan, from where they got exported to Kashmir.

Prime Minister Modi's bold and swift response to the February 14 terrorist attack was a major factor in his and his party's landslide victory in the May 2019 parliamentary election. That victory brought them to a second five-year term in power and emboldened them to fulfill a campaign promise they had made vis-à-vis Kashmir. They had promised to repeal Article 370, if they won.

On August 5, 2019, the Modi government made good on the promise. It issued a presidential proclamation that Article 370 of the Indian Constitution had been repealed and that the special status given to Kashmir under that article had been withdrawn.

The Genesis of Article 370

The genesis of Article 370 was the assurance given to the ruler of Kashmir that his state would be accorded a special status in India once it merged with it. The assurance became necessary because he was still vacillating on the merger question. Once a special status provision was inserted in the Instrument of Accession, the ruler felt comfortable signing it. In terms of that provision, until the people of Kashmir decided on whether to join India or Pakistan through a referendum, the ruler would continue to enjoy jurisdiction over all areas of the state's administration, except defense, foreign affairs and communications. Kashmir's special status also prevented non-Kashmiris from buying properties in the state. The special status provision in the Instrument of Accession was the main ingredient of Article 370, which was added to the Indian Constitution as an amendment.

It was added on the insistence of Prime Minister Nehru, over the objections of many other leaders, especially Bhimrao Ambedkar, the man who presided over the drafting of the Constitution and who became independent India's first law minister. During the drafting, Dr. Ambedkar was approached by Sheikh Abdullah, the most popular leader of Kashmiri Muslims at the time and one of the three representatives from Kashmir in the Indian Constituent Assembly, with a message from Nehru. The message was that Nehru was keen on an article, giving Kashmir a special status, being incorporated in the Constitution. Dr. Ambedkar reportedly retorted: "You want India to defend Kashmir, feed its people, give Kashmiris equal rights all over India. But you want to deny India and Indians all rights in Kashmir. I am the law minister of India. I cannot be a party to such a betrayal of national interests."

Despite Ambedkar's objection, Nehru's wish was carried out. The proposed article did get drafted. It was done by Gopalaswamy Ayyangar, who was a minister without portfolio in the Nehru cabinet and, before that, the *diwan* (the title given to the chief administrator of a princely state) of Kashmir. Ambedkar, the chairman of the drafting committee, did not even attend the Constituent Assembly session that discussed the draft and voted for its approval.

The foregoing, in a nutshell, is the story of the evolution of Article 370 of the Indian Constitution. It was inserted as an amendment, in Part XXI of the Constitution, under "Temporary and Transitional Provisions." Mark the words: It was temporary and transitional.

The controversy Article 370 sparked then has continued to this day. It took a turn for the worse on August 5, 2019, when the BJP government announced its abrogation. Most Kashmiris are upset as much by the abrogation as by the hush-hush way it was done. Before the abrogation was announced, all internet, phone and social media channels linking Kashmir to the rest of the world were shut down. Government sources explained later that if those channels had been kept open, terrorists would have wreaked havoc on the entire state in the wake of the announcement. Before the announcement, the government had also taken into custody or put under house arrest all leading politicians of the state. Their number is said to be over 2,000. The government had also deployed thousands of additional security forces and imposed a curfew on the state. Mr. Khan's article says that a "blood bath is feared in Kashmir when the curfew is lifted." Let's hope that he wouldn't be disappointed if it doesn't happen.

Most people in the rest of India agree with the Modi government's contention that Article 370 was a historical blunder and support its repeal. They found the government's argument that the constitutional provision that prevented non-Kashmiris from investing in Kashmir was the main reason for the state's economic backwardness convincing. However, they don't agree with the way it was abrogated. It was done by ramming a bill – the Jammu and Kashmir Reorganization Bill – through Parliament where the BJP enjoys a very comfortable majority and getting it signed into law by the president of the country. Theoretically, the government did follow the established procedures in passing federal laws in India. But repealing an article in the Constitution is not the same as passing a law, critics say. The process of doing it is different. Because the Modi government did not follow the process, the new law enacted by Parliament is ultra vires the Constitution, they say.

Legal scholars and critics of the government have challenged the law in the Supreme Court of the country. Let's wish the judges of the court Solomon's Wisdom in reaching a verdict. The destiny of Kashmir and of its 12 million people will depend on their verdict.

Khan's Suggestion for Dialogue

Let me now turn to Prime Minister Khan's suggestion in the article for a dialogue that "must include all stakeholders, especially the Kashmiris." Admittedly, the other stakeholders are India and Pakistan. It's a welcome suggestion. But how can he expect India to participate in any dialogue if it "can start only when India reverses its illegal annexation of Kashmir, ends the curfew and lockdown, and withdraws its troops to the barracks"?

The curfew and lockdown will end very soon. No doubt about it.

The Indian troops will go back to the barracks the moment all terrorists in Kashmir go back to Pakistan or Pakistan annihilates them. But what about the lie that Pakistan has been repeating for seven decades, which Mr. Khan has parroted now – that India illegally annexed Kashmir?

I invite Mr. Khan to read the Instrument of Accession with India that the ruler of Kashmir signed in 1947. Then he will know how and why Indian troops entered Kashmir. Every student of the history of the Subcontinent knows that if Pakistan had not invaded Kashmir in violation of the Stand-Still Agreement it had signed with the Kashmiri ruler, there wouldn't be a Kashmir problem now. India would have waited until the ruler decided on which country to join and accepted his decision.

Again, there wouldn't be a Kashmir problem now, if Pakistan had met the condition set in the Security Council resolution for the conduct of the plebiscite. The plebiscite would have been conducted and India would have accepted Kashmiris' preference.

If Pakistan's claim to Kashmir is based on its being a Muslim-majority state, which in turn is based on the two-nation theory propounded by Pakistan's founding father Mohammed Ali Jinnah, it is forgetting the fact that the theory died on the battlefield of erstwhile East Pakistan, in 1971, giving rise to another Muslim nation called Bangladesh. According to Jinnah's two-nation theory, the Hindus and the Muslims of the Subcontinent are two separate nations, deserving two separate states. Before the theory died, it had claimed the lives of tens of thousands of fellow Muslims, simply because they happened to be ethnically and culturally different from those who fought to enforce the theory. The powers that be in West Pakistan looked down upon the Bengalis of East Pakistan as racially inferior. Does Pakistan need another battle, and does it have to engage in another genocide, as it did to the Bengalis, to realize that the Kashmiris are ethnically and culturally different, too?

Now let's examine the question from India's standpoint. Today, for India, Kashmir is not just another state. As the only Muslim-majority state in a Hindu-majority country, it has become the testing ground for secularism to which India is steadfastly committed. The country that had never accepted Jinnah's two-nation theory cannot be expected to concede Pakistan's claim to Kashmir based on that theory. Once religion is recognized as the basis for nationhood, more than 170 million Muslims living in India would automatically become non-national. It would also make a mockery of India's proud claim to be a secular nation.

Kashmiris' Grievances

The unfortunate victims of this ongoing hostility between India and Pakistan are the Kashmiris. Their grievances are further aggravated by terrorists roaming their state and the excesses committed by India's security forces in their fight against terrorism and in their efforts to maintain law and order in the state. What the terrorists are engaged in is a guerrilla-type of war. In guerrilla-type wars, it is difficult to tell who the enemy is. The guerrillas blend with civilians and often use them as human shields. That explains why innocent Kashmiris are getting killed in large numbers.

Of the 14 million Kashmiris, only a small percentage want their state to join Pakistan, which they know is controlled by the military. The number of those opposed to the state's being part of India, which was tiny in the beginning, has steadily grown over the years. Many of them turned militant in the late 1980s.

Apart from meddling by Pakistan, and the influx of foreign weapons and terrorists, another important factor contributed to it: the short-sighted policies followed by the late Indira Gandhi and her son Rajiv Gandhi during their tenures as prime minister, together lasting 21 years. They set one Kashmiri faction against another and interfered in the state's elections to put their favorite faction in power. The anti-India militancy took a turn for the worse in 1987, when then-Prime Minister Rajiv Gandhi's Congress (I) party and its electoral ally in Kashmir, the National Conference, headed by Dr. Farooq Abdullah, rigged that year's election to the state legislature. The blatant violation of democratic norms made many Kashmiris feel betrayed. A senior Kashmiri official expressed the betrayal this way: "India had initially held two great attractions for the Kashmiris: democracy and secularism. But the 1987 Assembly polls destroyed whatever faith Kashmiris had in the Indian democracy."

Some of the anti-India militants later joined the terrorist movement launched by the Islamic State (IS) in various Muslim countries. The terrorists belonging to the IS have been waging a war to establish what they call an Islamic caliphate. The Kashmiris who are fighting for total independence for their state should bear in mind that in the unlikely event of their achieving that goal, it would be only a question of time before their state becomes an outlying province of the caliphate the terrorist are dreaming of establishing. Is it something the Kashmiris, most of whom have been raised in the Sufi tradition of Islam, can be proud of?

The Kashmiri separatists should try to understand the dilemma India is in. If Kashmir is granted independence, it will have a domino effect. There are many other states waiting in the wings to demand the same. No country in the world would want to preside over its own disintegration.

A Realistic Solution

Is there a solution to the Kashmir problem? The problem has been festering for over seven decades now. No solution is possible unless the parties involved – India, Pakistan and the Kashmiris accept the reality on the ground. The reality on the ground is that for over seven decades, two-thirds of Kashmir has been under the control of India and one-third under that of Pakistan. Each country has been administering the area under its control as its integral part, while staking claim to the area under the other's control. As stated earlier, three of the four wars the two countries fought so far, and the numerous skirmishes they have had, have been over those conflicting claims. The wars and skirmishes have claimed thousands of lives and drained vast resources from both sides. In the unfortunate event of another war breaking out, it could turn nuclear, though not in the manner in which Prime Minister Khan envisages it. It could turn nuclear if just one of the terrorists operating in Pakistan in collusion with the rogue elements in its military gains access to its nuclear arsenal. That is, just one terrorist can trigger a nuclear war between India and Pakistan. So, it is imperative for both countries and the Kashmiris to find a solution that is feasible and realistic. For starters, Pakistan should cleanse its soil of all terrorists.

It is unrealistic to expect India and Pakistan to give up the parts of Kashmir they each have been administering for seven decades. Let the Line of Control in Kashmir that has been in existence for seven decades be the permanent border between the two countries. That is the only realistic solution that I can think of. The Kashmiris and the leaders of India and Pakistan should ask themselves this important question: Do they want a solution that can be made to work, though with great difficulty, or do they want perennial bloodshed?

41

Democratic-Led House Impeaches Trump; Republican-Led Senate Acquits Him

February 7, 2020

Speaker Nancy Pelosi of the U.S. House of Representatives leaving the news conference she held soon after the House impeached President Donald Trump, on December 18, 2019. (*The picture is reproduced courtesy Alyssa Schukar/*The New York Times.)

•

Republican members of the U.S. Congress are a pathetic lot. They have been conducting themselves as courtiers of President Trump, not as representatives of the people who elected them. In doing so, they have disgraced the Constitution which they have sworn to "support and defend."

Facts: On December 18, 2019, the House of Representatives completed its months-long inquiry into the crimes Trump was charged with, and passed two articles of impeachment against him. The crimes, as spelled out in the articles, were his abuse of power as president and obstruction of Congress during its inquiry into that abuse.

In normal circumstances, the speaker of the House submits the articles to the Senate majority leader soon after they are passed, and the Senate begins the trial of the impeached president without any delay. It didn't happen so this time because of the abnormal behavior of the present Senate majority leader, Mitch McConnell. Just a day after the House passed the articles, McConnell dismissed the House inquiry as "rushed and rigged." He went on to say: "If the Senate blesses this slap-dash impeachment, if we say that from now on this is enough, then we invite an endless parade of impeachable trials. The Senate must put this right."

His reckless remarks made clear that the Senate trial would be anything but fair. This plus another irresponsible statement he had made earlier – that he would be deciding on the rules of the trial in "total coordination" with the White House – made Speaker Nancy Pelosi delay forwarding the articles of impeachment to the Senate until she could be sure what the rules would be. McConnell's statements were not only stupid and irresponsible but also an insult to the U.S. Constitution.

Abuse of Power

As spelled out in House Resolution 755, the first article of impeachment, the one that pertains to abuse of power, reads thus:

(1) President Trump – acting both directly and through his agents within and outside the United States Government – corruptly solicited the Government of Ukraine to publicly announce investigations into –

(A) a political opponent, former Vice President Joseph R. Biden, Jr.; and

(B) a discredited theory promoted by Russia alleging that Ukraine – rather than Russia – interfered in the 2016 United States Presidential election.

(2) With the same corrupt motives, President Trump – acting both directly and through his agents within and outside the United States Government – conditioned two official acts on the public announcements that he had requested –

(A) the release of $391 million of United States taxpayer funds that Congress had appropriated on a bipartisan basis for the purpose of providing vital military and security assistance to Ukraine to oppose Russian aggression and which President

Trump had ordered suspended; and

(B) a head of state meeting at the White House, which the President of Ukraine sought to demonstrate continued United States support for the Government of Ukraine in the face of Russian aggression.

(3) Faced with the public revelation of his actions, President Trump ultimately released the military and security assistance to the Government of Ukraine, but has persisted in openly and corruptly urging and soliciting Ukraine to undertake investigations for his personal political benefit.

Obstruction of Congress

As detailed in the same House resolution, President Trump committed obstruction of Congress, which is the subject of the second article of impeachment, by:

(1) Directing the White House to defy a lawful subpoena by withholding the production of documents sought therein by the Committees.

(2) Directing other Executive Branch agencies and offices to defy lawful subpoenas and withhold the production of documents and records from the Committees – in response to which the Department of State, Office of Management and Budget, Department of Energy, and Department of Defense refused to produce a single document or record.

(3) Directing current and former Executive Branch officials not to cooperate with the Committees – in response to which nine Administration officials defied subpoenas for testimony, namely John Michael "Mick" Mulvaney, Robert B. Blair, John A. Eisenberg, Michael Ellis, Preston Wells Griffith, Russell T. Vought, Michael Duffey, Brian McCormack, and T. Ulrich Brechbuhl.

What a shame, not a single Republican lawmaker has so far shown the guts to call the president out for these egregious violations! The president's hostility to the inquiry notwithstanding, witness after witness, some of them with first-hand knowledge of the president's abuse of power, testified before the House committees. The committees also collected reams and reams of documents that back up the witnesses' testimony.

The Democratic leadership in the House could have challenged the president's order that prevented witnesses from appearing before it. It decided not to mainly for two reasons: one, a prolonged court battle would leave enough time for the president and his henchmen to continue their illegal activities and manipulate the next election to their advantage; and two, the evidence the Democrats have already collected was more than enough to make their case for impeachment.

Despite the mountain of evidence and testimony, part of it from Trump-appointed administration officials themselves, not a single Republican House member voted for impeachment. They kept repeating the mantra that the impeachment inquiry was an insult to the 63 million Americans who voted for Trump in the 2016 election. Every time they did it, they were reinforcing the fact that but for the antiquated, undemocratic American institution called the Electoral College, his Democratic opponent Hillary Clinton would be sitting in the White House today. She won three million more votes than Trump did. Trump stooges may please note that many of those who voted for him in 2016 have started regretting their votes now.

To get back to the "rushed and rigged" charge McConnell leveled against the House inquiry. If he thought so, wasn't it all the more reason why he should have supported the Senate trial and made sure that it was thorough and fair? Shouldn't he have complied with the Democrats' demand that, in light of the stunning new revelations that emerged after the House completed the inquiry, witnesses and documents that are central to those revelations be subpoenaed?

New Evidence Emerges

Soon after Chuck Schumer, the leader of the Democratic minority in the Senate, submitted the demand, news broke out which further corroborates the first article of impeachment. At the heart of the first article is President Trump's July 25, 2019, phone call to President Volodymyr Zelensky of Ukraine, seeking dirt on his political opponent. The newsbreak was about a bunch of emails the Pentagon released on December 20, 2019. According to one of the emails, about 90 minutes after the phone call, the White House budget office ordered the Pentagon to suspend all military aid to Ukraine that Congress had already passed. Trump and his minions had persistently denied any connection between the July 25 phone call and the withholding of the aid. The emails released by the Pentagon were the most authentic poof that they were lying.

In another email, Michael Duffey, an official at the White House budget director's office, told the Pentagon to keep quiet about the aid freeze because of the "sensitive nature of the request." Was he referring to the "do us a favor" request in Trump's phone call to the Ukrainian president? We will find out if and when he testifies at the Senate trial. He is one of the four White House officials Schumer wants to be called as witnesses. The other three are Mick Mulvaney, the president's acting chief of staff; Robert Blair, Mulvaney's senior adviser; and John Bolton, the president's former national security adviser. Remember Bolton's characterization of the Ukraine episode as a "drug deal" being cooked up by Trump's personal attorney Rudy Giuliani, which he refused to be part of?

And then came another explosive information contained in the manuscript of Bolton's soon-to-be published book, which reconfirmed the quid-pro-quo demand Trump made on President Zelensky during the phone call. As Trump's national security adviser at the time, Bolton had firsthand knowledge of the phone call. And Bolton had conveyed his willingness to testify. Mitch McConnell would have none of it. He adamantly stuck to his predetermined goal of ending the Senate trial in a hurry – with no new witnesses and documents.

Rules of Senate Trial

Apart from the controversy over calling new witnesses, there was another reason why Speaker Pelosi delayed submitting the House's impeachment resolution to the Senate: McConnell wouldn't respond to her request that the rules governing the Senate trial be established in consultation with the Democratic minority in the Senate. McConnell and Trump kept saying that they had nothing to hide. If that's the case, why can't they accede to the very reasonable requests made by Schumer and Pelosi? As Schumer said at his news conference in New York City, on December 22, 2019, "What is a trial with no witnesses and no documents? It's a sham trial."

If it were a regular court trial, McConnell could be charged with obstruction of justice, too. Again, if it were a regular court, the facts presented in the House were more than enough to declare Trump guilty. It will remain a mystery forever that, based on the same set of facts, Democratic members of the House voted to impeach the president and their Republican colleagues voted against it. The latter would have succeeded in exonerating Trump, but for the fact that Democrats enjoyed a comfortable majority in the House. What happened to the logic and basic commonsense ordinary human beings are supposed to have? What happened to their conscience? Will these Republicans be able to live with this travesty of justice the rest of their lives? What message are they sending to other countries which still look up to the American political system as the ideal model to emulate?

Fast-Forward to Senate Trial

After the prolonged controversy over the procedure and need to call more witnesses, the Senate trial formally began on January 16, 2020, with the swearing in of Supreme Court Chief Justice John Roberts and the senators who would act, respectively, as the judge and jurors in the case. It concluded on February 5, with Trump's acquittal.

Of the nasty exchanges between Democrats and Republicans that took place in the interim, a tweet issued by Speaker Pelosi, on February 1, 2020, deserves special mention. The subject of her tweet was the vote in the Senate the day before that defeated the Democrats' demand to call additional witnesses. In the 53-47 Republican-majority Senate, only two Republicans – Mitt Romney of Utah and Susan Collins of Maine – were principled and conscientious enough to break with their party and vote with Democrats. Referring to the 51-to-49 vote that rejected the Democrats' demand, Speaker Pelosi's tweet said: "It is a sad day for America to see Senator McConnell humiliate the Chief Justice of the United States into presiding over a vote which rejected our nation's judicial norms, precedents and institutions which uphold the Constitution and the rule of law."

Going by the way the Trump acquittal was accomplished, one couldn't help observing that the trial of a case in a kangaroo court has more legitimacy than the one conducted by the Republican-led U.S. Senate from January 16 to February 5, 2020. Where else than in a kangaroo court are witnesses and documents that are pivotal to the case prevented from being produced? Let's hope those who brought this infamy to the U.S. Senate would be penalized by their constituents at the appropriate time.

42

Pro-Trump Conspiracy Theorists Blame Covid-19 on Bill Gates

April 23, 2020

Bill Gates
(*The picture is reproduced courtesy* Getty Images)

•

    Bill Gates "has now become the star of an explosion of conspiracy theories about the coronavirus outbreak," according to an April 18, 2020, news article in *The New York Times*. The story, by Daisuke Wakabayashi, Davey Alba and Marc Tracy, goes on to say: "In posts on YouTube, Facebook and Twitter, he is being falsely portrayed as the creator of Covid-19, as a profiteer from a virus vaccine, and as part of a dastardly plot to use the illness to cull or surveil the global population."

    The basis for the right-wing zealots' accusation is a speech Mr. Gates gave in 2015, in which he had issued a warning that the greatest risk to humanity was not nuclear war but an infectious virus that could threaten the lives of millions of people. Isn't it sickening that instead of congratulating Gates for being so prescient about the kind of pandemic the world is currently reeling from, some pro-Donald Trump propagandists decided to give a twisted interpretation to his warning and use it to advance the latest conspiracy theory they concocted to attack him.

They say he had advance knowledge about the pandemic and planned to make more money by exploiting the global health system.

Gates Spends Half His Wealth on Philanthropy

Bill Gates, 64, the co-founder of Microsoft, is now the second-richest person in the world. His net worth is over $106.7 billion. The authors of the latest conspiracy theory should know that if he makes more money by selling vaccine to fight the coronavirus, the beneficiary would be the entire world. Since 2008, he has been spending half his wealth and most of his time on philanthropic activities. The Bill and Melinda Gates Foundation, which he started with his wife Melinda in 2000, is said to be the largest philanthropic organization in the world. It is engaged in various humanitarian activities, especially in developing countries of Africa and Asia. Maybe the conspiracy theorists, at the forefront of whom are those adamantly opposed to vaccination, are annoyed that the foundation has promised to fund factories for seven most promising potential vaccines and to spend $250 million to curb the coronavirus's spread.

The first mention of a baseless conspiracy connecting Bill Gates to the coronavirus outbreak occurred on January 21, says the *Times* story, "when a YouTube personality linked to QAnon suggested on Twitter that Mr. Gates had foreknowledge of the pandemic. The tweet was based on a coronavirus-related patent from the Pirbright Institute, a British group that received funding from the Gates Foundation."

The fact that the patent was not for Covid-19 but connected to a potential vaccine for a different coronavirus, one that affects poultry, did not make any difference. The damage had already been done. Two days later, another conspiracy website, Infowars, inaccurately said the patent from the Pirbright Institute was for "the deadly virus," the *Times* story says. Thanks to conspiracy theorists active on Infowars and QAnon, anti-vaccinators, and anti-Gates propogandists in the right-wing media, his 2015 speech attracted 25 million new viewers on YouTube, says the *Times* story.

"The idea spread," the *Times* story continues. "From February to April, conspiracy theories involving Mr. Gates and the virus were mentioned 1.2 million times on social media and television broadcasts, according to Zignal Labs. That was 33 percent more often, it said, than the next-largest conspiracy theory: that 5G radio waves cause people to succumb to Covid-19."

Zignal Labs, formerly known as PolitEar, is a media-monitoring and -analyzing company. QAnon is a pro-Trump, anti-Democratic Party digital platform started by an anonymous individual known as Q. The very first conspiracy theory on Covid-19 which Q posted on QAnon says that the virus was a Chinese bioweapon released jointly by China and the Democratic Party to stop Trump's re-election by destroying the economy.

The FBI called conspiracy theories spread by QAnon and others a "potential domestic terrorism threat." The fabricators of these theories can be happy about one thing, though: While all rational-minded people have discarded their sick theories with the contempt they deserve, they have been embraced with great enthusiasm by the conspiracy theorist-in-chief of the United States, Donald Trump. According to a February 10, 2020, report in *nytimes.com*, "Recently, during a daylong Twitter binge, Mr. Trump retweeted more than 20 posts from accounts that had trafficked in QAnon material."

The same day *The Times* published the report highlighting conspiracy theories connecting Bill Gates to the coronavirus, Mr. Trump sent out tweets, exhorting his Republican base in three Democratic-controlled states to "liberate" their states from the shutdown imposed in the wake of the virus's outbreak. Like Mr. Trump, his right-wing base in these states – Virginia, Minnesota and Michigan – has been chafing at the restrictions imposed by the states' Democratic governors, in compliance with the guidelines issued by health experts. And the restrictions, like social distancing and shutting down all activities, have been yielding results in terms of saving human lives. But to Trump, appeasing his political base, which would help him get re-elected, is more important than saving lives.

A Trump Stooge in the Kennedy Family?

Most of the conspiracy theories against Bill Gates are premised on the outlandish claim that he is planning to exploit the pandemic to make money. Most of the theorists are Trump's obeisant followers in the Republican Party and his cheerleaders in the right-wing media, especially Fox News. To the dismay of many, myself included, one of them is from outside these two groups, or at least not openly allied with either. He is Robert Kennedy Jr.

I never thought that I would one day have the unpleasant task of calling the son of the late Senator Robert Kennedy and nephew of the late President John F. Kennedy a Trump stooge. Unfortunately, in the present saga, Kennedy Jr. has acted as one. I wish he had found some other way to express his opposition to vaccines without saying on his Instagram page, as the *Times* story says he did, that Mr. Gates pushes vaccines to feed his other business interests.

As for the cartoon the *Times* story says he posted – of a smiling Mr. Gates with a syringe and a caption: "Your Body, my choice" – I can assure him that I will not even look at it. The reason? I don't want to throw up. I didn't expect a member of the respected Kennedy family – the son of a famous U.S. Senator and nephew of a more famous U.S. President to boot – to be this uncouth.

Talking about uncouthness, I don't expect anything other than that in a couple of other conspiracy theorists against Gates mentioned in the *Times* story. One of them is Roger J. Stone Jr., a Trump confidant and an official in his 2016 presidential campaign, who was sentenced to 40 months in prison for seven counts of felony – obstruction of justice, lying to investigators under oath, etc. He said in a radio interview, according to *The Times*, that whether Mr. Gates "played some role in the creation and spread of this virus is open for vigorous debate."

And when it comes to uncouthness, nobody can outsmart Laura Ingraham of Fox News, a Trump stooge masquerading as a political pundit. The whole world knows that the coronavirus crisis in the country would not have become this worse if President Trump had not derisively dismissed health experts' early warnings about it and treated it as a minor problem well under control. When concerned people in the country, some even from his own administration, and non-conservative media criticized the president's disdainful attitude toward what was threatening to be a pandemic, Ms. Ingraham and some of her colleagues on Fox News ridiculed it as a continuation of the president's impeachment which the House of Representatives had just completed.

Their attitude has not changed much even after several Fox News employees tested positive for the virus. I have not heard Ms. Ingraham's reaction to the report that several of her own staffers have been suspected to be Covid-19 cases and quarantined until tests are completed. Her latest anti-Bill Gates conspiracy theory questions the motive behind his call to track and identify who had received a Covid-19 vaccine. "Digitally tracking Americans' every move has been a dream of the globalists for years," Ms. Ingraham wrote on Twitter on April 7.

Ever since President Trump started promoting hydroxychloroquine, a medicine used in the treatment of malaria, for use against the coronavirus, Ms. Ingraham and her two Trump propagandist colleagues, Sean Hannity and Tucker Carlson, have been acting as salesmen for the drug. And this, despite the fact that leading medical experts in the country, including Dr. Anthony Fauci, director of the National Institute of Allergy and Infectious Diseases since 1984, and respected around the world as a leading expert on infectious diseases, openly said that more tests need to be conducted before its efficacy as an anti-coronavirus medicine can be determined. The Food and Drug Administration (FDA) in the Trump government has not yet approved the medicine.

People are anxious to know what makes President Trump recommend so strongly a medicine whose name he couldn't even pronounce properly. It was pathetic to watch him, at press briefings, struggling even to read its name off teleprompter. And the viewers of Fox News have a right to know what makes three leading commentators on the network promote the drug so vociferously when medical experts are skeptical about its efficacy in anti-coronavirus treatment.

All these points are significant, given that most pro-Trump conspiracy theorists in the country have been too quick to attribute monetary motive to Bill Gates's criticism of the Trump administration for its lack of preparedness to handle the crisis. Gates has been writing and speaking about how Trump failed in the first serious test of his leadership since he came to office. In an opinion piece in *The Washington Post*, on March 31, 2020, Bill Gates wrote:

"There's no question the United States missed the opportunity to get ahead of the novel coronavirus. The choices we and our leaders make now will have an enormous impact on how soon case numbers start to go down, how long the economy remains shut down and how many Americans will have to bury a loved one because of Covid-19."

Many more Americans have buried their loved ones since Mr. Gates wrote those words.

43

Trump Has Deplorably Failed in His First Test as Commander-in-Chief

November 1, 2020

Dr. Anthony Fauci (right) and President Donald Trump at a coronavirus task force briefing on April 22, 2020. (*The picture is reproduced courtesy Drew Angerer*/Getty Images.)

•

The United State is at war right now. The enemy is the coronavirus pandemic. The war is also President Trump's first test as commander-in-chief. His performance so far has been deplorable.

Underestimating the enemy is the biggest mistake a soldier can make. In this case, it is not a lower-level soldier who has made that mistake. It's the commander-in-chief of the armed forces who did it. He didn't just underestimate the strength of the enemy; he has been persistently lying about it, to the surprise and disappointment of those who are actually fighting the war. In a war in which an infectious disease is the enemy, the soldiers who fight it are medical professionals and other scientists.

Nine months ago, when the war had just begun, the president treated the enemy as nothing more than a flu. As the weather warmed up, it would go away, he said. He ridiculed the scientists who did not share his self-serving optimism. He didn't stop at that. He pooh-poohed the simple precautionary measures the scientists recommended on how to control the spread of the virus. Once it was established that the virus was transmitted through the air, measures like mask wearing and social distancing were considered sensible ways of controlling its spread. It's just a matter of commonsense.

There is only one explanation for Mr. Trump's contempt for those simple measures: They don't fit the macho image of himself he has been projecting all his adult life. The courtiers in his administration made a show of sharing his contempt. It seems that his followers in the rest of the country also shared that contempt. They are seen jostling with one another, most of them without masks, at the campaign rallies he has been holding lately throughout the country. They are also seen cheering him when he ridicules those who wear the mask. His Democratic opponent Joe Biden, who always insisted on following scientists' advice on how to fight the virus, has been a frequent target of his ridicule. We'll soon find out how many of these rallies were super-spreaders of the virus and what explanation Mr. Trump gives when he is held to account for that.

The consequences thus far of his callous attitude to the virus are there for all to see. When testing for the virus began nine months ago, there were only 15 cases of infection, with zero death. That number grew exponentially and, as of October 31, it stood at 9,024,298 cases of infection, with 229,109 deaths. Which means that on average, 850 Americans died of coronavirus every day. All these numbers are the highest for any country in the world. And they are from the records kept by the U.S. government's Centers for Disease Control and Prevention (CDC). It started recording them on January 21, 2020. They are based on testing done on people with obvious symptoms. There are asymptomatic people who carry the virus, health experts say. Which means that the actual number of those infected will be much higher, and it is rapidly rising, they add.

Trump Ridicules COVID Victims

Despite these alarming figures, President Trump keeps ridiculing those who are frightened by the pandemic and the news media for truthfully reporting what it is doing to the country. This is how he did it at a campaign rally on October 28: "With the fake news, everything is COVID, COVID, COVID, COVID." Then he went on to boast, to applause from his amen crowd at the rally: "I had it. Here I am, right?"

Does he realize that many of those who died would be alive today, if they had access to the expensive treatment he received at Walter Reed National Military Medical Center, at taxpayers' cost? But then, such thoughts occur only to those who have the things called empathy and compassion.

'COVID' stands for Coronavirus Disease. Because the outbreak occurred in 2019, the disease is commonly referred to as COVID-19.

On October 30, the U.S. set another world record, with 99,000 new cases reported. The same day, as on days before and after, the president kept lying at his campaign rallies that "we are turning the corner" in the fight against COVID.

In the beginning, the infection was confined to a few areas in the country. It soon became pandemic, encompassing the whole country. It sent a chill down my spine when I read a few minutes ago that one American is infected with the virus every second and one is killed by it in every two minutes – another frightening record for any country in the world. All scientists, except a few Trump stooges, say that thousands of lives could have been saved if the administration had not ignored the deadly virus in the beginning and if it had adopted a uniform strategy on how to fight it. Such a strategy would have resulted in a countrywide mandate on mask wearing and social distancing, the two important precautionary measures recommended by scientists.

At the forefront of Trump stooges among scientists is Dr. Scott W. Atlas, a neuroradiologist with no experience in infectious disease or epidemiology. He got his job as White House coronavirus adviser after he challenged the restrictions – mask wearing and social distancing – Democratic governors enforced in their states. He did the challenging during his appearances on Trump's favorite news channel, Fox News.

Just a few minutes ago, I heard that, in a 27-minute interview with RT, Russia's state-owned TV, Dr. Atlas called the lockdown ordered by some states in the U.S., in the wake of alarming spike in COVID cases, an "epic failure of public policy." President Trump might have found those words exhilarating, but not his friend, President Vladimir Putin of Russia. In Russia, a countrywide shutdown has been ordered by Putin because the spread of the virus there has gone out of control.

Dr. Atlas's ideas pitted him against Dr. Anthony Fauci, director of the National Institute of Allergy and Infectious Diseases, and an internationally recognized authority on infectious diseases; and Dr. Deborah L. Birx, the White House coronavirus response coordinator. With Dr. Atlas's induction into the White House coronavirus task force by the president, Dr. Fauci and Dr. Birx feel sidelined from it. President Trump recently called Dr. Fauci a "disaster" because he wouldn't go along with the stupid things Trump has been saying about the pandemic.

We now learn, from the recently released audio recording of a conversation author and journalist Bob Woodward had with Jared Kushner, President Trump's son-in-law and senior adviser, that the administration had decided early on not to have a federal policy on how to tackle the pandemic. It decided to leave the unpleasant task of imposing restrictions on people's lives to the states. The federal government would come into the picture when a vaccine to fight the disease was ready. Many Democratic-controlled states saw in this a cleverly devised plan to blame the states if things went wrong and to take credit for coming to their rescue with the vaccine when it is ready.

How COVID Split the Country

Most Republican-controlled states welcomed the idea. Apart from their own opposition to the restrictions proposed by medical experts, it would enable them to return to the pre-pandemic pattern of doing things. Trump's opposition to the restrictions and the Democratic-controlled Sates' embrace of them split the country into two camps in its fight against the disease. The Trump policy even endangered the life of one Democratic governor, Gretchen Whitmer of Michigan. Michigan is one of the states in the country worst affected by the pandemic.

On October 9, news broke out in the country of the arrest of 13 people belonging to two extremist militia groups in Michigan who had been plotting to kidnap Governor Whitmer and other government officials over the state's coronavirus restrictions. It was an FBI sting operation that exposed the plot and resulted in the arrests. On hearing the news, Governor Whitmer said that she "never could have imagined anything like this" and accused the president of encouraging extremism. "Just last week, the president of the United States stood before the American people and refused to condemn white supremacists and hate groups like these two Michigan militia groups," she added.

She was referring to the first presidential debate, held on September 29, at which Mr. Trump hemmed and hawed when asked by moderator Chris Wallace whether he would denounce white supremacy in the country. And when he mustered enough courage to say a few words, all that he could say was: "Stand back and stand by."

Some denunciation that is! It served as a "rallying cry, as a call to action," Ms. Whitmer said. "When our leaders speak, their words matter," she added. "They carry weight. When our leaders meet with, encourage or fraternize with domestic terrorists, they legitimize their actions. And they are complicit."

Mr. Trump knew that he could condemn white supremacists in the country only at his own peril. It was their unwavering support that got him to the White House last time. He needs their support more this time.

At a campaign rally in Lansing, Michigan, on October 27, he blasted Whitmer for the stay-at-home order she had issued when the virus broke out. The moment he mentioned the governor's name, Trump's henchmen at the rally started chanting, "Lock her up. Lock her up. ..."

Because the terrorist plot exposed only a few days earlier was very much on everyone's mind, the president decided to say something about that, too. This is what he said: "Maybe it was a problem, maybe it wasn't."

Bah! Governor Whitmer might have found those words so soothing. Those were the words the president of the country used to describe what the FBI called a clear case of domestic terrorism. Ms. Whitmer's response to Mr. Trump's description couldn't have been better. "[It] tells you everything you need to know about the character of this president," she said.

Trump's Conduct of the War

Let's take our discussion back to how Mr. Trump is conducting the first-ever war he was called upon to fight as commander-in-chief, the war against COVID-19. In times of war, the commander-in-chief comes up with a uniform strategy to fight it and orders unit commanders under him to follow that strategy. In this case, unfortunately, the commanderin-chief left it to unit commanders – read state governors – to put together strategies which they thought would work for them. The result was utter confusion.

To put it in terms of the politics of the country, most Republican governors adopted a strategy that would please Mr. Trump, that would reflect his attitude toward the virus. They knew how vengeful the president could get if they displeased him. The president's attitude toward the virus, in turn, reflected the utter contempt he has for the strategy recommended by most health experts and other scientists. At one of his rallies, he even called the scientists "idiots."

In times of war, again, the president of the country brings all political parties together and presents a united front to the enemy. In this case, the president used the threat posed by the enemy to widen the split between Republicans and Democrats. All Democratic governors listened to the scientists, and some even mandated in their states the precautionary measures recommended by them. The scientists, on their part, kept insisting that the precautionary measures they recommended were just that, precautions against the sickness, not a cure for it. The cure would come only when a vaccine was found, they said.

Sickening Lies

More sickening than the sickness itself are the lies the president has been saying about it. He keeps repeating what he said in the early stage of the sickness: "it's nothing"; "it will disappear" soon; "don't let it dominate you"; and so on. He even told his gullible followers not to trust their doctors on this. "Doctors get more money if someone dies from COVID," he said. People all over the world were appalled that the president of the U.S. should speak in such disparaging terms about the doctors in his country who are among the best in the world in their profession.

Among most medical doctors and other scientists, and among most Democratic governors in the country, there was no confusion about how to fight this war and what weapons to use. The enemy being a virus, the most effective weapon against it is a vaccine. None in the world, least of all the scientists, were impressed when the president suggested that various medicines used for other illnesses be tried on

COVID patients. He made a fool of himself when he suggested that bleach be injected into them as an experimental measure.

Mr. Trump, who was more interested in getting re-elected than finding a cure for COVID, has been putting pressure on scientists to come up with a vaccine before the election, which is on November 3.

The scientists have been working at breakneck speed and putting in extra hours to meet his demand. But they are not willing to compromise their professional integrity. Hence the president's constant attack on them.

On October 27, the White House science office outdid all Trumpian lies, when it declared that one of the administration's major achievements was "ending the Covid-19 pandemic."

It is by now known to the entire world that Donald Trump is a compulsive and impulsive liar. One doesn't have to be a psychiatrist or psychologist to conclude that his problem is pathological. The way he conducted himself as president in the past four years has made the country the laughingstock of the world. The way he conducted the first war as commander-in-chief is a total failure.

He doesn't deserve a second chance.

44

How to Prevent the Likes of Trump from Becoming President

December 31, 2020

The New York Times, in its December 20, 2020, editorial, has offered several valuable suggestions on how to prevent the likes of Donald Trump from becoming president of the United States in the future. Let's examine the feasibility and urgency of some of them.

The editorial says that Joe Biden, soon after he takes over as president on January 20, 2021, should first make an honest appraisal of "the damage wrought by the departing president" and hold him accountable for it. The next step, the editorial adds, should be to "enact laws and policies aimed at preventing the same thing from happening again."

The editorial goes on to say: "There is ample evidence already that Mr. Trump and some of his top allies may have broken multiple federal laws by committing campaign-finance violations, lying to federal investigators and obstructing justice, to name a few. Even if he is not prosecuted by federal authorities, Mr. Trump and his businesses face at least two separate tax-fraud investigations in New York. Many of Mr. Trump's associates have already been convicted of various crimes.

"Yet there are still many lingering questions, foremost among them: Did the president's business interests influence his conduct of foreign and domestic policy? The American people have a right to know if that was so."

That foremost lingering question mentioned above wouldn't arise once "[n]ew laws compelling all presidential candidates to release at least 10 years of their tax returns, as well as a comprehensive list of any possible conflicts of interest, financial and otherwise," and "bar[ring] presidents from being involved in overseeing any business while serving in office," which the editorial recommends, are enacted.

As the editorial says, "Four years into Mr. Trump's presidency and nearly five years since he promised to release his full tax returns, the American people still don't know how much his personal financial interests and entanglements are intertwined with his administration's domestic- and foreign-policy decisions." Though they have been able to figure out by now that his fondness for strongmen has something to do with his peculiar mind-set, they still don't know whether his "solicitousness toward leaders like Russia's Vladimir Putin, Turkey's Recep Tayyip Erdogan and Saudi Arabia's Mohammed bin Salman [is] a result of something more mercenary."

The reason Mr. Trump gave for his refusal to release the tax returns was that it was under audit by the IRS. Has anyone heard of an IRS audit that lasts five years?

Abuse of Presidential Pardon

Another important reform the editorial advocates relates to the president's pardoning power. There are few limits to a president's power to issue pardons. But Mr. Trump has pushed those limits, so he could pardon his close allies involved in politically sensitive cases.

One of the senior leaders in the Trump coterie that benefited from this was retired Lt. Gen. Michael T. Flynn, his national security adviser for 23 days. He had pleaded guilty twice to charges, including lying to the F.B.I., about his contacts with Russians. The F.B.I. was investigating the 2016 Trump presidential campaign's alleged collusion with Russia, which was later taken over by special counsel Robert Mueller III. The president formally pardoned Mr. Flynn on November 25, 2020.

It may be Gen. Flynn's way of showing gratitude for the pardon he received that he advised Mr. Trump to put the country under martial law, so the campaign he had started to get Joe Biden's victory in the November 3, 2020, election overturned would be beyond any legal challenge. The reason Trump gave for the campaign was that he lost the election because it was riddled with fraud. So far, 60 such challenges have been dismissed by various court in the country, including the Supreme Court, for reasons of their being baseless.

Another prominent Trump crony that benefited from his clemency was Roger J. Stone Jr., his longtime campaign adviser, who was convicted on seven felony crimes, including lying to investigators and obstruction of justice, all related to the special counsel's probe into Russian interference in the 2016 election to help Trump. On July 10, 2020, just days before Mr. Stone was to report to a federal prison to serve his 40-month sentence, the president announced its commutation.

On the evening of December 22, 2020, a newsbreak flashed across the country saying that the president had pardoned 15 people and commuted the sentences of five more. ABC News called it "a move that further cements his legacy of exercising his sweeping powers to benefit his political allies." According to a report, by Maggie Haberman and Michael S. Schmidt, in *The New York Times*'s online edition the next day, "more than half of the cases did not meet the [Justice] department's standards for consideration" of pardon. Among the recipients of these 'Christmas gifts' were George Papadopoulos, an aide to Trump's 2016 presidential campaign; three former Republican members of Congress, Duncan D. Hunter of California, Chris Collins of New York and Steve Stockman of Texas; and four former employees of Blackwater Security Consulting, a private military contracting firm engaged in security operations in Iraq at the height of the infamous Iraq war. The four had been accused of killing 17 Iraqi civilians, two of them children, nine and 11 years old.

Mr. Papadopoulos worked for Mr. Trump's 2016 campaign as an unpaid foreign policy adviser. He became the first member of the campaign to be arrested as a result of Mueller's Russia probe. In 2018, he was sentenced to 14 days in prison, after pleading guilty to lying to the F.B.I. about his interactions with Russians. At his trial, he had told the judge that he "made a dreadful mistake." After serving his sentence, though, he "pivoted away from contrition and took to denouncing the Russia investigation as, in his words, 'the deep state's attack on our president,'" according to ABC News that broke the story of his pardon.

Duncan Hunter, former Republican congressman from California, had pleaded guilty, in December 2019, to one count of conspiracy in a case that arose from his alleged misuse of $250,000 from his campaign kitty. He had used part of it to pay for family vacations, oral surgeries, etc., according to ABC News. He also used "some of that money to finance romantic trysts with multiple congressional aides and lobbyists, according to court filings from federal prosecutors," ABC News added. Mr. Hunter was sentenced to 11 months in prison and set to begin serving it next month. Thanks to the president's pardon, he won't be serving it.

Chris Collins, former congressman from New York and the first member of Congress to endorse Trump in the 2016 election, was indicted in August 2018 for alleged insider trading involving an Australian biotechnology company, Innate Immunotherapeutics. He began serving his 26-month prison term in October. Trump's December 22 pardon set him free and erased his criminal record.

Steve Stockman, former Republican congressman from Texas, also known as a conservative firebrand, was convicted in 2018 on charges of fraud and money laundering. He was charged with misusing $1.25 million from what he had received as political contributions. He used them to pay kennel bills and for hot air balloon rides, a new dishwasher and such other things that had nothing to do with politics. He was also accused of planting an undercover intern in the office of a political rival. He had been serving a 10-year sentence when the president commuted his remaining sentence.

Of all the December 22 presidential pardons, it was the ones granted to four former employees of Blackwater Security Consulting that stirred worldwide condemnation. The four – Nicholas Slatten, Paul Slough, Evan Liberty and Dustin Heard – were convicted for killing 17 Iraqi civilians, including two children, in Nisour Square, Baghdad, on September 16, 2007. As security guards working for Blackwater, they were escorting a U.S. embassy convoy.

"These pardons violate U.S. obligations under international law and more broadly undermine humanitarian law and human rights at a global level," said Jelena Aparac, chair of the U.N. working group on the use of mercenaries, according to a Reuters report from Geneva. What they committed were war crimes and, under the Geneva Conventions, the perpetrators should be held to account as war criminals, even when they act as private security contractors, the U.N. statement said.

News reports have linked these four pardons to President Trump's close association with two individuals: Erik Prince, who owned Blackwater at the time the crime occurred, and Mr. Prince's sister Betsy DeVos, the education secretary in Trump's cabinet. Mr. Prince had contributed $250,000 to Mr. Trump's 2016 presidential campaign, and $100,000 to Make America Number 1, a super political action committee (PAC), formed primarily to oppose the candidacy of Trump's Democratic Party opponent, Hillary Clinton.

On December 23, 2020, the president doled out pardons to another group of loyalists. There were 26 pardons and three commutations, in all. Two names from the group stood out for the prominent roles they played in Mr. Trump's 2016 presidential campaign and a third one for his close relationship with the president. The two were Paul Manafort, his 2016 campaign chairman, and Roger J. Stone Jr. The third prominent figure that benefited from the December 23 pardon spree was Charles Kushner, the father of President Trump's son-in-law, Jared Kushner.

The crimes Charles Kushner was charged with involved tax evasion, retaliating against a federal witness and lying to the Federal Election Commission. The case against him, to quote from the *New York Times* report cited above, "was also a lurid family drama." He was charged with hiring a prostitute to have sex with his brother-in-law William Schulder, who, along with his wife, Mr. Kushner's sister, was cooperating with federal officials in a campaign finance investigation against him; videotaping the sex act; and then sending the tape to his sister. His blackmail tactic boomeranged on him. His sister and brother-in-law handed the tape to the prosecutors. Former Governor Chris Christie of New Jersey, who was U.S. attorney at the time that prosecuted the crime, called Mr. Kushner's crime most "loathsome" and "disgusting," even by the standards applied to New Jersey criminals at the time. Mr. Kushner served two years in prison before being released in 2006.

In Donald Trump's book, tax-dodging, lying to authorities, witness tampering, etc., have never been major crimes. His December 23, 2020, pardon absolved his son-in-law's father of all federal crimes, while petitions for pardon from hundreds of others charged with less serious crimes were still pending.

What Mr. Stone received on December 23 made the commutation of his 40-month sentence, which Mr. Trump had proclaimed on July 10, 2020, formal and final. Pardoning Stone was Trump's way of thanking him for all the dirty things he did for him during their decadeslong association, including as an adviser in the 2016 presidential campaign. He told ABC News, on December 28, that "[m]y wife and I both had the opportunity to thank the president personally for righting the injustice of my conviction in a Soviet-style show trial... ." DailyMail. com quotes him as saying that "Donald Trump is the greatest President since Abraham Lincoln."

Paul Manafort, who served as Trump's campaign chairman from June to August 2016, was convicted of bank fraud and tax evasion, and he also pleaded guilty to illegally lobbying for Ukraine. Although he was sentenced to more than seven years in prison, he has been under home confinement because of the spread of coronavirus in federal prisons.

Responding to the news of his pardon, Mr. Manafort tweeted: "Mr. President, my family & I humbly thank you for the Presidential Pardon you bestowed on me. Words cannot fully convey how grateful we are." Another tweet said that President Trump had accomplished more than any of his predecessors.

The December 23 pardons raised eyebrows even among many Republicans. Senator Ben Sasse of Nebraska issued a statement, saying: "This is rotten to the core."

More pardons can be expected before he leaves office on January 21, 2021. As *The Times*'s December 20 editorial says, "he has floated granting pre-emptive pardons to family members and even himself.… ."

Whether a president's pardoning power, guaranteed under the Constitution, is so broad as to include self-pardoning has lately become a hotly debated issue in the country. Settling the issue may require the lengthy process of a constitutional amendment.

Politicization of Justice Department

Another area of presidential abuse of power, which the *Times* editorial has discussed and which the incoming Biden administration should put on its reform agenda, pertains to Trump's "politicization of law enforcement." The abuse stems from his "belief that the Justice Department should do his bidding," the editorial says. "He pressured his attorneys general, from Jeff Sessions through William Barr, to protect him and his allies and prosecute his perceived enemies. Sometimes they consented. Other times they resisted."

We know the fate that befell Sessions and Barr when they resisted. "But if law enforcement is to operate fairly and effectively," the editorial continues, "the American people have to see it as independent from politics."

The surest way of doing it is to put in place laws that would make it impossible for the likes of Donald Trump to become president. The task facing Joe Biden will be herculean. To quote from the *Times* editorial, again, "With every act he takes, he will send an important message to the American people, and the world, about what a president should do – and, perhaps more important, what a president should not do, even if he technically has the power to do it."

45

Conservative Majority on the U.S. Supreme Court May Bring Back Back-Alley Abortions

September 20, 2021

The decision made by five conservative justices on the U.S. Supreme Court, on September 1, 2021, to allow the clearly unconstitutional antiabortion law passed by Texas State to go into effect will be laughed at by legal scholars for all time to come. More than the decision, it is the disingenuous reason for it, which the court's 5-to-4 majority gave that makes it laughable.

The decision was made in response to an application submitted to the court by abortion providers in Texas, requesting that the state's law be blocked. The majority said that they did not go into the constitutionality of the Texas law before arriving at their decision. They decided not to block the law because of the procedurally improper manner in which the application for blocking it was submitted, they said.

The decision being rushed, made without full briefing or oral argument, was the main criticism leveled against it by Elena Kagan, a liberal member of the court and one of the four who dissented from the majority decision. The rushed, hush-hush manner in which the Supreme Court has been resolving important issues, came to be called "shadow-docket" decision making. "Today's ruling illustrates just how far the court's 'shadow-docket' decisions may depart from the usual principles of appellate process," Justice Kagan wrote in her dissenting opinion. "That ruling, as everyone must agree, is of great consequence."

The rushed decision was "shameful," said Jerrold Nadler, Democratic Congressman from New York. The congressional hearings he plans to hold "to shine a light on the Supreme Court's dangerous and cowardly use of the shadow docket" will be fully justified.

The impression one gets from the majority's reason for their decision is that they were looking for just any excuse to allow the Texas law to go into effect. If they had deliberated on the constitutionality of the law, they would be compelled either to uphold the landmark decision the Supreme Court made in 1973, in Roe v. Wade; or overrule it.

In Roe v. Wade, the court had decided that a woman's right to have an abortion is a fundamental right guaranteed under the U.S. Constitution. In terms of the Supremacy Clause of the Constitution, it or any federal law passed in pursuance thereof takes precedence over all state laws and state constitutions. Upholding the Roe verdict would mean declaring the Texas law ultra vires the Constitution. And that may as well be the reason why five conservative justices on the present Supreme Court decided not to rule on the constitutionality of the Texas law. They wouldn't dare to anger their political patrons to whom they owe their positions on the court.

It may be noted that the political patron to whom three of the five justices – Neil M. Gorsuch, Brett M. Kavanaugh and Amy Coney Barrett – owe their positions on the court is former President Donald Trump. He had repeatedly said that his main criterion for nominating a person for the Supreme Court was the person's willingness to overrule Roe v. Wade. Letting the Texas law go into effect being the immediate goal of the five justices, they decided that the best way to achieve it was to avoid examining its constitutionality. They knew such an examination would be lengthy and controversial.

Justices 'opted to bury their heads in the sand'

Their timid, partisan, time-serving decision invited this well-deserved reproach from Justice Sonia Sotomayor, another liberal member of the court who dissented from the majority opinion: "Presented with an application to enjoin a flagrantly unconstitutional law engineered to prohibit women from exercising their constitutional rights and evade judicial scrutiny, a majority of justices have opted to bury their heads in the sand." Alluding to Roe, she added, "The court should not be so content to ignore its constitutional obligations to protect not only the rights of women, but also the sanctity of its precedents and of the rule of law."

If one is looking for an example of partisan preferences trumping jurisprudence, one doesn't have to look further than the performance of the present conservative majority on the court. The laudable exception is Chief Justice John G. Roberts, Jr. Though conservative on most issues, he refused to overlook the provision in the Texas law, which its crafty Republican architects inserted in it with a view to gaming the system. This is how the chief justice expressed, in his dissenting opinion, his disgust for the dubious provision in the law: "The legislature has imposed a prohibition on abortions after roughly six weeks, and then essentially delegated enforcement of that prohibition to the populace at large. The desired consequence appears to be to insulate the state from responsibility for implementing and enforcing the regulatory regime."

Under the Texas law, doctors who perform abortions, staff members at abortion clinics, counselors, people who help pay for the procedure, and even an Uber driver who takes a patient to an abortion clinic are all potential defendants. Plaintiffs don't have to be Texas residents and don't have to prove that they suffered any personal injury because of the abortion. If they win, the law says, they are entitled to collect from the defendant $10,000 plus the legal expenses they incurred. None should be surprised if the antiabortion law of Texas sets bounty hunters on the prowl.

The possibility of this deplorable outcome of the enforcement provision in the law should have been reason enough for the Supreme Court to strike it down. But the majority chose to ignore it. There's one more thing that they chose to ignore: the well-known fact that antiabortion laws, like laws banning alcohol, have been a flop. When there was a legal ban on alcohol in most states, and even when there was a constitutional ban on it, those who wanted to drink always found ways of getting their liquor. Wasn't it the reason why bootlegging and liquor smuggling flourished all over the country during the period of Prohibition? The loser was the State. It lost a rich source of revenue.

Ditto has been the case with antiabortion laws. Those who were determined to terminate their pregnancies always found ways of doing it. But unlike in the case of Prohibition, antiabortion laws disproportionately hurt the poor. The rich could afford to leave their state where abortion was illegal and travel to another state or another country where it was legal and safe. They got the abortion with no hazard to their health.

The poor who couldn't afford to travel and pay for the procedure were compelled to resort to abortions performed by quacks in their own state. What they performed were often called back-alley abortions, because of the secrecy in which they were performed. Back-alley abortions, often causing irreparable damage to women's bodies, and sometimes even deaths, were numerous in the country before Roe. Weren't the five Supreme Court justices, who refused to block the draconian Texas law, in a way giving their blessings to back-alley abortion? Plans are underway in seven more Republican-controlled states to enact anti-abortion laws patterned after that of Texas.

No Exception for Rape or Incest

The Texas law makes no exception even in the case of pregnancy resulting from rape or incest. Governor Greg Abbott of the state, the chief architect of the law, gave this explanation for the absence of exception: "It doesn't require that at all because obviously it provides at least six weeks for a person to be able to get an abortion. … That said, however, let's make something very clear. Rape is a crime and Texas will work tirelessly to make sure that we eliminate all rapists from the streets of Texas by aggressively going out and arresting them and prosecuting them…. . So goal number one in the state of Texas is to eliminate rape so that no woman, no person, will be a victim of rape."

The stupidity in Gov. Abbott's explanation evoked this response from the Democratic congresswoman from New York, Alexandria Ocasio-Cortez: "Well, I find Governor Abbott's comments disgusting. …I don't know if he's familiar with a menstruating person's body. … [I]n case no one has informed him before in his life, six weeks pregnant means two weeks late for your period." Many women, even those who are not sexually active, have experienced it. Ms. Ocasio-Cortez gave her response while on CNN's "Anderson Cooper 360," on September 7, 2021.

After tutoring the governor on menstruation, she directed her ridicule at his 'remedy' for the rape problem: "The majority of people who are raped, and who are sexually assaulted, are assaulted by someone that they know. These aren't just predators that are walking around the streets at night. They are people's uncles, they are teachers, they are family friends. And when something like that happens, it takes a very long time, first of all, for any victim to come forward. … They don't want to re-traumatize themselves when they go to court." Ms. Ocasio-Cortez concluded her chastising of the governor with these strong words: "He speaks from a place of such deep ignorance and it's not just ignorance, it's ignorance that is hurting people across this country."

The Texas governor's ignorance hurting people goes beyond the area of abortion. If Texas is one of the states in the country where the number of victims claimed by the coronavirus is rapidly increasing, his ignorance of, or adamant refusal to accept what science says about, the cause of the virus is largely to blame. The campaign he has launched in his state against the federally mandated measures to control the spread of the virus is also attributable to his ignorance and adamance.

Ditto is the case with many other Republican-controlled states. The reason they have given for their opposition to federal mandates is that mandates interfere with their personal freedom guaranteed under the Constitution. And these are the same people who are at the forefront of the antiabortion campaign in the country. Do they think that telling a woman what she should do with her body is not interference with her personal freedom?

It was Texas's antiabortion law that initiated the lawsuit that resulted in the Roe verdict. Since the Supreme Court issued the widely acclaimed verdict in 1973, Texas has been working hard to get the verdict overturned. Many other Republican-controlled states have followed the Texas example. Their efforts have continued to this day despite the fact that most of them have been rebuffed at the federal appeals court level, before they reached the Supreme Court.

Even the Department of Justice has sued Texas for passing a law that violates the Constitution. The DOJ case is scheduled for hearing on October 1, 2021.

The Boldest Challenge to Texas Law

The boldest challenge to the Texas law so far came from Alan Braid, a medical doctor from San Antonio, Texas. In an article published in *The Washington Post* of September 19, 2021, he said that he had performed an abortion after the law went into effect. He knew he was "taking a personal risk" by doing it, he said in the article. He did it because "it's something I believe in strongly." He went on to say in the article: "I have daughters, granddaughters and nieces. I believe abortion is an essential part of health care. … I can't just sit back and watch us return to 1972." He was referring to the pre-Roe v. Wade period in the country.

What Dr. Braid has done, and a few more conscientious medical doctors may do, in defiance of the Texas law are not going to do anything to reverse the damage the conservative justices of the Supreme Court have done. Their inaction or, to put it more accurately, condonation of the Texas law, would take the country back to the days of back-alley abortions.

46

Slow Pace of Capitol Attack Probe May Pave the Way for a Trump Comeback

April 11, 2022

Pro-Trump rioters clashing with police while forcing their way into the U.S. Capitol building, on January 6, 2021. (*The picture, by Lev Radin/Pacific Press/LightRocket, is reproduced courtesy* Getty Images.)

•

Unless the United States Department of Justice acts fast, the remarkable work so far done by the Select Committee of the House of Representatives investigating the January 6, 2021, insurrection at the U.S. Capitol will come to naught. And that, in turn, may pave the way for a comeback for the man who instigated the insurrection. The man, of course, is former President Donald Trump.

To briefly go into what led to the insurrection: On January 6, 2021, the U.S. Congress was in session at the Capitol in Washington, D.C. Its only agenda for the day was to discharge its constitutional duty of certifying the victory of Joseph Biden, the Democratic Party candidate, in the November 2020 presidential election. On the same day, instigated by President Trump who spread the lie that he lost the election because it was rigged, thousands of his supporters descended on the Capitol to get the Biden victory overturned by force. In the confrontation that followed between the Trump mob and the security personnel guarding the Capitol, five people were killed and 140 police officers were injured. Many of the security personnel are still undergoing treatment for the trauma they suffered on that day.

On January 13, 2021, the Democratic-controlled House of Representatives impeached the president for the crime of inciting the mob that assaulted the Capitol. Though there was only a week left for Trump's presidential term to end, the Democrats deemed the crime too egregious to ignore. The 2021 assault on the Capitol has been recorded as the worst since the assault on it during the War of 1812.

Unfortunately, as in the case of Trump's first impeachment, in 2019, he was acquitted after the Senate trial this time, too. Under the U.S. Constitution, it's the responsibility of the House to impeach a president. But whether or not to convict him is decided by the Senate, by a two-third vote, after a trial presided over by the chief justice of the Supreme Court. Which means that, to convict an impeached president, 67 senators must be voting "guilty." At the first impeachment trial, only one Republican senator, Mitt Romney, had the courage of conviction to break with his 52 Republican colleagues and vote to convict Trump. But his one vote didn't make any difference.

At the 2021 impeachment trial, though seven of the 50 Republican senators crossed the party line and voted to convict Trump, the 57-43 "guilty" vote was far shorter than the required 67. If he were convicted then, he would have been permanently barred from seeking any public office again.

Though acquitted by the Senate, the House Democrats decided to conduct a thorough investigation of the insurrection, and to hold to account all those responsible for it. On July 1, 2021, the House passed a resolution to create an investigation committee. The Democrats had only a razor-thin majority in the 435-member House. But, with 19 Republican members abstaining from voting, the resolution was passed with a comfortable 222-to-190 vote.

Representatives Liz Cheney and Adam Kinzinger were the only two Republicans who voted for it. Unlike many of their party colleagues, they have been very critical of Donald Trump for the role he played in the insurrection and the lie he has been spreading that the victory in the 2020 presidential election was stolen from him. The two principled Republicans also accepted House Speaker Nancy Pelosi's invitation to be on the nine-member committee. For their vote to create the committee and decision to join it, they were censured by the Republican Party leadership.

The committee, with Democratic Representative Bennie Thompson as chair and Republican Liz Cheney as vice chair and officially called the U.S. House Select Committee to Investigate the January 6th Attack on the United States Capitol, began its work with public hearings on July 27, 2021. With more and more damning pieces of evidence emerging almost daily, the scope of the committee's inquiry steadily expanded. More and more people and organizations, both within and outside the Trump administration, are coming under the committee's radar. As of this writing, more than 700 people have been interviewed by the committee. They include Trump's daughter, Ivanka, and her husband, Jared Kushner. They worked for the Trump administration as senior advisers to president.

Claim of Executive Privilege to Cover Up Crime

Not all those in the Trump administration, from whom the committee sought testimony and documents, have been readily coming forward. Many refused to cooperate with it, claiming executive privilege. It goes without saying that they did it on the advice of their former boss.

He also claimed executive privilege to block the release of documents from the National Archives to the committee. Whether a former president can claim executive privilege over documents lying in the National Archive is an issue that has not yet been resolved definitively. In this case, the present president, Joe Biden, has issued statements waiving it. There has not been any case of even a sitting president, other than the late Richard Nixon of the Watergate notoriety, claiming executive privilege over documents out of fear that their disclosure would reveal the illegal activities he was engaged in. Let's thank counsel Dana Remus of the Biden White House for tutoring Trump on the stupidity of his executive privilege claim. She let it be known to him, through a letter sent to the National Archives, that "constitutional protections of executive privilege should not be used to shield ... information that reflects a clear and apparent effort to subvert the Constitution itself."

Thanks to the committee's persistent work, often resulting in orders from court, the National Archives has made available to the committee thousands of emails and other documents pointing to Trump's responsibility for the January 6 insurrection. This past week, there was a report in the press about another email-related incident linking him to it. According to the report, a law professor by the name of John Eastman, working as an adviser to Trump, had sent him more than 100 emails on how to get his election defeat overturned; and a draft memo to his personal attorney Rudy Giuliani, laying down what he claimed to be the legal basis for it. The legal basis, in Eastman's warped thinking, was that Vice President Mike Pence could decertify Joe Biden's victory by rejecting the Electoral College votes from the states whose election results Trump had challenged in courts. Trump, who has utter contempt for the laws and time-honored institutions of the country, enthusiastically embraced the idea. But in putting it forth, the law professor was not only disgracing the legal profession and academe, but also showing ignorance of the fact that all the challenges his client had lodged – 60 in lower courts and one in the U.S. Supreme Court – had already been dismissed as baseless.

Claiming attorney-client confidentiality, he had refusal to honor the House committee's subpoena for the emails and the memo. The case ended up in a California district court. Judge David Carter's March 28, 2022, verdict ordered that the documents in question be released to the committee. It also said: "Dr. Eastman and President Trump launched a campaign to overturn a democratic election, an action unprecedented in American history. Their campaign was not confined to the ivory tower – it was a coup in search of a legal theory."

'Be there, will be wild!'

This past week, again, there was another revelation in the press, which also established Trump's responsibility for the attack on the Capitol. According to a report in the March 30, 2022, edition of *The New York Time*, a tweet issued by him in the early hours of December 19, 2020, "served as a crucial call to action for extremist groups that played a central role in storming the Capitol." The tweet said: "Big protest in D.C. on January 6th. Be there, will be wild!"

The "will be wild" part of the tweet and the "fight like hell" exhortation to his followers, in his January 6 speech on the Ellipse near the

White House, belied Trump's later claim that the call he gave was for a peaceful demonstration.

His followers did get the message in his tweet right. The Oath Keepers, the Proud Boys, the Three Percenters Original, and other far-right groups marched on the Capitol, fully prepared for an armed insurrection. Citing court filings, the *Times* story says that by the end of December, "the Oath Keepers had reserved three hotel rooms in Arlington, Va. The rooms were meant as a staging ground for three teams of armed militiamen poised to rush across the river into Washington on Jan. 6 if needed."

After having been rebuffed in his 60-plus court attempts to get the Biden victory overturned, Trump had decided that an armed insurrection was the only option left for him. Of course, he was careful not to spell it out in so many words. As an anonymous Trump supporter has been quoted in the *Times* story as having posted on TheDonald.win, a pro-Trump chat board, he "can't exactly openly tell you to revolt. This is the closest he'll ever get."

Gaming the System

Those who are familiar with the career path of Donald Trump, both in business and in politics, know that gaming the system is second nature to him. He knew that the defiance of subpoenas from the committee would lead to contempt of Congress charges, which in turn would lead to court orders to honor the subpoenas. The trove of text messages and emails exchanged between him and his minions; the White House log showing who went in and out on the day of, or immediately before, the insurrection; and the record of phone calls to and from Trump; which are now in the possession of the House committee, are the results of its determined effort to establish who the chief architect of the insurrection was. By making the committee's work difficult and time-consuming, Trump has been able to buy time. And that's part of his game plan, too.

In terms of jurisdiction, the responsibility of the House panel ends with collecting evidence from those who participated in, or were involved in the planning of, the insurrection; and then submitting its findings to the Justice Department. It is the responsibility of the Justice Department to act on those findings and start criminal proceedings against the suspects. A lot of time will have already elapsed before a case reaches the Justice Department because of the procedural requirements that each be first approved by the Rules Committee and then by the full House. That puts an added burden on the Justice Department to act fast when a case against a suspect finally reaches it.

It is very unfortunate that Attorney General Merrick Garland is made to bear the brunt of lawmakers' criticism for the slow pace of his department's work. Representative Elaine Luria of Virginia, one of the members of the House committee, has been reported as saying, "Attorney General Garland, do your job so we can do ours." Her frustration is shared by Rep. Adam Schiff of California, who is also the chairman of the House Intelligence Committee. Schiff has reportedly said, "We are upholding our responsibility. The Department of Justice must do the same." Luria and Schiff were echoing the frustration not only of most Democratic members of Congress, but also of all apolitical people in the country. All of them are anxious to see the culprits responsible for the capitol assault brought to book as fast as possible.

The Justice Department's slowness is also blamed on the overly cautious approach of the attorney general. Critics of Garland do understand that he is working hard to reestablish the integrity and independence of the Justice Department. His predecessor Bill Barr, a toady of Donald Trump, had converted the department into an appendage of the Trump White House. Those who work closely with Garland say that he is determined not to be pressured by Democrats who control the present Congress and even by the Democratic president who appointed him. He has been quoted as saying that the only pressure he feels is "to do the right thing," meaning "follow the facts and the law wherever they may lead."

That's an admirable quality in normal circumstances. The situation in the country right now is anything but normal. A president who was voted out of office in a free and fair election tried to regain the presidency through an armed insurrection. Having failed to do that, he is now planning to secure it though the next presidential election. He knows that the main obstacle in his path is the investigations undertaken by the Justice Department and the House committee.

It is almost certain that the control of Congress would switch from Democrats to Republicans after the November 2022 midterm election. The first thing that a Republican-controlled House of Representatives would do is disband the Select Committee created by its Democratic-controlled predecessor. Trump stooges in the House will make it very easy to accomplish. Once that happens, Trump will have to worry only about the investigation by the Justice Department. He will continue to put all sorts of obstacles on its path until the 2024 election. If he is not indicted by then, he will surely be the Republican Party candidate for president.

If he loses again, we can expect from him a repeat performance of what he did after his 2020 defeat. If he wins, that will mark the beginning of the end of democracy in America. The concern expressed by Democratic members of the January 6 panel about the slow pace of the Justice Department's investigation against the former president is shared by most Americans, Attorney General Garland may please note.

www.ingramcontent.com/pod-product-compliance
Ingram Content Group UK Ltd.
Pitfield, Milton Keynes, MK11 3LW, UK
UKHW020244240426
12048UKWH00026B/1609